MEXICO IS PEOPLE

MEXICO IS PEOPLE
Land of Three Cultures

Edited by
BARBARA NOLEN

With an Introduction by
CONCHA ROMERO JAMES
Former Councilor for Cultural Affairs
Mexican Embassy, Washington, D.C.

ILLUSTRATED WITH PHOTOGRAPHS

Charles Scribner's Sons, New York

Acknowledgments

Permission to use the following material is gratefully acknowledged by Barbara Nolen and the Publishers. Every effort has been made to locate all persons having any rights or interests in the material published here. If some acknowledgments have not been made, their omission is unintentional and is regretted.

THE AZTEC EMPIRE by Miguel Leon-Portilla; THE MESSENGERS REPORT TO MONTEZUMA; MONTEZUMA WELCOMES THE SPANIARDS; and BROKEN SPEARS: From *The Broken Spears: The Aztec Account of the Conquest of Mexico*, edited by Miguel Leon-Portilla. Copyright © 1962 by the Beacon Press; reprinted by permission of Beacon Press. Originally published in Spanish under the title of *Visión de los Vencidos;* copyright © 1959 by Universidad Nacional Autonoma de Mexico.

MALINCHE, THE TONGUE OF CORTÉS by Margaret Shedd: From *Malinche and Cortés*, copyright © 1971 by Margaret Shedd Kisich. Reprinted by permission of Doubleday & Company, Inc.

ARRIVAL OF THE CONQUISTADORS and THE SIEGE AND FALL OF MEXICO by Bernal Díaz del Castillo: Abridged from pp. 88–92, 289, 293–294, 266–299 of *The Conquest of New Spain*, by Bernal Díaz del Castillo, translated by J. M. Cohen. Copyright © J. M. Cohen, 1963. Penguin Books Ltd.

THE GREAT MONTEZUMA by Francisco López de Gómara: From *Cortés: The Life of the Conqueror by his Secretary Francisco López de Gómara*, translated and edited by Lesley Byrd Simpson. Originally published by the University of California Press; reprinted by permission of The Regents of the University of California.

THE ART OF THE FIESTA by Octavio Paz: From *The Labyrinth of Solitude*, by Octavio Paz; reprinted by permission of Grove Press, Inc. Copyright © 1961 by Grove Press, Inc.

[vi]   ACKNOWLEDGMENTS

FIESTA OF THE FLYERS by Gustav Regler: From *A Land Bewitched*, by Gustav Regler. Putnam & Company, London, 1955.

BLESSING OF THE ANIMALS and WOMEN WHO LED THE WAY by J. W. F. Stoppelman: Abridged from *People of Mexico*, by J. W. F. Stoppelman. Copyright © 1966 by Joseph W. F. Stoppelman. Reprinted by permission of Hastings House, Publishers, New York, and J. M. Dent & Sons Ltd., London.

PILGRIMAGE by Dane Chandos: From *House in the Sun*, by Dane Chandos; reprinted by permission of the author.

THE DAY OF THE DEAD and OUR LADY OF GUADALUPE by Frances Toor: Taken from *A Treasury of Mexican Folkways*, by Frances Toor. © 1947 by Crown Publishers, Inc. Used by permission of Crown Publishers, Inc.

THE BULLFIGHT, OR "LA FIESTA BRAVA" by True Bowen: From *Men and Bulls*, by True Bowen; reprinted by permission of the author.

THE CRY FOR INDEPENDENCE by Dana Catharine de Ruiz; used by permission of the author.

REVOLUTION IN MEXICO CITY, 1841 by Frances Calderón de la Barca: Abridged from the book *Life in Mexico*, by Frances Calderón de la Barca. Published by E. P. Dutton & Co., Inc. and used with their permission. Everyman's Library text published by J. M. Dent & Sons Ltd., London.

RETURN FROM EXILE by Nina Brown Baker: From *Juárez: Hero of Mexico*, by Nina Brown Baker. Vanguard Press, New York, 1942. Copyright 1942 by Nina Brown Baker. Renewed 1969 by Nina Sydney Ladof. Reprinted by permission of the publisher.

THE DICTATORSHIP OF DON PORFIRIO by Lesley Byrd Simpson: From *Many Mexicos*, by Lesley Byrd Simpson. Originally published by the University of California Press; reprinted by permission of The Regents of the University of California.

REVOLUTIONARY WITH A PAINTBOX by Diego Rivera: From *My Art, My Life*, by Diego Rivera. Citadel Press, New York, 1960.

VIVA THE REVOLUTION! by Anita Brenner: From *The Wind that Swept Mexico*, by Anita Brenner. University of Texas Press, Austin, 1943, 1971; reprinted by permission of the author and the publisher.

FLIGHT FROM CUERNAVACA by Rosa E. King: From *Tempest Over Mexico*, by Rosa E. King. Little, Brown and Company, 1935.

PANCHO VILLA AND THE PRISONERS by Martin Luis Guzman: From *The Eagle and the Serpent*, by Martin Luis Guzman and translated by Harriet DeOnis. Copyright 1930 and renewed 1958 by Alfred A. Knopf, Inc. Reprinted by permission of the publisher.

REVOLT OF YOUTH, 1968 by Octavio Paz: From *The Other Mexico: Critique of the Pyramid*, by Octavio Paz. Reprinted by permission of Grove Press, Inc. Copyright © 1972 by Grove Press, Inc.

MY FATHER, JARANO by Ramón Beteta: From *Jarano*, by Ramón Beteta, translated by John Upton. University of Texas Press, Austin, 1970.

INDIAN MARKET by D. H. Lawrence: From *Mornings in Mexico*, by D. H. Lawrence. Copyright 1927 by D. H. Lawrence and renewed 1955 by Frieda Lawrence Ravagli. Reprinted as abridged by permission of Alfred A. Knopf, Inc. *Mornings in Mexico and Etruscan Places*, by D. H. Lawrence. William Heinemann Ltd., London. Reprinted by arrangement with Lawrence Pollinger Ltd. and the Estate of the late Mrs. Frieda Lawrence.

COURTSHIP—OLD STYLE by Elizabeth Borton de Treviño: From *My Heart Lies South*, by Elizabeth Borton de Treviño. Copyright © 1972, 1953 by Elizabeth Borton de Treviño. Reprinted with permission of Thomas Y. Crowell, Inc.

THE MINERS OF GUANAJUATO by Dana Catharine de Ruiz; used by permission of the author.

PITO, THE WANDERER by José Rubén Romero, translated by William O. Cord: From *The Futile Life of Pito Perez*, by José Rubén Romero, translated by William O. Cord. Prentice-Hall, Inc., New Jersey, 1967. © 1966 by William O. Cord. Copyright under International and Pan-American Copyright Conventions. Library of Congress Catalog Card Number 67–12200.

BLACK GOLD by Carleton Beals: From the book *Mexican Maze*, by Carleton Beals. Copyright 1931, Renewal © 1959 by Carleton Beals. Reprinted by permission of J. B. Lippincott Company.

THE CHILDREN OF SANCHEZ by Oscar Lewis: From *The Children of Sanchez*, by Oscar Lewis. Copyright © 1961 by Oscar Lewis. Reprinted as abridged by permission of Random House.

THE WONDER KIDS OF MONTERREY by Michael Scully: From *The "Wonder Kids"—Pint-Size Baseball Heroes* by Michael Scully. Reprinted with permission from the June 1958 Reader's Digest. Copyright 1958 by The Reader's Digest Assn., Inc.

MAYA ART by Miguel Covarrubias: From *Indian Art of Mexico and Central America*, by Miguel Covarrubias. Copyright © 1957 by Alfred A. Knopf, Inc. Reprinted as abridged by permission of the publisher.

POET NUN OF THE NEW WORLD by Carlos González Peña: From *History of Mexican Literature*, by Carlos González Peña, translated by Gusta Barfield Nance and Florene Johnson Dunstan. Southern Methodist University Press, Dallas, 1968. LOVE LYRICS by Sor Juana Inés de la Cruz, translated by Peter H. Goldsmith: From "The Poet Nun," by Ermilo Abreu Gómez, *Américas*, October, 1951. Reprinted from *Américas*, monthly magazine published by the General Secretariat of the Organization of American States, in English, Spanish, and Portuguese.

MADE IN MEXICO by Patricia Fent Ross: From *Made in Mexico*, by Patricia Ross. Copyright 1952 by Alfred A. Knopf, Inc. Reprinted by permission of the publisher.

FOLKLORE IN WAX by Carmen C. de Antúnez: From "Folklore in Wax," by Carmen C. de Antúnez, *Américas*, November 1951; and ALIAS DR. ATL by Alice Raine: From

[viii]   ACKNOWLEDGMENTS

"Alias Dr. Atl," by Alice Raine, *Américas,* July 1951. Reprinted from *Américas,* monthly magazine published by the General Secretariat of the Organization of American States, in English, Spanish, and Portuguese.

THE FOLKLORE BALLAD by Lysander Kemp: From *Fly Away, Little Dove,* by Lysander Kemp, Evergreen Review; reprinted by permission of the author.

MODERN MURAL PAINTERS by John A. Crow: Abridged from pp. 155–161 from *Mexico Today,* Rev. Edition by John A. Crow. Copyright © 1957, 1972 by John A. Crow.

THE FOUR HUNDRED YOUNG MEN from the Popol Vuh, translated by Delia Goetz and Sylvanus G. Morley: From *Popol Vuh: The Sacred Book of the Quiché Maya,* From the Translation of Adrián Recinos. Copyright 1950 by the University of Oklahoma.

THE EAGLE AND THE SERPENT by William H. Prescott: From *The Works of William Hickling Prescott,* Montezuma Edition, Edited by Wilfred Harold Munro. Copyright 1904 Renewal 1932 by J. B. Lippincott Company. Reprinted as abridged by permission of J. B. Lippincott Company.

THE WORLD AND OTHER FOLKTALES by Américo Paredes: From *Folktales of Mexico,* edited and translated by Américo Paredes. University of Chicago Press, 1970. Copyright by University of Chicago.

THE SMOKING MOUNTAIN by Maurice Boyd: From *Tarascan Myths and Legends,* by Maurice Boyd. Texas Christian University Press, Fort Worth, Texas, 1969.

LEGENDS OF THE CITY OF MEXICO by Thomas A. Janvier: From *Legends of the City of Mexico,* by Thomas A. Janvier. Copyright 1910 by Harper & Row Publishers, Inc., copyright renewed 1938 by H. S. Drinker.

Editor's Note

To complete this book, research was carried out in many pleasant places, with the help of friends, librarians and authors who shared the editor's enthusiasm for a fascinating country. My serious interest in Mexico goes back to student days at Stanford University. It was strengthened during the editing of twenty-four small volumes on Latin America produced during World War II, and reinforced during several international workshops. Finally, it resulted in four trips to Mexico and extensive reading of books by Mexican authors and others who know Mexico well.

The search for appropriate material began at the Benjamin Franklin Library in Mexico City and continued at the National University of Mexico and the University of the Americas. The Department of Cultural Affairs at the U.S. Embassy in Mexico City, and the editor of the bulletin of the Society of Mexican Writers helped to select from the great mass of Mexican literature and history some of the most significant authors and themes. Librarians everywhere, and friends who have spent years in Mexico, suggested unusual and out-of-print titles. Excellent suggestions came from provincial Mexican cities: from Guanajuato, San Miguel de Allende, Chapala, San Miguel de Regla, and Oaxaca.

In Washington, D.C., the Hispanic Society of the Library of Congress and the Columbus Memorial Library of the Pan American Union provided excellent guidance and reference services. Universities in California, Texas and other states also provided useful bibliographies in Mexican culture. Finally, Mexico City's magnificent National Museum of Anthropology made available to me their photographic files in the section on ethnography.

To all these sources I am grateful for information and encouragement, but especially to Hazel Wilson, author, librarian and friend, who shared in my four winters in Mexico and the endless search for excellence.

BARBARA NOLEN

Connecticut, 1973

Contents

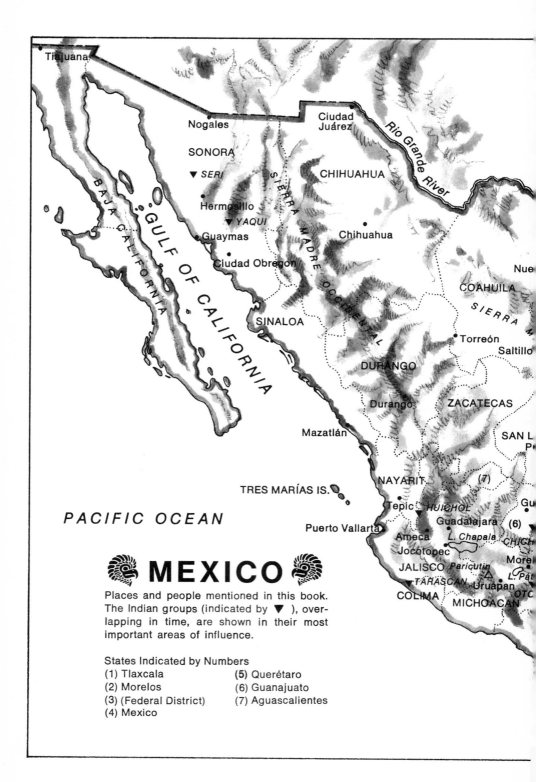

PACIFIC OCEAN

🐍 MEXICO 🐍

Places and people mentioned in this book.
The Indian groups (indicated by ▼), over-
lapping in time, are shown in their most
important areas of influence.

States Indicated by Numbers
(1) Tlaxcala   (5) Querétaro
(2) Morelos   (6) Guanajuato
(3) (Federal District) (7) Aguascalientes
(4) Mexico

Tiajuana

Nogales   Ciudad
                 Juárez   Rio Grande River

SONORA

▼ SERI   CHIHUAHUA

Hermosillo

▼ YAQUI   Chihuahua

Guaymas

Cludad Obregon   Nue

                                COAHUILA
                                        SIERRA

SINALOA   Torreón
                                        Saltillo

                 DURANGO

                 Durango   ZACATECAS

                                        SAN L
                                        P

Mazatlán

TRES MARÍAS IS.   (7)

NAYARIT

                 Tepic HUICHOL   Gu

Puerto Vallarta   Guadalajara (6)

                 Ameca   L. Chapala CHICH

                 Jocotopec

                 JALISCO Paricutin   More

                 TARASCAN Uruapan   L. Pát

COLIMA   MICHOACAN   OTC

BAJA CALIFORNIA

GULF OF CALIFORNIA

SIERRA MADRE OCCIDENTAL

UNITED STATES

GULF OF MEXICO

Rio Grande River

aredo

EVO
LEÓN

Monterrey

E ORIENTAL

TAMAULIPAS

SÍ

HUASTECA

Tampico

Luis Potosí

uato

(5)

TOTONAC

TEC   HIDALGO

Tula

Pachuca

(4)

AZTEC

Teotinuacan

Mexico City

(1)

TLAXCALAN

ro.

(3)   Ixtaccihuatl   Orizaba   Vera Cruz (San Juan
de Ulua)

oluca

Puebla

(2)   Popocatépetl

Cuernavaca

PUEBLA

Taxco

VERA CRUZ

ERRERO

OAXACA

OLMEC

SIERRA MADRE DEL SUR

Oaxaca

MIXTECA

Isthmus of
Tehuantepec

apulco

Mitla

ZAPOTEC

N

BAY OF
CAMPECHE

Papantla

Mérida   Chichen-Itza

Uxmal   YUCATÁN

Campeche   MAYA

QUINTANA
ROO

CAMPECHE

COZUMEL IS.

TABASCO

Palenque

BRITISH
HONDURAS

LACANDON

CHIAPAS

GUATEMALA

Introduction

We are living in an era when most of us, but particularly the young, irrespective of our national roots have an opportunity to become involved in acts of world citizenship. More than ever before, people must communicate with each other across the barriers of distance, language and custom. In order to bring about the kind of people-to-people relationship that can provide a solid foundation for the formal contacts established by governments, it is essential to gain an appreciation of the cultural heritage, life style and aspirations of the various members of the family of nations.

A glimpse of Mexican life is no small contribution to the understanding of a good neighbor of the United States. In this connection, I would like to emphasize that the stature of a country cannot be measured by the size of its territory, natural resources, defense establishment or scenic wonders. Its quality rests on the eagerness of its inhabitants to serve the nation and contribute their individual gifts to the community. These may not necessarily be material in nature, but rather different manifestations of pride in their membership—acts of courage, patience, dignity, imagination, and willingness to share in events and projects of communal interest.

Happily, Mexicans have a tradition of community service going back to pre-Hispanic times, when every member of the group participated in efforts such as planting and harvesting the crops.

After the conquest, the Spanish missionaries were quick to appreciate this cooperative spirit and put the Indians to work on the enormous task of building churches. The Spanish also recognized the creative capacity of the Indians and taught them to carve the stones and decorate the walls and altars of the thousands of churches that were erected in plazas and on hillsides all over Mexico. The Indians learned the techniques very rapidly and soon began to create their own designs and motifs in paintings and sculptures. Whole families participated in the task of church building, and even children carried small stones or containers of water.

In modern Mexico the same spirit has been shown in the building of rural schools and other public facilities such as athletic fields, roads and dispensaries. The termination of each is celebrated with a fiesta in which everybody takes part, irrespective of age. Much has been written about the variety and frequency of Mexican fiestas; but none is more joyous than the celebrations held on the occasion of the raising of the Mexican flag on a new rural school made possible by the government which provides prefabricated parts, and the labor of the villagers who do all the necessary work to erect it.

Mexicans are great believers in miracles, because, after all, Mexico today is a miracle. In no other way can we explain the evolution of a country that gained political independence after three hundred years under Spanish rule, during which our people had no voice in public administration and acquired no experience for independent life.

Our War of Independence lasted eleven years (1810–1821) and practically all the nineteenth century was marked by political instability. We even had three wars, one with the United States, and two empires. Following a period of peace that lasted thirty years, a social revolution broke out in 1910 but it was not until 1920 that a constructive period of that great movement was initiated. A new constitution was promulgated in 1917 when the revolution was still in progress, and this was nothing short of a miracle because this notable document pointed the way to basic changes in educational and labor policies, as well as in the concept of public ownership of natural resources. Strong systems of social security and revenue sharing as well as agrarian laws are among the great accomplishments of the legislators of 1917. Most of them were not ideologists but rather men who had suffered deprivation and poverty and had felt the most pressing needs of the country in their own lives.

Since 1920, Mexico has attracted much attention for the impulse given to the arts, and several Mexican painters enjoy an international reputation, among them Diego Rivera, José Clemente Orozco, David Alfaro Siqueiros and Rufino Tamayo. Among the composers, the best known are Carlos Chavez who has been a guest conductor and played some of his works in the United States and Europe, and the late maestro Julian Carillo, exponent of new musical theories and highly respected at home and abroad.

Folk artists have been encouraged and it is in their products that the genius of Mexico is perhaps most evident. Colorful costumes and rugs, lacquered trays and boxes, clay animals and pottery, kitchen utensils and furniture are individually designed. No self-respecting folk artist will duplicate any of his creations because making one thing is a pleasure, but copying it several times is a sacrifice.

Folk musicians are quick to react to unusual occurrences and compose *corridos* (a sort of ballad) to record the exploits of bull fighters, heroes or bandits, crimes, and accidents. Floods, strikes, and natural phenomena are also featured. In fact any dramatic event is a suitable subject, such as the death of Rosita Alvirez who was killed because she refused to dance with a suitor. The *corrido* singer might be called a singing reporter.

In the years that have elapsed since the end of the revolution of 1910, Mexico has witnessed the rise of great buildings housing institutions such as the National University, the National Institute of Cardiology and the National Museum of Anthropology. A magnificent subway system was planned and built in less than two years.

One of the most inspiring sites in Mexico City is the *Plaza de las Tres Culturas*, the Plaza of the Three Cultures, the place where the Aztecs lost the last battle for the defense of their empire. The three civilizations coexisting in Mexico today—the pre-Hispanic, the colonial and the modern—are proudly represented there by pyramids, a colonial church and the imposing building of the Ministry of Foreign Affairs. A bronze plate on the church contains an inscription proclaiming that a new race, neither Spanish nor Indian, had its birth on that spot. The mestizo, the full-blooded Indian and the full-blooded Spaniard are equally respected and we can justly say that Mexicans have never been guilty of institutionalized racial prejudice. Education and higher standards of living automatically make an Indian the equal of any other man. We have had two Indian presidents, Benito Juárez and Porfirio Díaz, but there is no record that in their political career either one of them ever experienced discrimination because of his race.

An American visitor to the National Museum of Anthropology observed a boy who was busily taking notes and innocently asked him: "Are you of Spanish or Aztec descent?" The boy's back stiffened and he replied with a flash of fire in his eyes: "I am Mexican." And probably he felt ten feet tall.

A new generation is moving into positions of responsibility in government, business and the professions. Half the population of Mexico is under seventeen years of age. Sixty-five percent is under twenty-five.

There are other important indices of national strength: Mexico has stepped permanently out of the ranks of underdeveloped countries. Ten thousand new classrooms are being built every year in rural areas, and free textbooks are distributed by the government to elementary and secondary school pupils. Prefabricated schoolhouses have been exported by Mexico to nine Latin American countries, Italy, India, Indonesia, Yugoslavia and the Philippines. In 1900 only one quarter of the population could read and write. Today the literacy rate is eighty-five percent.

The determination and faith that have been shown by the people of Mexico in the presence of incredible obstacles truly reveal their quality and the stature of the country.

CONCHA ROMERO JAMES

Washington, D.C.
January 1973

MEXICO IS PEOPLE

PART 1
THE PAST IS PROLOGUE

The Aztec Empire
by Miguel Leon-Portilla

Mexico City, 8000 feet above sea level, surrounded by mountains, has long been a center of great peoples. Today in the 1970s, with a population of about eight million, it is the fifth largest city in the world. Founded in 1325, it was the largest city in the New World in 1519 when the Spanish conquerors saw it for the first time. Tenochtitlán, as the Aztecs called it, was then a metropolis of a quarter of a million people. It was the capital of the Aztec Empire of close to several millions, ruled over by the Emperor Montezuma—who exacted tribute from many subject tribes.

The Aztecs or Mexicas were the last of the many nomadic tribes to enter the Valley of Mexico from the north. They arrived during the middle of the thirteenth century, and attempted to settle in one or another of the flourishing city-states, but wherever they appeared, they were violently driven away as undesirable foreigners. It is true that they spoke the same language as the old Toltecs, but otherwise they were almost totally uncultured. The only heritage they brought with them, besides the Náhuatl tongue, was an indomitable will.

After a whole series of defeats and humiliations, the Aztecs succeeded in establishing themselves on an island in the lake; the ancient codices state that their city was founded in the year 1325.

1

A little more than a century later, incredible as it may seem, this destitute tribe had been able to assimilate the old cultural traditions and, at the same time, to achieve complete independence. Then they began their career as conquerors, extending their rule from the Gulf Coast to the Pacific and as far south as Guatemala —and again they accomplished all this in only one century. Their capital grew rich and powerful, much more powerful than Teotihuacán or Tula had ever been. Its temples, palaces and gardens were so magnificent that the Spanish conquistadors gaped in astonishment.

When the Old World and the Aztecs in the New World met face to face on that November day in 1519, their attitudes toward each other were very different. The Aztecs thought the strangers were Quetzalcoatl and other gods returning from over the sea, while the Spaniards—despite their amazement at the splendors of Tenochtitlán—considered the Aztecs barbarians and thought only of seizing their riches and of forcing them to become Christians and Spanish subjects.

This confrontation, vividly described both by the conquistadors and the natives, was something more than a meeting between two expanding nations; it was the meeting of two radically dissimilar cultures, two radically different modes of interpreting existence. Spain had recently brought the long wars of reconquest against the Moors to a triumphant conclusion and was now the greatest power in Europe. The Aztec state had also reached a climax, and its magnificence was evident in its capital city and its vigorous religious, social, economic and political structure. To understand more clearly the tragic loss that resulted from the destruction of this indigenous culture, it will be useful to view the great city as the "gods" viewed it before they leveled it to the ground.

Tenochtitlán, the Aztec Metropolis

The beginnings of the Aztec capital were very humble. It was founded on a low-lying island so undesirable that other tribes had not bothered to occupy it. The indigenous chronicles describe the difficulties with which the Aztecs managed to build a few miserable huts and a small altar to their supreme deity, the war-god Huitzilopochtli. But their fierce will overcame every obstacle. Less than two centuries later, the Spanish conquistador Bernal Díaz del Castillo thought that the wonders he beheld must be a dream. The

Spaniards had been welcomed into the city as guests of Montezuma, and a party of them—led by Cortés—climbed up to the flat
top of the pyramid on which the main temple was built. They were
met by the Aztec king himself, who pointed out the various sights.

"So we stood looking about us, for that huge and cursed temple
stood so high that from it one could see over everything very well,
and we saw the three causeways which led into Mexico, that is the
causeway of Iztapalapa by which we had entered four days before,
and that of Tacuba, and that of Tepeaquilla, and we saw the fresh
water that comes from Chapultepec which supplies the city, and we
saw the bridges on the three causeways which were built at certain
distances apart through which the water of the lake flowed in and
out from one side to the other, and we beheld on that great lake
a great multitude of canoes, some coming with supplies of food
and others returning loaded with cargoes of merchandise; and we
saw that from every house of that great city and of all the other
cities that were built in the water it was impossible to pass from
house to house, except by drawbridges which were made of wood
or in canoes; and we saw in those cities Cues [temples] and oratories like towers and fortresses and all gleaming white, and it was
a wonderful thing to behold; then the houses with flat roofs, and
on the causeways other small towers and oratories which were like
fortresses.
    "After having examined and considered all that we had seen we
turned to look at the great market place and the crowds of people
that were in it, some buying and others selling, so that the murmur
and hum of their voices and words that they used could be heard
more than a league off. Some of the soldiers among us who had
been in many parts of the world, in Constantinople, and all over
Italy, and in Rome, said that so large a market place and so full of
people, and so well regulated and arranged, they had never beheld
before."

The Spanish soldier had good reasons for describing the city in
such enthusiastic terms. Almost nothing remains today of what he
saw, but his account is corroborated by other writings, ancient
maps and archaeological investigations.
    The two most important places in the capital were the sacred
precinct of the main temple, with its related temples, schools and

other structures (in all, it contained seventy-eight buildings), and the huge plaza in Tlatelolco that served as the principal market place, offering an astonishing variety of products from far and near. The walled precinct of the main temple formed a great square measuring approximately five hundred yards on each side. Today nothing is left of the temple except a few remains that can be seen near the eastern walls of the Cathedral of Mexico.

The palace of Axayacatl, who ruled from 1469 to 1481, stood on the western side of the main temple, and it was here that the Spaniards were lodged when they arrived in the city as Montezuma's guests. The palace of Montezuma, facing a broad plaza, stood on the site now occupied by the National Palace of Mexico. And in addition to these and other structures, there was a large number of lesser temples and stone and mortar buildings reserved as living quarters for the nobles, merchants, artists and other persons. The streets of Tenochtitlán were comparatively narrow, many of them with canals through which canoes from the lake-shore could reach the center of the city. The capital boasted many other attractions, and the Spaniards were particularly impressed by the botanical and zoological gardens, as nothing of the kind existed at that time in their native land.

The population of Tenochtitlán at the time of the Conquest has been the subject of considerable controversy, but beyond question it must have amounted at least to a quarter of a million. The activities were many and colorful. Fiestas, sacrifices and other rituals were celebrated in honor of the gods. Teachers and students met in the various *calmecac* and *telpuchcalli,* the pre-Hispanic centers of education. The coming and going of merchant canoes and the constant bustle in the Tlatelolco market impressed the Spaniards so much that they compared the city to an enormous anthill. The military exercises and the arrival and departure of the warriors were other colorful spectacles.

In brief, the life of Tenochtitlán was that of a true metropolis. The city was visited by governors and ambassadors from distant regions. Gold, silver, rich feathers, cocoa, bark paper and other types of tribute, along with slaves and victims for the human sacrifices, streamed in along the streets and canals. The Spaniards were right: Tenochtitlán was indeed an anthill, in which each individual worked unceasingly to honor the gods and augment the grandeur of the city.

PEOPLE OF THE SUN

Most important of all is the exalted praise given to what can only be called a mystical conception of warfare, dedicating the Aztec people, the "people of the sun," to the conquest of all other nations. In part the motive was simply to extend the rule of Tenochtitlán, but the major purpose was to capture victims for sacrifice, because the source of all life, the sun, would die unless it were fed with human blood.

There is good evidence that human sacrifices were performed in the Valley of Mexico before the arrival of the Aztecs, but apparently no other tribe ever performed them with such frequency. The explanation seems to be that Tlacaélel persuaded the Aztec kings that their mission was to extend the dominions of Huitzilopochtli so that there would be a constant supply of captives to be sacrificed. Fray Diego de Durán wrote that Itzcoatl "took only those actions which were counseled by Tlacaelel," and that he believed it was his mission "to gather together all the nations" in the service of his god. It was also Tlacaelel who suggested the building of the great main temple in Tenochtitlán, dedicated to Huitzilopochtli, God of the Sun and Giver of Life. Before the Spaniards destroyed it, it was the scene of innumerable sacrifices of captives, first from nearby places and later from such distant regions as Oaxaca, Chiapas and Guatemala.

WARFARE IN ANCIENT MEXICO

As in other cities in central Mexico, military training in Tenochtitlán began during early youth. The army was made up of squads of twenty men, which were combined to form larger units of about four hundred, under a *tiachcauh* who came from the same clan as the warriors he commanded. The more important leaders were usually Eagle or Jaguar Knights, with such titles as *tlacatecatl* (chief of men) and *tlacochcalcatl* (chief of the house of arrows).

The most important offensive weapon of the Aztecs was the *macana*, a sort of paddle-shaped wooden club edged with sharp bits of obsidian. It was so awesomely effective that on more than one occasion during the Conquest warriors beheaded Spanish horses at a single stroke. Other widely used arms were the *atlatl*, or spear thrower, bows and arrows of different sizes, blowguns and a variety of spears and lances, most of them with obsidian points. The defensive weapons were shields made of wood or woven fibers—

often elaborately painted and adorned with feathers—and quilted cotton armor. Some of the warriors also wore various types of masks and headdresses to show that they were Eagle or Jaguar Knights or belonged to the higher military ranks.

A war or battle always commenced with a certain ritual: shields, arrows and cloaks of a special kind were sent to the enemy leaders as a formal declaration that they would soon be attacked. This explains the Aztecs' surprise when the Spaniards, their guests, suddenly turned on them without any apparent motive and—more important—without the customary ritual warning.

Malinche, the Tongue of Cortés
by Margaret Shedd

Malinche, called Doña Marina by the Spaniards, was the slave girl who became the "tongue of Cortés," his interpreter and also his mistress. Without her the story of the Conquest would have been very different. Cortés had a difficult mission. He could not have succeeded so well, against such odds, without the skills of Malinche to translate his thoughts into words. To the "tongue of Cortés" must go the blame or the credit for many of the Spanish victories.

Malinche was a daughter of the chief of a lowland town subject to the mighty highland Aztecs. At twelve she was sold into slavery at the demand of her stepmother, which suggests that even as a child she was powerful enough to be a threat to certain adults. When she was about fifteen she was given, with eighteen other slave girls, to Hernán Cortés and his captains. These Spanish warriors and colonizers had just landed on Mexican soil, in the Bay of Campeche.

No one knows what happened to the other girls, but Malinche, who spoke two Mexican languages, learned Spanish rapidly and she was put to help Cortés' translator. Soon after that she became Cortés' mistress. She bore his first son, Martín. Her seven years with Cortés were the time of his greatest success, and the indigenous peoples marked this joint triumph by calling woman and man by the same name, Malinche. During the days of glory they were Malinche together. She had other names: Marina, her baptized Christian name, and Malintzin, which may have been the Náhuatl pronunciation of Marina with the conventional last syllable of respect. The name first given her by her parents is unrecorded.

Obviously she betrayed her own people; she could not have had so important a part in the Conquest had she not betrayed them. Today in Mexico the word Malinche, which has come to refer alone to her and not to both of them, means servant and defender of the conquering enemy, and *malinchismo* is a noun of treachery.

However there is also a volcano named after her, paradoxically, so she represents more than simply a figure of hate. In her lifetime those people she helped to destroy, the Aztecs, treated her with respect. Those other people, the Spaniards, in whose great campaign of destruction she served, respected her too, and their leader chose her for himself, and took their son with him on his first triumphant return to Spain after the Conquest. But in a way she is outside history.

She left behind her name, her descendants through Cortés' son, and a riddle: who is the betrayer and who the betrayed and why have they become so? The formalized drawings of her in the chronicles show a handsome woman, usually standing behind a seated Cortés, her hand raised, the Náhuatl curlicue meaning words coming from her mouth. She is no brawny Amazon, although she rode beside Cortés in battles. If she was feminine, eloquent, beautiful, cruel, courageous, brilliant, she was also subtle and wily.

The Conquest of Mexico, in which Malinche participated from beginning to end, started with eleven Spanish sailing vessels seen off the southeastern shore of Mexico, at Tabasco, in March 1519. Aboard those ships there were five hundred and fifty soldiers, a hundred sailors, sixteen horses and a few dogs. The Spaniards landed in Tabasco and fought a battle won for them by their horses, first seen in Mexico on that day; they took on board the slave girls including Malinche, and went to a better harbor which they named Villa Rica de la Vera Cruz. What happened in the next seven months is extravagant and difficult to believe even now.

This band of miscellaneous warriors burned their ships, left a hundred and fifty of their men to guard the new town while the rest of them marched into the mountains over passes ten thousand feet high to capture the most beautiful city of its time as well as one of the richest, the Aztec capital, Tenochtitlán. They entered it, took it over, and made the Aztec emperor captive, who had at his instant command no less than fifty thousand Aztec and mercenary soldiers. This brilliant, precarious campaign was a compound of Spanish courage (which must never be downgraded), a lust for gold, the astute use Cortés made of the Aztecs' angry subjects, and Christian fanaticism.

And what was it the conquerors supplanted with their Spanish civilization? At the time few men thought about what was being destroyed, because since it was unchristian it must be savage—although their eyes told them differently. The Aztecs ruled Mexico, which was made up of many tribes. The Aztecs had built a great empire rapidly and ruthlessly. They had high arts well developed because they had taken them from their predecessors. Very complicated ritual was what intrigued them most; when the Spaniards arrived Aztec civilization was a sophisticated, doctrinaire dictatorship. Rules regarding every aspect of life were precise and strict—how many cactus thorns to be run through the tongue as penance for various sins. And there is no doubt that the capital city was utterly beautiful, shining forth from its islands in the lakes.

The emperor, Montezuma, from all accounts, was charming, witty, prudent, but he believed that he and his people had come to the end of their rule. He was confronted with many signs and dreams that told him so, and perhaps he also knew it from the spreading revolt of the subject tribes. The omens he saw had to do with the fall of his city, pillars of unquenchable fire, the birth of monsters; and finally they brought him a bird caught in a fishnet, with a kind of mirror in its head and the mirror showed him men riding great deer. Disaster was also presaged by the appearance of the *llorona*, a legendary night woman heard wailing in despair for the children she herself had drowned.

Arrival of the Conquistadors
by Bernal Díaz del Castillo

The Spanish fleet of eleven vessels under Hernán Cortés which reached the shores of Mexico in 1519 was not the first to explore this coast. Two other Spanish captains, Hernandez de Córdoba (1517) and Juan de Grijalva (1518), arrived earlier, stopping in Yucatán and the island of Cozumel. They had several encounters with natives who were not always friendly. They noted the Indians' temples, their custom of human sacrifices, and the presence of gold objects and jewelry for trade.

Bernal Díaz, born in 1492, had served under both Córdoba and Grijalva, so that he was a man of experience when he signed up with Captain-General Cortés for the expedition of 1519. Later, he summed up their purpose: "to serve God and His Majesty, to give light to those who sat in darkness, and also to acquire that wealth which most men covet."

O n Holy Thursday 1519 we arrived with all the fleet at the port of San Juan de Ulua.* Knowing the place well from his previous visit under Juan de Grijalva, the pilot Alaminos at once ordered the vessels to anchor where they would be safe from the northerly gales. The royal standards and pennants were raised on the flagship, and within half an hour of our anchoring two large canoes or pirogues came out to us full of Mexican Indians.

Seeing the large ship with its standards flying, they knew that it was there they must go to speak with the Captain. So they made straight for the flagship, went aboard and asked who was the *Tatuan*, which in their language means the master. Doña Marina, who understood them, pointed him out; and the Indians paid Cortés great marks of respect in their fashion. They said that their lord, a servant of the great Montezuma, had sent them to find out what kind of men we were and what we were seeking, also to say that if we required anything for ourselves or our ships, we were to tell them and they would supply it.

*The Spaniards founded a city here, Villa Rica de la Vera Cruz, which became the city of Vera Cruz.

Cortés thanked them through our interpreters, and ordered that they should be given food, wine, and some blue beads. After they had drunk the wine he told them that he had come to visit and trade with them, and that they should think of our coming to their country as fortunate rather than troublesome.

The messengers went ashore very contented, and next day, which was Good Friday, we disembarked with our horses and guns on some sandhills, which were quite high. For there was no level land, nothing but sand dunes; and the artilleryman Mesa placed his guns on them in what seemed to him the best positions. Then we set up an altar, at which mass was said at once, and built huts and shelters for Cortés and his captains. Our three hundred soldiers then brought wood, and we made huts for ourselves. We put the horses where they would be safe, and in this way we spent Good Friday.

On Saturday, which was Easter Eve, many Indians arrived who had been sent by a *Cacique* called Pitalpitoque, whom we afterwards named Ovandillo and who was one of Montezuma's governors. They brought axes, and dressed wood for Cortés' hut and the others near it, which they covered with large cloths on account of the sun. For since it was Lent, the heat was very great. They brought fowls and maize cakes and plums, which were then in season, and also, I think, some gold jewels; all of which they presented to Cortés, saying that next day a governor would come and bring more provisions. Cortés thanked them warmly, and ordered that they should be given certain things in exchange, with which they went away well pleased.

Next day, Easter Sunday, the governor of whom they had spoken arrived. His name was Tendile, a man of affairs, and he brought with him Pitalpitoque, who was also an important person among them. They were followed by many Indians with presents of fowls and vegetables, whom Tendile commanded to stand a little aside on a hillock, while according to their custom he bowed humbly three times, first to Cortés and then to all the other soldiers standing near by.

Cortés welcomed them through our interpreters, embraced them, and asked them to wait, as he wished to speak to them presently. Meanwhile he had had an altar set up as well as could be done in the time, and Fray Bartolomé de Olmedo, who was a fine singer, chanted mass with the assistance of Padre Juan Díaz, while the two governors and the other *Caciques* who were with them looked on.

After mass Cortés and some of our captains dined with the two officers of the great Montezuma, and when the tables had been removed, he took these two and our two interpreters aside, and explained to them that we were Christians, and vassals of the Emperor Don Carlos, the greatest lord on earth, who had many great princes as his vassals and servants, and that it was at his orders we had come to their country, since for many years he had heard rumors of it and of the great prince who ruled it. Cortés said that he wished to be friends with this prince, and to tell him many things in the Emperor's name, which would greatly delight him when he knew and understood them. Moreover he wished to trade with their prince and his Indians in a friendly way, and to know what place this prince would appoint for their meeting.

To this Tendile replied somewhat proudly: "You have only just arrived, and already you ask to speak with our prince. Accept now this present that we give you in our master's name, and afterwards tell me whatever you wish."

He took out of a *petaca*—which is a sort of chest—many golden objects beautifully and richly worked, and then sent for ten bales of white cloth made of cotton and feathers—a marvelous sight. There were other things too that I do not remember, and quantities of food—fowls, fruit, and baked fish.

Cortés received all this with gracious smiles, and gave them in return some beads of twisted glass and other little beads from Spain, begging them to send to their towns and summon the people to trade with us, since he had plenty of these beads to exchange for gold. They replied that they would do as he asked.

Cortés next ordered his servants to bring an armchair, richly carved and inlaid, and some moss agates pierced and intricately worked, and packed in cotton scented with musk to give them a good smell, also a string of twisted glass beads, and a crimson cap with a gold medal engraved with a figure of St. George on horseback, lance in hand and slaying the dragon. He told Tendile that he would send the chair to his prince Montezuma—for we already knew his name—so that he could sit in it when Cortés came to visit and speak with him, and that he should wear the cap on his head.

These stones, he said, and all the other things were in token of friendship from our lord the King, for he was aware that Montezuma was a great prince. Cortés then asked that a day and a place might be fixed for his meeting with Montezuma. Tendile accepted the present. Observing that his great master would be glad to know our great king, he promised to deliver it promptly and return with Montezuma's reply.

It appears that Tendile brought with him some of those skilled painters they have in Mexico, and that he gave them instructions to make realistic full-length portraits of Cortés and all his captains and soldiers, also to draw the ships, sails, and horses, Doña Marina and Aguilar, and even the two greyhounds. The cannon and cannon balls, and indeed the whole of our army, were faithfully portrayed, and the drawings were taken to Montezuma.

Cortés ordered our gunners to load the lombards with a big charge of powder, so that they should make a great noise when fired, and told Pedro de Alvarado that all his horsemen must be ready with little bells tied to their breastplates, to gallop in front of Montezuma's servants. He too mounted his horse.

"It would be a good thing," he said, "if we could gallop on these dunes. But they will see that even on foot we get stuck in the sand. Let us go down to the beach when the tide is low and gallop there two by two." And he put all the horsemen under the command of Pedro de Alvarado, whose sorrel mare was a great runner and very quick on the rein.

The display was carried out in the presence of the two ambassadors, and in order that they should see the shot leave the gun Cortés pretended that he wished to speak to them and some other *Caciques* again, just before the cannon was fired. As it was very still at that moment, the balls resounded with a great din as they went over the forest. The two governors and the rest of the Indians were frightened by this strange happening, and ordered their painters to paint it, so that Montezuma might see.

The Messengers Report to Montezuma
from the *Codex Florentino*

When Montezuma heard of the arrival of the Spaniards, he sent five messen-gers, Jaguar Knights, to greet them and to bring them gifts. He thought the strangers were indeed gods, the great Quetzalcoatl and other deities, whose return had been foretold by many omens. He told his messengers: "It is said that our lord has returned to this land. Go to meet him. Go to hear him. Listen well to what he tells you; listen and remember." What follows is the messen-gers' report, from the Codex Florentino, *a document in Náhuatl, the Mexican language, set down by Fray Bernardino de Sahagún between the years 1555 and 1585.*

While the messengers were away, Montezuma could neither sleep nor eat, and no one could speak with him. He thought that everything he did was in vain, and he sighed almost every moment. He was lost in despair, in the deepest gloom and sorrow. Nothing could comfort him, nothing could calm him, nothing could give him any pleasure.

He said: "What will happen to us? Who will outlive it? Ah, in other times I was contented, but now I have death in my heart! My heart burns and suffers, as if it were drowned in spices . . . ! But will our lord come here?"

Then he gave orders to the watchmen, to the men who guarded the palace: "Tell me, even if I am sleeping: 'The messengers have come back from the sea.'" But when they went to tell him, he immediately said: "They are not to report to me here. I will receive them in the House of the Serpent. Tell them to go there." And he gave this order: "Two captives are to be painted with chalk."

The messengers went to the House of the Serpent, and Mon-tezuma arrived. The two captives were then sacrificed before his eyes: their breasts were torn open, and the messengers were sprin-kled with their blood. This was done because the messengers had completed a difficult mission: they had seen the gods, their eyes had looked on their faces. They had even conversed with the gods!

When the sacrifice was finished, the messengers reported to the king. They told him how they had made the journey, and what they had seen, and what food the strangers ate. Montezuma was astonished and terrified by their report, and the description of the strangers' food astonished him above all else.

He was also terrified to learn how the cannon roared, how its noise resounded, how it caused one to faint and grow deaf. The messengers told him: "A thing like a ball of stone comes out of its entrails: it comes out shooting sparks and raining fire. The smoke that comes out with it has a pestilent odor, like that of rotten mud. This odor penetrates even to the brain and causes the greatest discomfort. If the cannon is aimed against a mountain, the mountain splits and cracks open. If it is aimed against a tree, it shatters the tree into splinters. This is a most unnatural sight, as if the tree had exploded from within."

The messengers also said: "Their trappings and arms are all made of iron. They dress in iron and wear iron casques on their heads. Their swords are iron; their bows are iron; their shields are iron; their spears are iron. Their deer carry them on their backs wherever they wish to go. These deer, our lord, are as tall as the roof of a house.

"The strangers' bodies are completely covered, so that only their faces can be seen. Their skin is white, as if it were made of lime. They have yellow hair, though some of them have black. Their beards are long and yellow, and their mustaches are also yellow. Their hair is curly, with very fine strands.

"As for their food, it is like human food. It is large and white, and not heavy. It is something like straw, but with the taste of a cornstalk, of the pith of a cornstalk. It is a little sweet, as if it were flavored with honey; it tastes of honey, it is sweet-tasting food.

"Their dogs are enormous, with flat ears and long, dangling tongues. The color of their eyes is a burning yellow; their eyes flash fire and shoot off sparks. Their bellies are hollow, their flanks long and narrow. They are tireless and very powerful. They bound here and there, panting, with their tongues hanging out. And they are spotted like an ocelot."

When Montezuma heard this report, he was filled with terror. It was as if his heart had fainted, as if it had shriveled. It was as if he were conquered by despair.

Montezuma Welcomes the Spaniards
from the *Codex Florentino*

Leaving some of his men at Vera Cruz, Cortés marched cross-country toward Tenochtitlán, capital of Mexico. They marched through three hundred miles of rough country, through valleys and mountains, collecting as allies certain Aztec tribes who were hostile to Montezuma. There were conflicting reports of treachery from his new allies and from native spies. At Cholula, Cortés decided there really was a plot against him, and his soldiers fell on the unarmed natives, slaughtering three thousand Indians gathered in a great plaza and scattered around the city.

Afterwards, accompanied by their Tlaxcalan allies, the Spanish conquistadors approached the capital. They marched through the Eagle Pass between the twin volcanoes that rose above the city. It was barely six months since they had arrived in Mexico. Montezuma had continually requested Cortés not to approach the city because the omens were not favorable. When Cortés persisted, Montezuma prepared to greet him with all courtesy. But in his heart he felt despair. His envoys had reported the Spanish lust for gold, how "their bodies swelled with greed, and their hunger was ravenous; they hungered like pigs for that gold"!

The Spaniards arrived in Xoloco, near the entrance to Tenochtitlán. That was the end of the march, for they had reached their goal.

Montezuma now arrayed himself in his finery, preparing to go out to meet them. The other great princes also adorned their persons, as did the nobles and their chieftains and knights. They all went out together to meet the strangers.

When Montezuma had given necklaces to each one, Cortés asked him: "Are you Montezuma? Are you the king? Is it true that you are the king Montezuma?"

And the king said: "Yes, I am Montezuma." Then he stood up to welcome Cortés; he came forward, bowed his head low and addressed him in these words: "Our lord, you are weary. The journey has tired you, but now you have arrived on the earth. You have come to your city, Mexico. You have come here to sit on your throne, to sit under its canopy.

"This was foretold by the kings who governed your city, and now it has taken place. You have come back to us; you have come down from the sky. Rest now, and take possession of your royal houses. Welcome to your land, my lords!"

When Montezuma had finished, La Malinche translated his address into Spanish so that the Captain could understand it. Cortés replied in his strange and savage tongue, speaking first to La Malinche: "Tell Montezuma that we are his friends. There is nothing to fear. We have wanted to see him for a long time, and now we have seen his face and heard his words. Tell him that we love him well and that our hearts are contented."

Then he said to Montezuma: "We have come to your house in Mexico as friends. There is nothing to fear."

La Malinche translated this speech and the Spaniards grasped Montezuma's hands and patted his back to show their affection for him.

When the Spaniards entered the Royal House, they placed Montezuma under guard and kept him under their vigilance. They also placed a guard over Itzcuauhtzin, but the other lords were permitted to depart.

Then the Spaniards fired one of their cannons, and this caused great confusion in the city. The people scattered in every direction; they fled without rhyme or reason; they ran off as if they were being pursued. It was as if they had eaten the mushrooms that confuse the mind, or had seen some dreadful apparition. They were all overcome by terror, as if their hearts had fainted. And when night fell, the panic spread through the city and their fears would not let them sleep.

In the morning the Spaniards told Montezuma what they needed in the way of supplies: tortillas, fried chickens, hens' eggs, pure water, firewood and charcoal. Also: large, clean cooking pots, water jars, pitchers, dishes and other pottery. Montezuma ordered that it be sent to them. The chiefs who received this order were angry with the king and no longer revered or respected him. But they furnished the Spaniards with all the provisions they needed—food, beverages and water, and fodder for the horses.

When the Spaniards were installed in the palace, they asked Montezuma about the city's resources and reserves and about the warriors' ensigns and shields. They questioned him closely and then demanded gold.

Montezuma guided them to it. They surrounded him and

crowded close with their weapons. He walked in the center, while they formed a circle around him.

When they arrived at the treasure house called Teucalco, the riches of gold and feathers were brought out to them: ornaments made of quetzal feathers, richly worked shields, disks of gold, the necklaces of the idols, gold nose plugs, gold greaves and bracelets and crowns.

The Spaniards immediately stripped the feathers from the gold shields and ensigns. They gathered all the gold into a great mound and set fire to everything else, regardless of its value. Then they melted down the gold into ingots. As for the precious green stones, they took only the best of them; the rest were snatched up by the Tlaxcaltecas. The Spaniards searched through the whole treasure house, questioning and quarreling, and seized every object they thought was beautiful.

Next they went to Montezuma's storehouse, where his personal treasures were kept. The Spaniards grinned like little beasts and patted each other with delight.

When they entered the hall of treasures, it was as if they had arrived in Paradise. They searched everywhere and coveted everything; they were slaves to their own greed. All of Montezuma's possessions were brought out: fine bracelets, necklaces with large stones, ankle rings with little gold bells, the royal crowns and all the royal finery—everything that belonged to the king and was reserved for him only. They seized these treasures as if they were their own, as if this plunder were merely a stroke of good luck. And when they had taken all the gold, they heaped up everything else in the middle of the patio.

La Malinche called the nobles together. She climbed up to the palace roof and cried: "Mexicanos, come forward! The Spaniards need your help! Bring them food and pure water. They are tired and hungry; they are almost fainting from exhaustion! Why do you not come forward? Are you angry with them?"

The Mexicans were too frightened to approach. They were crushed by terror and would not risk coming forward. They shied away as if the Spaniards were wild beasts, as if the hour were midnight on the blackest night of the year. Yet they did not abandon the Spaniards to hunger and thirst. They brought them whatever they needed, but shook with fear as they did so. They delivered the supplies to the Spaniards with trembling hands, then turned and hurried away.

The Great Montezuma
by Francisco López de Gómara

The Emperor Montezuma and his court have been described by many who took part in the Conquest—by Cortés himself in his letters to the Emperor of Spain, by Bernal Díaz in his memoirs, and by others. This account by Gómara, secretary to Cortés, shows the respect which Montezuma commanded among his enemies as well as among his own subjects.

Montezuma was a man of middling size, thin, and, like all Indians, of a very dark complexion. He wore his hair long and had no more than six bristles on his chin, black and about an inch long. He was of an amiable though severe disposition, affable, well-spoken, and gracious, which made him respected and feared. Montezuma means a furious and solemn man.

His people endowed him with such majesty that they would not sit in his presence, or wear shoes, or look him in the face, with the exception of only a few great lords. But he would not permit the Spaniards to remain standing, either because he enjoyed their society, or because of his high regard for them.

When he took a notion to dress in the Spanish fashion, he would exchange garments with them. He changed his own four times a day and never wore the same garment twice. His used garments were saved and given as rewards and presents to servants and messengers, or, as a token of favor and privilege, to soldiers who had fought and captured an enemy. The many and beautiful mantles that he sent to Cortés were of such.

Montezuma was naturally clean and neat; he bathed twice a day. He seldom left his chambers except to eat, and always ate alone, but gravely and abundantly. His table was a cushion or a couple of dyed skins; his chair a bench of four legs, made from one piece, the seat hollowed out, very well carved and painted. His dishes were brought in by four hundred pages, gentlemen's sons, who served them all at once in his dining hall. Montezuma would enter and look them over, pointing to those he liked, whereupon they would be set on braziers of live coals, to keep them warm and

19

preserve their flavor. He would seldom touch other dishes, unless it was a well-prepared one recommended by his majordomo.

Before he sat down to eat, as many as twenty of his wives would enter, the most beautiful or shapely, or those serving their weekly turn, who very humbly brought him his food, after which he sat down. Then the steward would enter and draw a wooden screen to keep the people from crowding in, and only the steward could serve him, for the pages were not permitted to approach the table or utter a word; nor could any of those present speak while their master was eating, save only his jester, or someone who had a question to ask; and all waited on him barefoot. His drinking was not done with such pomp and ceremony.

Some six old men, with whom Montezuma would share portions of the dishes he liked, were always at the king's side, although somewhat withdrawn. They accepted the food reverently and ate it even more respectfully, not looking him in the face—which was the greatest mark of humility they could show him. During his meals he would listen to the music of pipes, flutes, conches, bone fifes, drums, and other instruments of the kind, for they have no better ones; nor can they sing, I say, because they do not know how, and their voices are bad besides.

Always present at his meals were dwarfs, hunchbacks, cripples, and so on, all for his entertainment and amusement, and these, along with the jesters and mountebanks, were given the leavings to eat at one end of the hall. Whatever else was left over was eaten by the three thousand men of the regular guard, who stayed in the courtyards and square—which is why it is said that three thousand dishes were always served, and three thousand pitchers of the beverage they drink, and that the cellar and pantry were never closed. It was a wonderful thing to see what they contained. Everything obtainable in the market was cooked and served daily without fail. There was, as we shall relate elsewhere, an infinite variety, in addition to what was brought in by hunters, tenants, and tributaries.

The plates, bowls, cups, pitchers, and the rest of the service were of very good pottery, as good as that of Spain, and were never used for more than one of the king's meals. He also had a large number of gold and silver vessels, which he seldom used, because to use them more than once would seem a low thing to do. Some have said that Montezuma cooked and ate babies, but the only human flesh he ate was that of sacrificed men, and this not commonly.

When the table linen was removed, the men and women, who were still standing, would approach to offer him water for his hands, which they did with equal respect, and then retired to their own chambers to eat with the others, as they all did, save only the gentlemen and pages who were on duty.

While Montezuma was still seated and the table had been taken away and the people departed, the merchants entered, barefoot, for all removed their shoes upon entering the palace, save only great lords such as those of Texcoco and Tacuba, and a few of his kinsmen and friends. All came very poorly dressed: if they were lords or great men, and it was cold, they wore old blankets, coarse and tattered, over their fine new mantles. They bowed three times, but did not look him in the face, and spoke humbly, always facing him. He answered them with great dignity, in a low voice and few words. He did not always speak or answer them, whereupon they would leave, walking backward.

AMUSEMENTS

Then Montezuma would amuse himself by listening to music and ballads, or to his jesters, as he was very fond of doing, or by watching certain jugglers who use their feet as ours do their hands. They hold between their feet a log as big as a girder, round, even, and smooth, which they toss into the air and catch, spinning it a couple of thousand times, so cleverly and quickly that the eye can hardly follow it. Besides this, they perform other tricks and comical acts with astonishing skill and art. They also perform grotesque dances, in which three men mount one above the other, resting upon the shoulders of the bottom man, while the top man does extraordinary things.

Sometimes Montezuma would watch the game of *patolli*, which closely resembles our game of *tabas*. It is played with broad or split beans, used like dice, which they shake between their hands and cast upon a mat, or upon the ground, where a grid has been traced. Gamblers will wager all their goods in this game, and at times will even put up their bodies to be sold into slavery.

At other times Montezuma went to the *tlachtli*, or ball court. The ball itself is called *ullamalixtli*, which is made of the gum of the *ulli* [*hule*], a tree of the hot country. This tree, when slashed, oozes thick white drops that soon harden, and are gathered, mixed, and treated. The gum turns as black as pitch, but does not stain. It is rolled into balls which, although heavy and hard to the hand, bounce and jump very well, better than our inflated ones. The game is not played for points, but only for the final victory, which goes to the side that knocks the ball against the opponents' wall, or over it. The players may hit the ball with any part of the body they please, although certain strokes are penalized by loss of the ball. Hitting it with the hips or thighs is the most approved play, for which reason they protect those parts with leather shields. The game lasts as long as the ball is kept bouncing, and it bounces for a long time. They play for stakes, wagering, say, a load of cotton mantles, more or less, according to the means of the players. They also wager articles of gold and featherwork, and at times even put up their own bodies, as in the game of *patolli*.

The ball court is a low enclosure, long and narrow, higher at the sides than at the ends, built so purposely for the game. It is kept always whitewashed and smooth. Stones resembling millstones are set into the side walls, with holes cut through them, hardly big enough to allow passage for the ball. The player who shoots the ball through them (which rarely happens, because it would be a difficult thing to do even if one threw the ball by hand) wins the game and, by ancient law and custom of the players, also wins the capes of all the spectators. He is then, however, obliged to sacrifice to the gods of the game and the stone. The spectators say that this fellow must be an adulterer or a thief, and will soon die.

Each ball court is also a temple, and images of the god of the game are set upon the two lower walls. This is done at midnight on a day of favorable omen, with certain ceremonies and magic rites, while the same rites are celebrated in the middle of the court, and ballads are sung to commemorate the occasion. Then a priest from the main temple, accompanied by other religious, comes to bless it. After speaking a few words, he throws the ball four times around the court, which is thus consecrated and can be used for playing, but by no means before. Montezuma took the Spaniards to see this game and showed the greatest pleasure at its performance, as he also showed at the Spaniards' games of cards and dice.

THE DANCES OF MEXICO
Another pastime of Montezuma's much enjoyed by the court and even by the whole city was a dance performed after he had dined, either at his command or by the townspeople for his service and pleasure. It was called *netotelixtli,* a dance of rejoicing and merri-

ment, and was performed in the following manner: Long before it began, a large mat was spread in the courtyard and upon it two drums were placed, a large one called a *teponaxtli,* made of a single piece of wood, very well carved, hollow, but without a skin or parchment head, although it is played with drumsticks like our own. The other is very large, tall, round, and thick, like our drums, hollow, carved, and painted. Over one end a tanned deerskin is very tightly stretched: the more tightly, the higher the tone; the more loosely, the lower. It is played with the hands, without sticks, and has a deep bass tone. The songs are joyful and merry, or they are ballads in praise of past kings, reciting their wars, victories, deeds, and the like. It is all done in rhyme and has a very pleasing effect.

When the time comes to start, eight or more men whistle very loudly and beat the drums softly. Then the dancers come on, dressed in rich mantles woven of many colors, white, red, green, and yellow; in their hands, bunches of roses or plumes, or fans of feathers and gold. Many carry wreaths of flowers, very fragrant; others wear feather caps or masks made to represent the heads of eagles, tigers, alligators, and other wild beasts.

At times there are as many as a thousand dancers, or at least four hundred, all of them noble and important persons, and even lords. They dance in rings, their hands joined, one ring within the other. They are led by two agile and skillful dancers, and all obey these two leaders: if the leaders sing, the whole chorus responds, sometimes more, sometimes less, just as is done here and elsewhere. It is done with no little grace, and with such a feeling for unity that no one gets out of step. So wildly do they dance, indeed, that it is quite amazing. At the beginning the dancers sing ballads and move slowly, playing, singing, and dancing quietly and with much gravity; but as they get warmer they sing popular ditties and gay songs; the dance is livelier, and they move quickly and vigorously. At times also the buffoons come out, mimicking other peoples in dress and speech, playing the drunk, the fool, or the old woman, to the vast entertainment of the spectators.

Everyone who has seen this dance says it is a fine thing to watch, better than the *zambra* of the Moors, which is the best dance we know here. It is much better when performed by women than by men, but in Mexico women do not dance it in public.

The Siege and Fall of Mexico
by Bernal Díaz del Castillo

*More than two years elapsed between the arrival of the Spaniards in 1519
and the end of the siege of Mexico in 1521. Bernal Díaz wrote later: "There
was never a time when we were not subject to surprises so dangerous that but
for God's help they would have cost us our lives. We never took off our armor,
gorgets, or leggings by night or day." Their Tlaxcalan auxiliaries and Doña
Marina warned Cortés that at any moment they might be attacked. In his
account of the Conquest of New Spain, Bernal Díaz describes some of these
scenes and battles.*

These battles lasted all day, and during the night, too, many
bands attacked us, hurling javelins, sling stones, arrows, and stray
stones in such numbers that they covered the courtyard and the
surrounding ground like corn on a threshing floor.

We spent the night dressing our wounds, repairing the breaches
the enemy had made in the walls, and preparing for next day. As
soon as dawn broke our Captain decided that we and Narvaez' men
combined should sally out and fight them, taking our cannon,
muskets, and crossbows, and endeavoring to defeat them, or at
least to make them feel our strength and valor better than the day
before. I may say that when we were forming this plan the enemy
was deciding on similar measures. We fought very well, but they
were so strong and had so many bands which relieved one another
by turns, that if we had had ten thousand Trojan Hectors and as
many Rolands, even then we should not have been able to break
through.

We were struck by the tenacity of their fighting, which was
beyond description. Neither cannon, muskets, nor crossbows were
of any avail, nor hand-to-hand combat, nor the slaughter of thirty
or forty of them every time we charged. They still fought on
bravely and with more vigor than before. If at times we were
gaining a little ground or clearing part of a street, they would
pretend to make a retreat, in order to lure us into following them.

By thus attacking at less risk, they believed they would prevent us from struggling back alive, for they did us most damage when we were retiring.

Then, as to going out and burning their houses, I have already described the drawbridges between them, which they now raised so that we could only get across through deep water. Then we could not stand up to the rocks and stones which they hurled from the roofs in such numbers that many of our men were hurt or wounded. I do not know why I am writing so calmly, for some three or four soldiers of our company who had served in Italy swore to God many times that they had never seen such fierce fighting, not even in Christian wars, or against the French king's artillery, or the Great Turk; nor had they ever seen men so courageous as those Indians at charging with closed ranks.

DEATH OF MONTEZUMA
In view of this situation, Cortés decided that the great Montezuma must speak to them from the roof and tell them that the attacks must cease, since we wished to leave the city.

While the fighting continued, Montezuma was lifted to a battlement of the roof with many of us soldiers guarding him, and began to speak very lovingly to his people, telling them that if they stopped their attacks we would leave Mexico. Many of the Mexican chiefs and captains recognized him and ordered their people to be silent and shoot no more darts, stones, or arrows, and four of them, coming to a place where Montezuma could speak to them and they to him, addressed him in tears: "Oh lord, our great lord, we are indeed sorry for your misfortune and the disaster that has overtaken you and your family. But we must tell you that we have chosen a kinsman of yours as our new lord." They said moreover that the war must be carried on, and that they had promised their idols not to give up until we were all dead.

Barely was this speech finished when a sudden shower of stones and darts descended. Our men who had been shielding Montezuma had momentarily neglected their duty when they saw the attack cease while he spoke to his chiefs. Montezuma was hit by three stones, one on the head, one on the arm, and one on the leg; and though they begged him to have his wounds dressed and eat some food and spoke very kindly to him, he refused. Then quite unexpectedly we were told that he was dead.

Cortés and all of us captains and soldiers wept for him, and there was no one among us that knew him and had dealings with him who did not mourn him as if he were our father, which was not surprising, since he was so good. It was stated that he had reigned for seventeen years, and was the best king they ever had in Mexico, and that he had personally triumphed in three wars against countries he had subjugated.

THE SAD NIGHT

Now we saw our forces diminishing every day, and the Mexicans increasing in numbers. Many of our men had died, and all the rest were wounded. Though we fought most valiantly, we could not drive back the many bands which attacked us by night and day, or force them to a standstill. We became short of powder, and then of food and water. We had sent to ask them for a truce, but because of Montezuma's death they would not leave us in peace. In fact we stared death in the face, and the bridges had been raised.

It was therefore decided by Cortés and all of us captains and soldiers that we should depart during the night, choosing the moment when their warriors were most careless. And to put them off their guard, on that very afternoon we sent one of their *papas* whom we had captured, a man of great importance among them, with some other prisoners, to propose that they should let us retire within eight days, leaving them all the gold. But this was only in order to distract their attention, so that we could get out that night.

Cortés ordered Cristóbal de Gúzman his steward, and other soldiers who were his servants, to have all the gold and jewels and silver brought out. He gave them many Tlaxcalans to do the work, and it was all placed in the hall. Cortés then told the King's officials, Alonso de Avila and Gonzalo Mejía, to take charge of the royal portion. He gave them seven wounded and lame horses and one mare and more than eighty of our Tlaxcalan allies, and they loaded men and animals alike with as much as each could carry. It was, as I have said, made up into very broad ingots, but much gold still remained piled up in the hall. Then Cortés called his secretary, and others who were the King's notaries, and said: "Bear witness for me that I can do no more with this gold. Here in this hall we have more than seven hundred thousand pesos' worth, and as you have seen, it cannot be weighed or brought to safety. I now give it over to any soldiers who care to take it. Otherwise we shall lose it to these dogs."

On hearing this, many of Narvaez' men and some of ours loaded themselves with it. I had no desire, I assure you, but to save my life. Nevertheless I picked up four *chalchihuites* from the little boxes in which they lay, and quickly stowed them in my bosom, under my armor. The price of them afterwards served to cure my wounds and buy me food.

As soon as we knew Cortés' plan that we should escape during the night, we prepared to move toward the bridges. Fearing that we should inevitably be killed, we pushed ahead along the causeway, where we found many bands with long spears awaiting us. They shouted abuse at us. "Villains," they cried, "are you still alive?" Although six of my companions were wounded, we cut and hacked our way through.

It was a destructive battle, and a fearful sight to behold. We moved through the midst of them at the closest quarters, slashing and thrusting at them with our swords. And the dogs fought back furiously, dealing us wounds and death with their lances and their two-handed swords.

The retreat took four days. Cortés made a final stand at Otumba, where he was met by his allies, the Tlaxcalans; and the Mexicans followed them no farther. When Cortés counted their losses, more than two-thirds of the Spaniards had been killed or sacrificed. They had lost most of their gold and treasure. Doña Marina had survived, but many other women and slaves had not.

Cortés spent the next eight months planning to recapture the city. He obtained supplies and reinforcements from Cuba and built a fleet of thirteen sloops with which to lead the attack.

Guatemoc, or Cuauhtemoc, a nephew of Montezuma, was now emperor of the Aztecs. The final siege was more bloody and devastating than all the other battles. This time the Spanish forces were overwhelming. Finally, Guatemoc was captured and taken before Cortés.

CAPTURE OF GUATEMOC

On appearing before him Guatemoc treated our Captain with great respect, and Cortés, embracing him joyfully, treated him and his captains with a great show of affection. "Lord Malinche," said Guatemoc, "I have assuredly done my duty in defense of my city and my vassals, and I can do no more. I am brought by force as a prisoner into your presence and beneath your power. Take the dagger that you have in your belt, and strike me dead immediately." He sobbed as he spoke and the tears fell from his eyes, and the other great lords whom he brought with him wept also. Cortés answered him very kindly through our interpreters that he admired him greatly for having had the bravery to defend his city, and did not blame him at all.

Guatemoc was very delicate, both in body and features. His face was long but cheerful, and when his eyes dwelt on you they seemed more grave than gentle, and did not waver. He was twenty-six, and his complexion was rather lighter than the brown of most Indians. They said he was a nephew of Montezuma, the son of one of his sisters; and he was married to one of Montezuma's daughters, a young and beautiful woman.

It rained and thundered that evening, and the lightning flashed, and up to midnight heavier rain fell than usual. After Guatemoc's capture all we soldiers became as deaf as if all the bells in a belfry had been ringing and had then suddenly stopped. I say this because during the whole ninety-three days of our siege of the capital, Mexican captains were yelling and shouting night and day, mustering the bands of warriors who were to fight on the causeway, and calling to the men in the canoes who were to attack the launches and struggle with us on the bridges and build barricades, or to those who were driving in piles, and deepening and widening the channels and bridges, and building breastworks, or to those who were making javelins and arrows, or to the women shaping rounded stones for their slings. Then there was the unceasing sound of their accursed drums and trumpets, and their melancholy kettledrums in the shrines and on their temple towers. Both day and night the din was so great that we could hardly hear one another speak. But after Guatemoc's capture, all the shouting and the other noises ceased, which is why I have made the comparison with a belfry.

Now to speak of the dead bodies and heads that were in the houses where Guatemoc had taken refuge. I solemnly swear that all the houses and stockades in the lake were full of heads and corpses. I do not know how to describe it but it was the same in the streets and courts of Tlatelolco. We could not walk without treading on the bodies and heads of dead Indians. I have read about the destruction of Jerusalem, but I do not think the mortality was greater there than here in Mexico, where most of the warriors who had crowded in from all the provinces and subject towns had died. As I have said, the dry land and the stockades were piled with corpses. Indeed, the stench was so bad that no one could endure it, and for that reason each of us captains returned to his camp after Guatemoc's capture; even Cortés was ill from the odors which assailed his nostrils and from headache during those days in Tlatelolco.

When the news spread through all these distant provinces that Mexico was destroyed their *Caciques* and lords could not believe it. However, they sent chieftains to congratulate Cortés on his victories and yield themselves as vassals to His Majesty, and to see if the city of Mexico, which they had so dreaded, was really razed to the ground. They all carried great presents of gold to Cortés, and even brought their small children to show them Mexico, pointing it out to them in much the same way that we would say: "Here stood Troy."

Broken Spears
by Anonymous Náhuatl Authors

For the Aztecs, the destruction of their city and the smashing of their idols was not only a battle lost. It was the end of a way of life. Their emperor Guatemoc was tortured after he surrendered, in spite of Cortés' promises. Other chiefs and leaders were killed or thrown to the dogs. Prisoners were branded as slaves. It was a terrible time for a proud people. According to their custom, Aztec poets composed songs of sorrow in the traditional manner. These poems, which have been preserved in a document called "Manuscript 22" in the National Library in Paris, were written down by anonymous natives of Tlatelolco within two or three years after the tragic fall of the city. The misfortunes of war were still fresh in their minds and hearts.

BROKEN SPEARS

Broken spears lie in the roads;
we have torn our hair in our grief.
The houses are roofless now, and their walls
are red with blood.

Worms are swarming in the streets and plazas,
and the walls are splattered with gore.
The water has turned red, as if it were dyed,
and when we drink it,
it has the taste of brine.

We have pounded our hands in despair
against the adobe walls,
for our inheritance, our city, is lost and dead.
The shields of our warriors were its defense,
but they could not save it.

We have chewed dry twigs and salt grasses;
we have filled our mouths with dust and bits of adobe;
we have eaten lizards, rats and worms. . . .

30

SONG OF SORROW

Nothing but flowers and songs of sorrow
are left in Mexico and Tlatelolco,
where once we saw warriors and wise men.

We know it is true
that we must perish,
for we are mortal men.
You, the Giver of Life,
you have ordained it.

We wander here and there
in our desolate poverty.
We are mortal men.
We have seen bloodshed and pain
where once we saw beauty and valor.

We are crushed to the ground;
we lie in ruins.
There is nothing but grief and suffering
in Mexico and Tlatelolco,
where once we saw beauty and valor.

Have you grown weary of your servants?
Are you angry with your servants,
O Giver of Life?

PART 2
EVERY DAY IS FIESTA TIME

The Art of the Fiesta
by Octavio Paz

Every day is fiesta time, somewhere in Mexico. A little fiesta may last for a day only, a big fiesta for as long as two weeks. If the fiesta is an important one, like the one before Lent, the whole town or village is decorated with colorful paper streamers, and people from the hills or nearby villages start coming into town several days in advance. Some stay with friends or relatives, but the greater number simply sleep in the main plaza or along the side streets. They may cook their meals on braziers, or buy tortillas and chili from itinerant vendors. At night, they sleep rolled up in their serapes or on straw mats called petates, *oblivious to any discomfort. After all, the joy of the fiesta is ahead.*

The art of the fiesta has been debased almost everywhere else, but not in Mexico. There are few places in the world where it is possible to take part in a spectacle like our great religious fiestas with their violent primary colors, their bizarre costumes and dances, their fireworks and ceremonies, and their inexhaustible welter of surprises: the fruit, candy, toys and other objects sold on these days in the plazas and open-air markets.

Our calendar is crowded with fiestas. There are certain days when the whole country, from the most remote villages to the largest cities, prays, shouts, feasts, gets drunk and kills, in honor of the Virgin of Guadalupe or Benito Juárez. Each year on the

32

fifteenth of September, at eleven o'clock at night, we celebrate the fiesta of the *Grito*, the cry for independence, in all the plazas of the Republic, and the excited crowds actually shout for a whole hour . . . the better, perhaps, to remain silent for the rest of the year. During the days before and after the twelfth of December, the fiesta of the Virgin of Guadalupe, time comes to a full stop, and instead of pushing us toward a deceptive tomorrow that is always beyond our reach, offers us a complete and perfect today of dancing and revelry, of communion with the most ancient and secret Mexico. Time is no longer succession, and becomes what it originally was and is: the present, in which past and future are reconciled.

But the fiestas which the Church and State provide for the country as a whole are not enough. The life of every city and village is ruled by a patron saint whose blessing is celebrated with devout regularity. Neighborhoods and trades also have their annual fiestas, their ceremonies and fairs. And each one of us—atheist, Catholic, or merely indifferent—has his own saint's day, which he observes every year. It is impossible to calculate how many fiestas we have and how much time and money we spend on them. I remember asking the mayor of a village near Mitla, several years ago, "What is the income of the village government?" "About 3,000 pesos a year. We are very poor. But the Governor and the Federal Government always help us to meet our expenses." "And how are the 3,000 pesos spent?" "Mostly on fiestas, señor. We are a small village, but we have two patron saints."

This reply is not surprising. Our poverty can be measured by the frequency and luxuriousness of our holidays. Wealthy countries have very few: there is neither the time nor the desire for them, and they are not necessary. The people have other things to do, and when they amuse themselves they do so in small groups. The modern masses are agglomerations of solitary individuals. On great occasions in Paris or New York, when the populace gathers in the squares or stadiums, the absence of people, in the sense of *a* people, is remarkable: there are couples and small groups, but they never form a living community in which the individual is at once dissolved and redeemed. But how could a poor Mexican live without the two or three annual fiestas that make up for his poverty and misery? Fiestas are our only luxury. They replace, and are perhaps better than, the theater and vacations, Anglo-Saxon week-ends and cocktail parties, the bourgeois reception, the Mediterranean café.

In all of these ceremonies—national or local, trade or family—the Mexican opens out. They all give him a chance to reveal himself and to converse with God, country, friends or relations. During these days the silent Mexican whistles, shouts, sings, shoots off fireworks, discharges his pistol into the air. He discharges his soul. And his shout, like the rockets we love so much, ascends to the heavens, explodes into green, red, blue, and white lights, and falls dizzily to earth with a trail of golden sparks.

This is the night when friends who have not exchanged more than the prescribed courtesies for months get drunk together, trade confidences, weep over the same troubles, discover that they are brothers, and sometimes, to prove it, kill each other. The night is full of songs and loud cries. The lover wakes up his sweetheart with an orchestra. There are jokes and conversations from balcony to balcony, sidewalk to sidewalk. Nobody talks quietly. Hats fly in the air. Laughter and curses ring like silver pesos. Guitars are brought out.

Now and then, it is true, the happiness ends badly, in quarrels, insults, pistol shots, stabbings. But these too are part of the fiesta, for the Mexican does not seek amusement: he seeks to escape from himself, to leap over the wall of solitude that confines him during the rest of the year. All are possessed by violence and frenzy. Their souls explode like the colors and voices and emotions. Do they forget themselves and show their true faces? Nobody knows. The important thing is to go out, open a way, get drunk on noise, people, colors. Mexico is celebrating a fiesta.

FIESTAS

Every day is fiesta time somewhere in Mexico. Fiestas for the most important religious holidays, such as the Day of the Dead, Holy Week, and Christmas, often last two weeks. There are fireworks, music, dancing, and pageants.

The Fiesta of the Flyers. The *Voladores* are men dressed in eagle feathers, who leap from a platform high in the air and swing from their feet in great circles. (*National Museum of Anthropology, Mexico City*)

Right: The Indians had no stringed instruments until the Spaniards came. The Spaniards introduced many new instruments which were adopted by the Mexicans. One of these is the guitar, which Mexicans use to accompany their folk ballads. The youth from San Luis Potosí is playing a lyre-type instrument. (*National Museum of Anthropology, Mexico City*)

Below: The flute and the drum were the most important of the old Indian instruments. This picture of a procession in Puebla shows one of the long horizontal drums. (*National Museum of Anthropology, Mexico City*)

Above: Flutes used by the Indians were made of wood, clay, reed, bone, or shell. This flute player also beats out the rhythm on a small drum. (*National Museum of Anthropology, Mexico City*)

The Dance of the Quetzal Bird goes back to pre-Conquest times. The enormous wheel-shaped headdresses are made of bamboo and colored paper or silk to imitate the plumage of the quetzal bird. The dance itself is very simple, the dancers marking the rhythm with rattles. (*National Museum of Anthropology, Mexico City*)

Tom Lea, in THE BRAVE BULLS, calls the *corrida*, or bullfight, "the only art form in which violence, bloodshed and death are palpable and unfeigned." Here are four scenes from a festival of the bulls in the world's largest bullring, the Plaza México, in Mexico City. *(William H. Field)*

In this opening procession, the matadors have just passed, and here come some of their *peónes*, the supporting cast that will play their traditional roles in the spectacle to come.

The *corrida* is a ballet of bravery and of "death in the afternoon," sometimes for the matador, always for the brave bull.

This time the matador was soon back in the fight, after attending to a bloody nose.

El toro, the bull, as always, starts his final journey to the butcher.

Above: The Dance of the Old Men of Patzcuaro, held on Saturday nights in villages around the largest lake in Michoacán, is actually performed by agile young men wearing masks and hats of Indian origin. Playing the part of decrepit old men, they stumble and clown their way through very energetic steps and jumps, pushing and tapping with their canes. (*National Museum of Anthropology, Mexico City*)

Right: The Deer Dance was originally designed to bring good luck in hunting. Now, it is a favorite at fiestas. One man impersonates the deer. He dances with bare torso and bare feet, shaking a gourd as he acts out the chase and the kill. (*National Museum of Anthropology, Mexico City*)

Left: Holy Week begins on Palm Sunday in San Luis Potosí with the blessing of palms. In churches all over Mexico, worshippers wear fiesta clothes and carry something to be blessed: palms, flowers, fruits, *pinole* balls, or decorated crosses. (*National Museum of Anthropology, Mexico City*)

The Dance of the Moors and the Christians was introduced after the Conquest. The costumes and masks use vivid Indian colors. The dance takes the form of sham battles, in which swords, lances, machetes, and guns produce a clashing noise to the beat of drums and the piping of flutes. *(National Museum of Anthropology, Mexico City)*

A painting of the Virgin of Guadalupe is carried by a fiesta procession in Puebla on December 12. *(National Museum of Anthropology, Mexico City)*

Fiesta of the Flyers
by Gustav Regler

One of the most spectacular sights in Mexico is the Dance of the Voladores, the flying men dressed in eagle feathers who leap from a platform high in the air and swing from their feet in great circles. This beautiful and dangerous spectacle goes back to the time of the Aztecs when it was the climax of the fiesta held at the end of the fifty-two-year cycle. In modern times, the Dance of the Flyers is performed only in the town of Papantla in the state of Vera Cruz.

For a long time I was unsure whether there remained a single peasant in the land who consciously invoked the old god. That was before I went to Papantla, to the Fiesta of the Flyers, the *voladores*. Years ago the peasants had noticed a certain tree growing deep in the jungle. This year it seemed to them tall enough to support their dance of invocation upon its crown. So they felled it and brought it to the district capital, where it was stripped and embedded firmly in the plaza immediately opposite the church, almost a bold defiance of the Christian temple by ancient heathendom. Did the peasants know this? Was their gesture deliberate?

I had never ascribed such knowledge to them; there are so many traditions in this country, many of which are mutually contradictory; idols merge; ancient cults are covered with a modern varnish; no one has attempted an analysis, and the Church is satisfied with the Indians' pious devotion to the new symbols.

On this occasion, however, I was proved wrong. One of the dancers taught me.

We were seated among a crowd of Totonacs, on the steps of the church, waiting for the spectacle to begin. The women wore white lace bonnets which provide a delicate frame to the nobility of their brown faces.

An American engineer was explaining that this fiesta would soon be a thing of the past. The dancers received 500 pesos, but the local authorities had discovered that it was no longer worth investing such a sum, since the central government had forbidden gambling in the market place, and therefore not enough Indians now came to the town. There may have been, and probably was, some truth in this materialistic explanation of the day's ceremony, but it was certainly no more than half the truth. The dancers were inspired by motives other than a simple desire to please the tourist bureau.

They were assembled on the platform which had been built upon the top of the tree trunk and which was so constructed that it could revolve. Four were seated awaiting the signal which would send them leaping outwards in all directions, each on the end of his rope. They now began to make the platform revolve and with it the principal dancer, who stood over them in his brilliant, red-and-blue-striped costume.

Almost as soon as the platform began to move, he started his dance. He bowed to the four winds, summoning them with his flute. He leaned over backward as though offering his body to Tlaloc for a sacrifice. From one of his fingers holding the flute there hung a little drum which he beat with his free hand. He bowed four times: there are four mansions of heaven.

He stood so indescribably alone, up there in the sky, utterly cut off from us spectators, in a space which we all seemed to have lost, and yet in his dance he re-created that space, for us as well as for himself.

As soon as he played his flute, *zopilotes* came out of the woods; they circled about him in great arcs.

He was already in complete ecstasy. But how minute was his world! A platform four feet squre, yet he stamped his feet like a stubborn animal demanding its rights. On his head there glittered countless small mirrors, heliographs directed at the mountain of the gods whence the rain must come. Sometimes he bowed so low that his body seemed to become a bow drawn against the sky. We gaped up at him, open-mouthed.

Then he fell silent. It was the signal for the four men crouching below him to hurl themselves out into space.

Their flight was like that of a family of eagles. The Mexican beside me, a highly educated photographer from the capital named Antonio Reynoso, remarked: "Hunting for men's hearts."

He raised his camera to catch their flight. Later he said, much to the astonishment of the American engineer: "It is very Mexican: the small space for dancing and all around the void that is death."

Then he placed a new film in his camera and, as though the movement of the spool had reminded him of the trick whereby a cinema reel can be run off backwards, added: "What great circles to finish in so small a space!" At that moment as it happened the dancers were ending their circles down below, leaping along the ground to the delight of the children. The photographer really saw it all backward; his eyes, being those of a true Mexican, followed the ropes up to that high point where death threatened; the security now reached by the flyers interested him not at all. Up above was death, the gamble with death, up above was the reality of life.

But only now did the excitement begin.

Normally, once the flyers have flown, the principal dancer climbs slowly and steadily down the tree trunk; when the "eagles" have left the nest below him his prayer is ended.

This year he began instead to play his flute once more. He stamped upon the platform, he leaned further over backward than ever, he beat his drum with mounting frenzy.

We knew that this was against the normal custom and were surprised. He went on more stubbornly than ever, almost with despair.

The town bosses had this year permitted two of the dancers to dress up in the costume of Cantinflas, the national clown. The principal dancer had reluctantly agreed to this.

But at the moment of their flight the two clowns had gone further. They had yelled and mimed, feigning fear; they had perverted the noble gestures of the eagle's glide into circus tumblings.

The dancer above them had seen this with angry eyes. The laughter of the tourists and of the children seemed to him to destroy all the magic power of his invocation. (Later he said as much in his own simple language to my Mexican friend, who had been equally disgusted at the sight of such profanation.)

Therefore, when it was all over, he took his flute in his brown fingers once again, threw his body backward in ever-bolder gestures and repeated his prayer in which he had a faith far deeper than had all those watchers down below.

He was the last, solitary incarnation of a peasant priesthood which believed that by music and by bodily surrender the forces of Nature could be convinced and compelled to kindness.

I shall never forget him, rising up against the heavens, begging, demanding, cursing, calling. There was so much space about him, so much that had vanished finally and forever.

And his faith was bitterly justified that year: the rains came later than usual. It is foolish to laugh at Tlaloc: such jokes do not go unpunished.

Blessing of the Animals
by J. W. F. Stoppelman

Among the many celebrations on the church calendar in Mexico, the Blessing of the Animals is one of the simplest and most enchanting. Ever since the time of St. Francis, the love of God has been extended to animals as well as people. At the Santa Prisca in Taxco, the beautiful church built by the silver king, José de la Borda, the blessing of the animals takes place in the name of St. Anthony.

Toward 3:30 Raquel came to warn me that it was time to go and see the animals blessed. She herself was taking her giant blue, green and yellow parrot Lolita to the portals of the Santa Prisca Cathedral. The bird cage had been painstakingly decorated with tiny festoons of pink and silver paper, and Lolita wore a green ribbon most unconcernedly around her right leg.

Together we walked down the Street of the Silversmiths, passed the Paco Bar that seems to watch over the Church Square, and went straight to the steps of the Santa Prisca. We were the first to arrive.

The January sun was shining hotly, and soon began to worry Lolita who, in a high, peevish voice, called upon all the world to witness her discomfort. But Raquel discovered shelter for her in the shadow of the cathedral, close to the makeshift altar at which the blessing of the animals was to take place.

A comfortable hush lay over the square. The benches were occupied by only a few relaxing citizens and tourists; the jukeboxes in the two open-air cafés were silent. Up on the hill, in front of the pink walls of the Taxco Art School, people had gathered: it is a good spot from which to see all that happens in the Zócalo and around the richly sculptured gates of the Santa Prisca.

At half past four there was a new arrival, a carefully groomed burro with a big drooping head. His master, a boy in tattered shirt and old denims, began to work hard and devotedly at fashioning a green paper collar for the burro's shaggy neck.

39

"Raquel—what's up?" I asked. "Where are the animals?"

"Ah, señor," she smiled, "San Antonio is in no hurry. This is *his* day, all day long. And when he's ready to bless our animals, it will happen!"

And so she, Lolita and I sat in the shade of the cathedral porch, looking at perilously maneuvering taxis, and at Gaspetta, the Taxco garbage collector, who sauntered around the square, flicking his palm-leaf broom at an occasional bit of refuse.

Then, all at once, the animals and their owners appeared from around every corner. They came along the path beside the church which leads steeply down to the covered booths of the market; they approached through the narrow lanes that emerge upon the Zócalo. They seemed to materialize out of nothing at all; and soon the open space within the church railings was completely filled with them.

There were dogs of all shapes and sizes: on the leash, pressed against the chests of their young owners or prancing along freely; all of them gaily beribboned, or wearing little bouquets of wild flowers in their collars. There were also tiny yellow canaries, one with miniature earrings somehow fastened at the sides of its head; parrots, some outside, some inside their steel prisons, making guttural protests against the crush in which they were caught. There were red-eyed rabbits, a couple of sharp-nosed badgers and an endless variety of chickens, their feathers neatly brushed, their legs bound together. They clucked nervously, jerking their heads; for them this was just another annoying trip to market. But the most attractive animal was a young white goat, dyed a russet-brown from its short tail to its melancholy face. Decorated with inch-wide blue ribbons that ran the length of his backbone and were fastened around his body, he resembled a parcel in special gift wrapping.

"Now the priest is coming soon!" Raquel assured me, and she added: "You understand, señor, I've got to stay right here near the altar. Lolita will be the very first to get blessed!" But others had meantime discovered our delectable shelter; and soon we found ourselves in the company of two white mice, a slate-blue pigeon, a black-and-white kitten with frightened yellow eyes and four assorted dogs.

But still no priest.

An Indian woman in a magenta blouse and yellow skirt pushed

her way through the crowd. Wrapped in her shawl was an object that from a distance resembled a very small baby. Her wrinkled face wore a determined expression. Her large black eyes smiled, but it was clear that she had made up her mind to join the front ranks of those waiting. When finally, with much jostling, she had reached that vantage point, she drew back her rebozo and proudly exhibited a most unhappy-looking cat.

Undoubtedly the poor thing had once been white, with black spots—still faintly visible—above both eyes. Now it had been dyed all the colors of the spectrum. Green and red and pale blue along its haunches and down its dainty legs; its tail was a muddy grey. In the middle of its forehead was a large red spot, and upon its chest an orange sun had been painted. To crown this work of art, the animal wore a fine gilt chain around its neck, with a tiny medal of St. Anthony. There were loud cries of admiration, and the children crowded round trying to stroke the little cat with affectionate hands.

Suddenly everyone pushed forward, so forcefully that a little boy with a white, wing-clipped dove upon his head narrowly missed being catapulted into the altar. Two donkeys, tired of waiting, had climbed the steps, poking their broad, flat faces into everything obstructing their progress.

It was a quarter past five. The sun still beat down upon the masses, and little girls in multicolored fiesta dresses tried to protect their pets against suffocation. Across the square came an aged Indian workman in white cottons, his broad-brimmed straw hat throwing a deep shadow upon his thin face. His sandals were covered with dust; he had come a long way down the mountain trails. Carrying two week-old piglets under his arms, he shyly remained in the background, but allowed a boy to fasten red paper ribbons around the fat necks of his animals.

All at once someone cried: "The priest's coming!" In one mighty heave the whole crowd surged towards the cathedral. "Por aquí," shouted hundreds of voices, "Por aquí"—and hands, small and large, smooth and gnarled, clean and dirty, held up high an enormous variety of birds and animals to receive St. Anthony's blessing.

The priest, young and good-looking, a broad smile on his brown Indian face, stood before the altar and besought the crowd to be calm. He then pronounced all these creatures of God, these friends and helpers of humanity, free of evil taint or diabolical influence. He sprinkled holy water over them, time and again, in wide, sweeping curves. An eager young girl, holding a gobbling turkey under one arm and balancing a brown chicken upon a shoulder, tried to lift a fat, baby-faced puppy high enough to get its share of the sprinkling.

Slowly the priest advanced, wielding his brush and endeavoring to reach as many animals as possible. The Indian woman with the colored cat walked backward as the priest advanced, and so managed to catch another few blessings for her pet. But now the crowd began to disperse. Excited and happy, the children showed off their animals, and argued among themselves as to which had had the most generous sprinkling, and thus the biggest blessing.

Meanwhile the group of larger animals at the side of the church had grown considerably. There were many mules now, and horses, and cattle with wreaths of purple and blood-red flowers around their horns. There were sheep with gilt hoofs, and two pitch-black lambs sporting red ribbons. The smiling priest approached, and the Indians who had led their beasts to Taxco from miles around bowed their heads and folded their hands. The gentle spray of the holy water descended not merely upon their animals but on them as well.

For a while the priest remained standing in front of the beautiful cathedral, so as not to disappoint the late-comers. At length he turned and went into the cool dimness of the church with short, hurried steps.

Raquel was awaiting me on a bench in the Zócalo. She held up the cage with Lolita for me to admire, and said, with a satisfied grin: "I told you, señor, Lolita would be the very first to be blessed —and she *was*!"

The bird looked at its mistress with sleepily closing eyes. It lifted its colorful head, intoning the first few notes of *La donn' è mobile*. And then, in its high, piping child's voice, it rasped, while winking at Raquel: "Oh, you stinker! . . . Oh, you stinker!"

Pilgrimage
by Dane Chandos

Our Lady of Guadalupe may be the most important virgin in Mexico, but there are others of great power and purity. One of these is Our Lady of Zapopan, a tiny doll-like virgin, only a foot high. Brought to Jalisco by the first settlers from Spain, she is loaded with jewels and antiquity. Ever since the seventeenth century, when terrible storms ravaged Guadalajara, she travels from church to church during the rainy season, staying two weeks in each. They say that storms have never been so violent since. In October each year, she is taken back to her own shrine at Zapopan, outside the city of Guadalajara, accompanied by a great pilgrimage.

Many Ajijic folk go to Zapopan every year, those who travel afoot or on donkeyback setting out three or four days in advance, for though it is no great distance and the fiesta lasts officially one day only, the whole jaunt takes a week. This year Venustiano had taken a vow to make the pilgrimage, goaded as usual, I think, by his wife. We found him in his yard pruning a castor-oil tree so as to let in the sunlight to a small, tired-looking begonia cutting.

"Oh yes, I'm going," he said, swinging his serape around him with the air of a Roman senator. "They say it's a very fine fiesta, if you care for things of that sort."

The Lady herself starts before dawn from the Church of San Felipe, riding in a carriage whose roof is surmounted by a huge crown of fresh flowers. Behind the carriage walk the plumed, caparisoned black horses, for they are never allowed to draw the Lady's coach but are always replaced by pious human muscle. For months now, in church after church throughout the city, she has stood in splendor, stiff and jeweled and adored, a flame of flowers and candles tiered in worship beneath her pedestal.

Now she was going home to her white church amid the quiet groves of Zapopan. And she did not go alone. Around her and after her came the pilgrims, and before her they streamed in their thousands down the dark road: poor women muffled in shawls, some praying as they went, some kneeling down every ten paces; rich girls, with hair elaborately arranged under the black chiffon veil, with mother and aunts hovering at their sides to help them over rough places, for they were barefoot, having taken a vow; Indios lying down, rising, lying down again, measuring the whole road out from the city with their bodies; others half naked, their flesh pierced by cactus thorns.

A well-dressed city boy went by, his face, in the flare of a torch, long and yellow and solemn, out of a Spanish picture, his eyes fixed ahead high up in the darkness and his bare feet bleeding. Then there were the dancers.

All the way down the road the groups were scattered, thirty or forty strong, unearthly under the fire of torches, magic under the rainbow-colored umbrellas of rocket-borne stars, each group in a different fancy dress, each doing a different step, each with its little band of musicians, fiddling, blowing horns and fifes, and drumming out on rattles its sharp, individual rhythm. The firecrackers snapped; the metal disks clattered. Nightmare faces appeared and vanished in the gloom—here, broad, Mongoloid features smothered in lipstick and glittering sequins; there, a flour-white vacuous mask, glassy-eyed, whose long black beard rippled over its wearer's brown chest. All the way amid gusts of incense and garlic, dancing and prancing, in faith and folly, wondrous and infantile and pathetic; all the way, out from the city to the wide gracious church in its great court among the cypresses; each year the Indios came dancing.

We were now more than halfway to Zapopan, and we climbed the high bank by the roadside to rest a little and watch the crowd go by. Already the eastern sky was smudged with the first streaks of tawny light. Behind us, sleek and green from the rains, calm and empty of people, stretched the most fashionable golf course in western Mexico. Before us, down the road, like a mountain river in spate, foamed and boiled the multitude of pilgrims. As the sun came up, the dark, sweaty Indio faces that had seemed masks became faces again, and the weird dresses—tinsel-banded trousers, shiny robes clasped on one shoulder, tinfoil crowns—seized real colors from the sunrise and stopped being momentary murky glitters. The twin spikes of turquoise light to our left, which had served as a beacon for the last two hours, faded into the ornate and silvery mass of Zapopan's domed and fretted towers.

And now we were at the end of our journey. Between ourselves and the massive carved portal milled ten or fifteen thousand people. All the way the road was lined with trophies of giant golden sunflowers bound up with sky-blue and white ribbons, the Lady's colors. On the sidewalk innumerable stall-keepers traded in soup, candles, ice cream, balloons, coffee, nuts, colored waters, tortillas, and confetti. Presently I was hailed from a rooftop by some Mexican friends. The door of the house was open, and the people were drifting in and out with the greatest self-possession in order to avail themselves of the drinking fountain, washbasins, and toilet. We went in and, finding a ladder, climbed up to the roof, where we were greeted by a number of kind people we had never seen.

From moment to moment the street presented scenes of ever-increasing animation. Fresh bands of dancers continually passed. Our host told us there were about sixty groups in all. Now, in daylight, it could be seen that for the most part the costumes followed the traditional patterns of Indio and conquistador, in endless permutations, though here and there was a Roman soldier. Still the crowd came pouring through. Little girls offered us streamers, flowers, and confetti to throw when the procession should arrive. A man with no legs went by, wielding his crutches with the utmost speed and agility, followed by his family of seven children, whose mother carried on her head a basket in which reposed a mountain of tortillas and a very small baby.

Smoke puffs filled the sky around us, and into the main street rode the first of the charros. They came in single file along either side of the street, horsemen of every age, and from every town in the state, their jackets frogged and embroidered, their sombreros laced with silver, whips in hand and lariats at the saddle bow, joking with the crowd and slowly closing their ranks to clear the center of the road for the procession that was to follow. Their horses were plump and glossy: blacks, chestnuts, bays, roans, and skewbalds, with here and there an elegant blond palomino. One or two women rode with the men, dressed mostly in the wide skirt and flower-embroidered blouse of the china poblana costume. They faced inward and dressed their ranks smartly. All the spectators on foot were now excluded from the center of the road, though at one moment, when the mayor's car edged its way through the barrier, it was followed amid shouts of laughter by a ragged urchin who capered gaily up the street, putting out his tongue at the dignified cavaliers to right and left.

Then came the procession. First a company of uniformed women—nurses, perhaps—came marching up the street followed by two bands and cars containing officials. When the bands had passed, we heard the singing, the stately solemn measure sung by the Lady's escort as they bore her through the kneeling crowds up the last slope into the town. Dancers preceded her, and a great company of singing Zapopanos bearing her blue and white flags; and these were followed by a concourse of women carrying baskets of every sort of flower, small bunches and huge trophies alike.

Then came the Lady herself. She rode in a modest four-wheeler, but two hundred youths drew her along with ropes of Mexican sisal. The carriage was almost hidden by banks of white flowers—camellias, roses, and gardenias—and a brightly jeweled crown of many-colored flowers adorned the roof. We could hear the clapping and cheers down the street, and, as the carriage passed, the watchers crossed themselves and bared their heads. And now we had a brief glance through the open window at the Lady herself. She was wearing no high coronet of diamonds, she was encased in no gemmed stomacher, and they had girt her with no jeweled sword. She wore a pilgrim's cloak and a little traveling hat tied beneath the chin with ribbons. So she journeyed home—gray-clad among her flowers, drawn by four hundred hands—home to the cool nave between the long columns that were fingers raised, not in admonition, but in triumphant thanksgiving for mercy, majesty, and glory.

Then we saw the American soldier. Among the drab clothes of the pilgrims and the gaudy costumes of the dancers, his uniform was the most exotic fancy dress of all. He stood there staring, and as the Lady went by, he gave her a military salute as if he knew she were a general. Maybe he should have bared his head like the rest. But he didn't. He saluted. Then, as the carriage rolled on and those who had lined the sidewalks swarmed to join the pilgrims, we lost sight of him.

Through the gates streamed the pilgrims, rich and poor, plenty of them people I knew. I saw the Governor and his staff go by. And then Venustiano came. He came with his free stride, this reader of Carlos Marx, and at the gate he knelt down, for that was the vow he had made, to go on his knees from the gates to the church

doors. Even on his knees he did not look humble, and his wrinkled
face gave no window to his thoughts. I looked at the turquoise-clad
group nearest me, where a man in a violet mantle of cheap satin
was dancing alone, and suddenly his gestures were significant and
his face was noble. After all, why not? All dedication is the same,
and the nostrils of heaven sniff impartially burnt offerings and
incense, sweat and gardenia.

I saw the American soldier watching, the dancers' parrot bright
beneath his khaki shoulders. He was tall and golden as a god, a
fair-haired Quetzal among his Indios, intent and solemn as they.
It was as though this were something he understood, this striving
and this dedication, as though the man in the violet mantle, and
the Indio there kneeling his way along, and he himself were all
pilgrims.

By now, inside the church, the Lady was enthroned again in a
misty glitter of prayer and diamonds. She was a high symbol, a flag,
and outside in her honor danced the Indios in their garish, gaudy
uniforms, and the American boy watching in his khaki dress stared
at them, and his eyes were huge as the ocean, solemn and lucid as
the eyes of Quetzal the god from across the sea.

The Day of the Dead
by Frances Toor

Religious fiestas in Mexico include many unique customs and beautiful cere-
monies which vary from village to village. There are special pageants and
processions for Holy Week and Christmas and for the Day of the Dead, which
involves a curious mixture of Christian and pagan traditions. On the Day
of the Dead, there are all-night ceremonies with candles or fireworks and
special foods for both the dead and the living. The ceremonies often continue
for days.

The Mexicans, fatalists that they are, accept death uncomplain-
ingly but also bravely. They fraternize, play, and joke with death
even while they weep. A typical attitude of the common man and
soldier is to be found in one of the most popular songs of the
Social Revolution of 1910–1920, entitled "Valentina." The lover
comes to see Valentina; he is in danger but his last words are: "If
I must be killed tomorrow, Let them kill me today."

The Day of the Dead, November 2, is a national holiday. For
days before and after, death is everywhere present. He leers invit-
ingly from bakery windows, where there are special *panes de muertos*
or the bread of the dead in animal and human forms; from candy
shops, in skulls with bright tinsel eyes. In the markets are sold
special candlesticks and censers and beautiful candles of all sizes
and shades; amusing toys for children—little coffins from which a
skeleton jumps when a string is pulled; funeral processions with
priests carrying a coffin, their bodies and hats made of shiny black
and colored paper, and heads made of chick-peas; miniature altars
with *ofrendas* or food offerings for the dead on them; dancing
skeletons on sticks with clay faces and feet; also many inexpensive
papier-mâché masks. Among other things, one can also buy there
skeleton necktie pins with weird shining eyes, dangling ribs, and
fleshless thigh bones. Young girls present them to their lovers.

Other amusing features of the Day of the Dead in cities are the
verses called *calaveras* printed on broadsides and sold on the

streets and in the market places for a few centavos apiece. They are satirical and mocking, addressed to well-known persons in public life and groups, such as the policemen, who are referred to as *tecolotes* or owls. There are times when no one is spared, not even the priests, of whom fun is made good-naturedly but with the tongue in the cheek.

Cemeteries are visited all day long. In the cities, the well-to-do, who can afford graves in first-class sections, take flowers to them and return home. But the poorer people who visit graves in the lower-class parts of the cemetery—in the Dolores of Mexico City there are as many as six, the last where the poor are buried free —take flowers, candles, perhaps a toy for a child. Priests are there with their attendants to serve those who wish to pay for responsories or to have a grave blessed. Outside of the cemeteries are vendors of candles, flowers, food, sweets, drinks. Many stay around, making a social event of the occasion.

The people who preserve the customs, whether in cities, towns or villages, expect visits from their dead and receive them as honored guests. They prepare *ofrendas* or altars of food for them, always trying to serve the dishes of which they were fondest in life. They believe that the dead partake of the food in spirit, and the living eat it afterward.

All Saints Day, November 1, is for the *angelitos* or little children. They do not have special *ofrendas* but candles, some special dish of food, or a toy are added to those of the adults. They are generally expected at night and parents often shoot off firecrackers outside to attract their attention to the house, so that they will be sure to find it.

All Saints Day is also the day for the adults' souls, but they may come any time on the night of the thirty-first of October. On that evening, it is customary for men and boys to go from house to house to sing *alabanzas* to the dead at the *ofrendas*. After they have finished, they are given drinks and something from that which is prepared for the souls. All the candles are lighted and the name of the one for whom each candle is intended is called. The following day the village folk visit the cemeteries as they do in the cities.

The Bullfight, or *La Fiesta Brava*
by True Bowen

Bullfighting was introduced to Mexico by the Spanish conquistadors, and soon became an important part of colonial life. The first fiesta brava, or bullfight, was held on San Juan Day in 1526 to celebrate the return of Hernán Cortés from Central America. From that time, the bullfight was a feature of all celebrations: a saint's day, the end of Lent, or the arrival of a new viceroy. The bullfighters were members of the upper classes who proved their bravery in this fashion.

After Mexican independence from Spain, several bullrings were built in and around Mexico City, each larger than the one before. The Plaza México, opened in 1950, is the largest in the world. Other cities in Mexico, and many small villages, have their own bullrings where favorite sons display their skill on Sunday afternoons and on special holidays or fiestas.

The spectacle of the bullfight has been for centuries one of the most important national pastimes of the Spanish-speaking peoples. Many Anglo-Saxons make the mistake of thinking of bullfighting as a sporting contest between men and bulls. It is, of course, no such thing. If there is any contest at all, it is within the matador himself: a contest of courage against fear.

The sounding of the trumpet signals the beginning of a *corrida de toros*—literally, running of the bulls. The wide gates at one end of the arena swing open and a mounted man, dressed usually in the manner of sixteenth-century Spain—black trousers, cape and a plumed hat—rides across the ring and doffs his hat to the Judge of the Plaza. He receives permission to start the fight, and collects the keys to the Gate of the Bulls, which bullfighters call the Gate of the Fright. Then he backs his horse across the ring; the band strikes up a dramatic *Paso Doble* (in Mexico it is the stirring *La Virgen de la Macarena*) and, with the constable at their head, the matadors and their assistants begin the *Paseo,* or parade.

The *Paseo* consists of all the men and horses who will participate in killing the six bulls used in the six fights that normally make up

50

an afternoon of bullfighting. All the men who fight bulls are called
toreros, but the stars, the men who actually kill the bulls, are known
as *matadores,* or matadors. Since each matador kills two bulls in an
afternoon, there will be three matadors in the *Paseo,* each accompanied by three *banderilleros* and two *picadores.* The *banderilleros,* or
peons, place the barbs in the bulls' shoulders and otherwise help
the matador during the course of the afternoon. The *picadores*
participate on horseback, placing the *varas* in the bulls' necks during the first act of the fight. After all these come the men who help
the *picadores* and clean the sand between fights, and the mule teams
used to drag the dead bulls from the ring.

According to the ritual, the bullfight is divided into three parts,
or acts, called *tercios.* The first is the Tercio of the Varas. The
second is the Tercio of the Banderillas. The third is the Tercio of
the Death.

It is all-important to remember that there is no manuever in
bullfighting which has as its object the infliction of pain upon the
bull. There is no "teasing" of the animal. Every step of the fight
has a definite purpose. There is no chance for the bull; it must die.
But the matador must kill it bravely and with skill, and in order to
kill it correctly he must prepare the animal for death in an artistic,
yet dominating manner, risking his own life. If there is any victor
in this "contest," then the victor is Death.

THE FIRST TERCIO

The bull comes into the arena in full possession of all its faculties
—it is confident, fast, vicious, out to sweep everything from the
ring. It would be almost impossible for a man on foot to kill it with
a sword, going in correctly over the horns, while the bull is in this
condition.

The first step is that taken by the peons of the matador, who
"run the bull," doing a few loose passes so that the matador can
see what horn the animal favors, if it has a charging fault, what side
is better for fighting, etc. Then the matador steps out from behind
the *burladero* (there are several of these wooden safety shields
jutting out from the fence enclosing the ring), and cites the bull's
charge. He almost always begins with a series of *verónicas* ended by
a *media-verónica.*

La Verónica is the Bible pass of bullfighting, the simplest in appearance and in reality the most difficult and dangerous in the

entire repertory of capework. The man profiles to the bull, holding the cape low and with both hands, then slowly and gracefully moves the cape as the bull charges, gliding the cape along in front of the horns until they are well past his body. The man's feet may be apart or together, but they should not move once he has taken his stance.

To have real value, the *verónicas* must be done in a series, and usually end with a *media-verónica,* in which the matador shortens the glide of the cloth into a fairly tight curve making the bull try to turn in a shorter space than is possible. This stops the animal and permits the man to walk calmly away, his back turned to the enemy.

After the first *puyazo* or "pic-ing" of the bull, in which the *picadores* place the *varas* in position, the matador in turn takes the bull away from the horse in what is known as a *Quite* (Kee-tay). After the second and third *puyazos* the other matadors of the day also alternate in performing series of brilliant and colorful cape figures.

The pic-ing of the bull has as its purpose the weakening of the animal's big tossing muscle, forcing the bull to lower its head. At the end of the first *tercio,* while the bull has been slightly weakened by the lancing and by its repeated charges at horses and capes, its courage is still high; it has been able to get its horns into something, even if only into the padding of the horses.

THE SECOND TERCIO

After the blowing of the trumpet, signaling the end of the first *tercio,* it is time for the placing of the *banderillas.* These are wooden sticks about 26 inches long, gaudily decorated with colored paper, with small iron harpoon points at the business ends. Usually peons place the barbs, one pair at a time, until three pairs have been put into the bull's shoulders. The object of this is to correct any fault in charging that the bull may have, and to continue the work begun by the *picador* in bringing the bull's head down.

Sometimes a matador, if he is a particularly good *banderillero,* will himself place the "sticks." Carlos Arruza, for example, one of the greatest modern stars, was fantastically good in the second *tercio.* The peons do not usually try anything fancy, being content to get in and get out without being caught by the horns.

The ideal placement of the six *banderillas* is in a cluster at the crest of the bull's shoulders. The matador may order them placed, or place them himself, in other positions in an attempt to correct a fault in the animal.

THE THIRD TERCIO

Now the matador takes up his *muleta,* the brilliant red cloth folded over a 25-inch stick, and his sword. Holding these in his left hand, he takes off his fighting hat, the *montera,* and walks to a spot in front of the box of the Judge of the Plaza. Looking up, *montera* raised, he makes the routine request for permission to kill his bull. After this is granted, the fighter then makes his dedication of the bull, to a friend in the stands, or to the entire audience or, if he thinks the bull is not good, to no one. If the dedication is for the public as a whole, the matador raises his hat and pivots slowly while standing in the ring, until he has faced all sides. Then he tosses his *montera* to the sand.

It is during this last section of the fight that the bravery of the bull and the courage of the man receive their greatest test. It is now that the man, using the scanty protection of the *muleta,* exposes his body more and more to the attack of the horns.

During this *tercio* the man should be alone in the ring with his enemy. He goes to face the bull alone, to perform the *faena,* the *muleta* work which brings the animal to the moment in which it must be killed.

If the bullfigher is artistic as well as brave, you will notice that he follows three basic formulas in his work. One, he stands still while the bull charges. Two, he moves smoothly and slowly, giving the utmost feeling of beauty, drama and danger to every pass that he performs. Three, he dominates the bull, becoming the aggressor because with his valiance and his skill he controls the beast.

During a good *faena,* the matador sometimes stands perfectly still on a small patch of sand, passing the bull back and forth, time after time, the horns grazing his body. The man stands contemptuous of danger. Yet he knows perfectly well that an error in timing, a false move, or even a gust of wind against the cloth may bring instant death or a horrible wound.

THE MOMENT OF TRUTH

It is during the *faena* that the man demonstrates his true worth as an artist, taking the risks that produce tremendous emotion in the crowd. With his physical grace and skill he creates the choreography that gives the fight its ballet-like quality. He brings the horns closer and closer to his body, creating danger by his own skillful action, yet always controlling and dominating the brute force of the animal. The functional purpose of all this is to condition the bull so that it can be killed, to "square" the animal so that its front feet will be together and its head held low. By bringing the front feet together, the shoulder blades will be open and apart, thus permitting the sword to penetrate and to cut the aorta artery—the largest artery in the body. If one foot is in front of the other, or if the feet are too wide apart, the sword will strike bone and fly out.

Once the bull is squared, its head down, eyes concentrated on the cloth, the man is ready for the tragic climax to which the Spanish-speaking peoples refer as The Moment of Truth. This means, really, the crucial moment when the man is expected to face the supreme test in a noble and honest manner. The Moment of Truth is, then, the moment of the kill, when the man has to give the maximum that is in him of courage and skill. He must go in as he should, over the right horn, truly risking his life to deliver the final thrust of the sword, when any false move may result in a serious goring or in death. This is the moment in which the man must most conquer himself and his fear.

If he goes in as he should, from in front of the bull with his left shoulder forward, the matador automatically comes within reach of the bull's horns. In fact, his body must pass over the right horn at the moment of putting in the sword, when he plants the steel in a spot between the shoulder blades not much bigger than a silver dollar. To accomplish this without being gored, the fighter must "cross" with his left hand holding the *muleta*, thus keeping the bull's head down almost to the ground until the man's body has passed over the horn and come out along the bull's flank.

If the matador has put up a good fight, the crowd will applaud and yell "*Olé!*" (O-lay, meaning Hurrah! or Bravo!) for him. If there is enough applause, the fighter will take a tour of the ring, while the crowd throws down flowers, hats, coats, cigars, etc. If the performance has been superior, the people wave handkerchiefs signifying that they want the Judge of the Plaza to award an ear to the man before the bull is dragged out. If there are enough hand-kerchiefs, the Judge waves his own, indicating that the fighter has been awarded an ear of his dead enemy. Sometimes a second ear is given, and, rarely, the bull's tail. If the bull has been extremely brave, it too may earn a round of the ring, or at least an ovation from the public. Sometimes the owner of the ranch from which the bull came is called out to take a bow.

The emotional thrill of seeing a truly brave and brilliant matador

working with a good bull cannot be described completely in words
—it must be felt. Imagine fifty thousand voices screaming "*Olé!*"
as if with one breath, and then chanting together, "*TO-RER-O!
TO-RER-O!*"—one of the highest honors that can be given a
bullfighter.

Inevitably, of course, even for the greatest matador and the
greatest bull, the applause fades away, the crowd quiets down, the
ring is cleared and the sand is smoothed. With a blast of the bugle
the signal is given, the gate of the bulls—The Gate of the Fright
—swings open, and another brave bull comes charging in, looking
for something to kill.

PART 3
VIVA THE REVOLUTION!

The Cry for Independence
by Dana Catharine de Ruiz

In Mexico, the period 1810–1821 is not called a revolution at all but rather "The War for Independence," the revolt against the mother country, Spain, which led to the establishment of Mexico as a free nation in the New World. Independence was declared at dawn on September 16, 1810, with the cry of Father Miguel Hidalgo: "Death to the Spaniards!" The movement did not end until many bloody battles had been fought. The first thrust was badly led and organized, and its leaders were captured and executed. For many years their heads hung in iron cages at the four corners of the granary in Guanajuato as a warning to other revolutionaries.

At the beginning of the nineteenth century, the structure of the Mexican colonial government was based on what was good for Spain, which was not always what was good for the growing country in the New World. New ideas on the freedom of man were entering the minds and hearts of the Mexican people. These ideas came from France and from their neighbor to the north, the United States. At the same time, Spain's domestic problem—the deposition of their king by Napoleon—caused unrest in the colony, already seething with dissatisfaction at the rule of the viceroys.

The scene was set. All that was lacking was the appearance of the principal player, Padre Miguel Hidalgo y Costilla, known from his student days as a man with advanced and dangerous ideas.

56

In the dark hours of the morning of September 16, 1810, Padre Hidalgo rang loud the bells of his parish church in Dolores and shouted the War for Independence into being with these words: "Long live the Virgin of Guadalupe. Death to the Spaniards!"

Hidalgo and his small band of insurgents crossed the mountains to the capital city of Guanajuato. The Spaniards held the rich mining city which had produced gold and silver for the Kings of Spain since the conquest. At the entrance to the city stood a large stone granary, the *Alhondiga de Granaditas*, built with tiny slit windows perfect for a fortress. As such, the Spaniards used it, confident that no one could enter.

When the rebel forces reached the granary, they discovered the one weak spot—the huge wooden door on the north side. It was impossible to think of scaling the walls, but if they could take that door, there was a chance of entering. However, the Spaniards, too, were well aware of the vulnerable door. It was heavily guarded on all sides. If someone could get to the door with a torch. . . .

Out of the ranks of the small insurgent army stepped a young Indian volunteer known by the doubtful nickname of "el pípila" (chicken neck). He would carry the torch to the door. His relatives and *compañeros* watched with awe and respect as a heavy slab of limestone was eased onto his back as protection against the Spanish bullets. He ran to the door amid shouts of encouragement and gunfire. The wooden door blazed and great cries of victory rose up from the band of Mexicans who poured into the Alhondiga. The battle raged fiercely, and in little time the Mexicans had killed most of the Spaniards and taken the granary.

Hidalgo rode off triumphantly to new victories at Valladolid, now Morelia, the old colonial capital where he had studied and served as rector of the university. He left behind part of his army holding the Alhondiga and some two hundred forty-seven prisoners and hostages, among them soldiers who had survived the battle, royalist merchants, and some few Spanish families. These unfortunate people were massacred when a member of the Mexican forces opened the gates of the Alhondiga—made prison to the angry populace. People swarmed in, refusing to heed the orders of the guards or the supplications of the chaplain of the nearby Church of Bethlehem.

This massacre provoked the retaliation of the Spaniards who were determined to retake the city and wipe out its inhabitants.

Félix María Calleja del Rey, a royalist general, rode furiously into Guanajuato, meeting no resistance, ordering the largest bell of the parish to sound the death knell. Calleja left his most severe man, the Count de la Cadena, Don Manoel Flon, in charge of carrying out his orders. Flon set up headquarters in the center of town, in front of the Church of San Diego, and prepared to begin the mass execution.

Suddenly there appeared on the scene a Franciscan friar, holding a crucifix in one hand, shouting and pleading:

"These people before you have committed no crime. If they had, they would be hiding out in the hills, as are so many others. Suspend the order for the execution, I beg you in the name of the Lord, who will on the last day of time ask for an account of the innocent blood that will be spilled here."

The brave words of the humble friar proved to have great effect on the Count. He realized that the townspeople were innocent and revoked the order for the mass execution. But the friar could not prevent the slaughter of some four hundred prisoners who paid the bloody price of revolt. Today, no one remembers the name of the Count, but that of the simple Franciscan, Padre Belaunzaran, is on the lips of all who pass through the magnificent underground street of Guanajuato which bears his name. He has become a cherished legend of mercy outstanding in a period when rivers of blood were spilled.

Revolution in Mexico City, 1841
by Frances Calderón de la Barca

In 1821 Mexico won her independence from Spain. In 1824 she adopted a constitution. The next fifty years saw a series of changing governments. There were plans, and pronunciamentos, *and the triumph of one general after another. Between 1843 and 1846, the presidency changed nine times. The evil genius of this period was Santa Anna, sometimes hero, more often a villain, who became dictator in 1853.*

In September, 1841, four generals were struggling for power in Mexico City: the incumbent president, Bustamante, and three rival generals, Santa Anna, Paredes, and Valencia. These events were recorded by Madame Frances Calderón de la Barca, wife of the first Minister of Spain to the Republic of Mexico.

1st September—This revolution is like a game at chess, in which kings, castles, knights, and bishops are making different moves, while the pawns are looking on or taking no part whatever.

Mexico looks as if it had got a general holiday. Shops shut up, and all business is at a stand. The people, with the utmost apathy, are collected in groups, talking quietly; the officers are galloping about; generals, in a somewhat party-colored dress, with large gray hats, striped pantaloons, old coats, and generals' belts, fine horses, and crimson-colored velvet saddles. The shopkeepers in the square have been removing their goods and money. An occasional shot is heard, and sometimes a volley, succeeded by a dead silence. The archbishop shows his reverend face now and then upon the opposite balcony of his palace, looks out a little while, and then retires. The chief effect, so far, is universal idleness in man and beast—the soldiers and their quadrupeds excepted.

The position of the president, however, is not so bad as at first sight it might appear, or as it will be, if his enemies are permitted to reunite. He has upwards of two thousand men; twelve pieces of ordnance, and, though his infantry are few, and he has little artillery, he has good cavalry. Valencia has twelve hundred men,

59

twenty-six pieces of ordnance, with good infantry, and almost all the artillery. The rebels have possessed themselves of the Acordada, and given liberty to those who were imprisoned for political opinions—a good loophole for the escape of criminals.

3rd—They are now keeping up a pretty brisk fire between San Agustín and the citadel. This morning the streets were covered with coaches, filled with families leaving the city.

4th—Every turret and belfry is covered with soldiers, and the streets are blocked up with troops and trenches. From behind these turrets and trenches they fire at each other, scarcely a soldier falling, but numbers of peaceful citizens; shells and bombs falling through the roofs of the houses, and all this for "*the public good.*"

The war of July had at least a shadow of pretext; it was a war of party, and those who wished to reestablish federalism may have acted with good faith. Now there is neither principle, nor pretext, nor plan, nor the shadow of reason or legality. Disloyalty, hypocrisy, and the most sordid calculation, are all the motives that can be discovered; and those who then affected an ardent desire for the welfare of their country have now thrown aside their masks, and appear in their true colors; and the great mass of the people, who, thus passive and oppressed, allow their quiet homes to be invaded, are kept in awe neither by the force of arms, nor by the depth of the views of the conspirators, but by a handful of soldiers, who are themselves scarcely aware of their own wishes or intentions, but that they desire power and distinction at any price.

Meanwhile, we pass our time very quietly. In the morning we generally have visitors very early, discussing the probabilities, and giving us the last reports. Sometimes we venture out when there is no firing, which is much less constant and alarming than it was last year. So far we continue to have visitors in the evening, and Señor B—— and I have been playing duets on the harp and piano, even though Mexico is declared "in a state of siege." The —— minister, who was here this morning, does, however, strongly recommend us to change our quarters, and to remove to Tacubaya; which will be so troublesome, that we are inclined to delay it until it becomes absolutely necessary. . . .

5th—We went upon the azotea [flat roof] this afternoon, to have a good view of the city. There were people on almost all the balconies, as on a fête day. A picturesque group of friars of the order of La Merced, in their white robes, had mounted up on the belfry of their church, and were looking out anxiously. The palace roof next our own had soldiers on it. Everything at that moment was still and tranquil; but the conduct of the people is our constant source of surprise. Left entirely uncurbed, no one to direct them, thousands out of employment, many without bread, they meddle with nothing, do not complain, and scarcely seem to feel any interest in the result. How easily might such a people be directed for their good! It is said that all their *apathetic sympathies* are in favor of Bustamante.

Some say that Santa Anna will arrive today—some that the whole affair will be settled by treaty; but neither reports nor bulletins can be depended on, as scarcely anyone speaks according to his true feelings or belief, but according to his political party. . . .

It appears that the conduct of congress in this emergency has given little satisfaction. They affect to give a declaration of the national will, and are as ambiguous as the Delphic Oracle; and it is said that their half-measures, and determination not to see that public opinion is against them, and that a thorough change can alone undermine this military revolution, will contribute more than anything to its eventual triumph. . . .

In listening to the different opinions which are current, it would seem that Bustamante, Santa Anna, and Valencia are all equally unpopular; and that the true will of the nation, which congress was afraid to express, was first for the immediate convocation of a Constitutional Congress; and secondly, that they should not be governed by Santa Anna, yet that Bustamante should renounce, and a provisional president should be named. . . .

Santa Anna writes, complaining that Bustamante, by assuming extraordinary powers, commanding the army and yet continuing president, is infringing the constitution. But as he is coming on to destroy it entirely, this is being rather particular. It is reported that the typhus fever is in the citadel, but there are many floating rumors which are not to be depended upon. . . . There is evidently a great deal of consternation beginning to be felt amongst the lower classes. Foreigners generally are inclined towards Santa Anna, Mexicans to Bustamante; but all feel the present evils.

Return from Exile
by Nina Brown Baker

Benito Juárez, the Zapotec Indian who became president of Mexico, has been called the "Lincoln of Mexico." The two leaders were alike in many ways. They were plain, homely men who took their responsibilities seriously. Juárez emerged the winner from Mexico's civil war, the War of Reform, in early 1861, and also from the terrible years of the French Intervention, 1864–1867, when Maximilian and his ambitious wife Carlota tried to establish an empire for themselves in the New World.

During the French Intervention, the United States could do little to help. Juárez did not despair, declaring, "It is enough for us that the North destroy slavery and do not recognize Maximilian." Confident of a common bond, Juárez sent his family into exile in the United States during the darkest hour of Intervention. In 1867, soon after Maximilian and his two most important generals had been captured and executed, Doña Margarita, wife of Juárez, sailed from the United States. She would return with her husband to the capital where he would issue his most important manifesto: "The people and the government," he said, "shall respect the rights of all. Between individuals, as between nations, respect for the rights of others is peace."

On a day in July, 1867, the port city of Vera Cruz was ablaze with flags. Most of them were Mexican, but there was a generous sprinkling of Stars and Stripes, too. The United States stood very high in Mexican esteem just now. American aid in ridding the country of the French had been real and important. Also the high honors shown the president's wife in Washington were a matter for national pride.

Doña Margarita, after living quietly in New York for two years, had visited Washington on her way home. She had been a guest at the White House, and President Johnson had assigned an American warship to take her back to Mexico. She was expected today, and the president had proclaimed it a day of national rejoicing.

The streets had been filling since dawn. Patiently they waited as the hot sun rose higher: mothers with babies in their arms, old men leaning on their staffs, village Indians stolidly sucking on lengths of sugar cane. These were humble folk. Some of them lived in the nearby houses, for this was not a fashionable street. But the well-to-do merchants and politicians had rented the houses for the day, bringing their own rocking chairs and cushions. With their wives and children they crammed the narrow balconies or clustered behind the barred windows.

A cheer rippled down the street. From the mayor's house in the heart of the town an empty carriage came into view, drawn by four white horses. And what a carriage!

The good citizens of Vera Cruz did not welcome home their First Lady every day. They proposed to do it in style. They had sent to Mexico City for the golden carriage of the Empress Carlota.

It is very like the state coach in which, in happier days, the King of England was wont to drive through the streets of London to open Parliament. The coachman's seat is draped in gold-fringed velvet, and the inside is a jewel case of softly tufted satin. Outside it is all gleaming gold; the harness is gilded, too.

The carriage, with two uniformed soldiers on the box, came to rest on the pier at the water's edge. A file of soldiers hurried out of the customs house to keep the inquisitive little boys from coming too close.

The day wore on, and nothing happened. The notables behind their windows rocked and chatted, fanning themselves with palm leaves. The sellers of sugar cane did a thriving trade among the thirsty street crowds. And always more and more people pressed in, until there was scarcely room to breathe in the stifling narrow street.

Then at last came the long-awaited sound, the boom of cannon from old Fort San Juan de Ulloa. Every head turned, and a deep-throated cheer went up. Slowly, majestically, decked with flags, the American gunboat *Wilderness* was steaming into the harbor.

The doors of the customs house opened now, and the cheers grew wilder. President Juárez, in his usual sober black, came down the steps and walked slowly to the gang-plank which had just been lowered. American bluejackets stood at attention as he stepped on deck, and the ship's band broke into a ragged but gallant rendering of the Mexican *Himno Nacional.* The music was drowned in the thunder of the ship's guns.

Bowing gravely to the officers who awaited him, Juárez shook Pedro Santacilia's hand. "This way, sir," his son-in-law said eagerly. "She asked to greet you in private, in her cabin."

She stood among her children, a thin, gray-haired figure in the heavy black of deep mourning. Her arms, which for so many years had cradled a sleepy baby, hung at her sides. They were empty now.

Don Benito clasped her close, his heart constricting to note how very thin and sharp were the shoulders under his hands. Margarita had been so prettily plump in the old days!

"Well, my dear ones, here you are," he said huskily.

"Here we are—those of us who are left!" Her voice broke, and she buried her head in his shoulder. "Oh, Benito, Benito—I have not brought you back your sons!"

"Hush, my sweet, I know, I know!" He stroked the soft gray hair, bound with its black ribbon. This was the moment which, much as he had longed for Margarita's return, he had most dreaded. Frail little José had died in New York, and so had the baby Antonio.

The Americans had been endlessly kind, Pedro had written. The finest doctors in New York had done their best. Sympathy had come from high and low all over the land, for the modest, unassuming Mexican lady had found her way into warm American hearts.

President Juárez, holding his sobbing wife, fruitlessly trying to find words of consolation, felt a tug at his coattails.

"I'm here, papa," young Benito reminded him in a stage whisper. "Maybe pretty soon you'll want to notice how I've grown?"

His mother raised her head, and automatically the life-long instinct of discipline asserted itself. "That is not nice, to speak English to papa," she said reprovingly. "Have you forgotten your Spanish, then?"

"*I* haven't!" "*We* aren't speaking English to him!" The girls, who had waited respectfully behind their mother, crowded around their father now.

Manuela, the married daughter, was in black like her mother, but they had dressed the others in white, with only black sashes and hair ribbons to mark the family mourning.

Doña Margarita dried her eyes on her black-bordered handkerchief. This, after all, was not the day for mourning. The grief that she carried always in her heart would be no lighter while life remained to her, but she was the mother of the living as well as of the dead. This was the day to which she had looked forward through the long, weary months of exile. With keen eyes she scanned her husband's face, marking the new lines, the thinning hair. Whatever happened, she promised herself, she would never leave his side again. That vow was not broken.

When they stepped ashore they found that a narrow lane had been cleared in the crowded street. A line of carriages waited, headed by Carlota's golden coach. By its open door stood the mayor of Vera Cruz, the city council, and those members of the president's cabinet who had come with him from the capital.

The mayor bustled forward. "If Your Excellency and lady will kindly take your places in the state coach, the rest of us will follow with the young people."

But Don Benito shook his head.

"Señor Mayor," he said gravely, "I know that this is meant in all kindness. I am deeply touched that the citizens of Vera Cruz desire to honor my wife. I offer you now her gratitude with my own. But she is a simple Mexican woman, the wife of your citizen president. Neither of us desires, or has ever desired, to assume the trappings of royalty. I hope that I will not be misunderstood when I ask you now to send that vehicle away. We have no use for it."

The golden coach was wheeled into a side street, and Doña Margarita stepped into the ordinary black carriage which had brought her husband from the capital. President Juárez took his place beside her; the one small son between their knees. The girls were helped into the following carriages, well distributed among the local dignitaries.

The procession had not gone a hundred feet when the shouting crowd surged forward and stopped the leading carriage. Eager hands fumbled at the harness; the horses were taken out and led away. And then up the long stony hill to the mayor's house the Juárez carriage rolled, pulled by the strong arms of citizens who knew no other way to show their homage.

The demonstration was unplanned, completely unexpected. These were no *léperos*, cynically ready to earn their fee. These were common people, working people. They were not honoring their president, although they loved him. They were the people who had known Doña Margarita when she lived in Vera Cruz during the Three Years' War. She had walked quietly among them, tending their sick, comforting their widowed, clothing their orphans. The golden coach had been the town council's idea. But the humble poor had found a better way to show her she was not forgotten.

The Dictatorship of Don Porfirio
by Lesley Byrd Simpson

In the beginning, Porfirio Díaz was not an enemy of Benito Juárez, nor of the Mexican people. He had Indian Zapotec blood in his veins and, like Juárez, he came from Oaxaca. He was an able general who supported Juárez during the War of Reform, 1858–1861, and through the French Intervention. Eventually, he turned against the idealistic, constitutionalist policies of Juárez. He seized the presidency in November, 1876, from Juárez' successor, Lerdo de Tejada.

Juárez and his Law had been rejected in favor of rule by force, and the astonished conservatives suddenly found themselves presented with a dictator, gratis. For the next thirty-four years they were to enjoy the most efficient despotism ever seen in the western hemisphere. Don Porfirio's slogan was "Bread and the Club": bread for the army, bread for the bureaucrats, bread for the foreigners, and even bread for the Church—and the club for the common people of Mexico and those who differed with him.

The nation was suffering from its endemic plague of banditry. Don Porfirio's solution was to set up a national gendarmerie called the Rurales, recruited from the gunmen of the cities and from among the bandits themselves. They were given showy uniforms, good salaries, and the power to shoot on sight, and no questions asked. Into their capable hands was placed the task of making Mexico safe for Don Porfirio and his friends. Troublesome Indian *caciques*, striking workmen, indiscreet speakers and writers, and honest bandits disappeared into the noisome dungeons of the fearful old Belén Penitentiary, or were shot "while attempting to escape," an effective device known as the *Ley Fuga*. In the course of a few years Mexico became the best policed country in the world. It was ruled by martial law, without courts, and the Rurales loved to shoot.

As the years rolled by and Mexico lay quiet in her straitjacket, foreign capital was encouraged to come in; manufactures and agriculture flourished; railroads pushed their way south from the border; American miners reopened the ancient *reales de minas* of the Spaniards, and smelters began to belch their yellow fumes into the desert air. Silver, gold, copper, lead, and zinc flowed north to feed the rapidly expanding commerce and industry of the United States; and coffee, sugar, bananas, and henequen found a ready market abroad.

For the Creole aristocracy the dictatorship of Don Porfirio meant the return of the Silver Age. The hacienda reverted to the pure type of the feudal estate, with the terrible Rurales to call on in the event of trouble. Elegant carriages drawn by high-stepping thoroughbreds again paraded up and down the Paseo on Sundays. The ladies discarded the graceful Spanish mantilla for the *dernier cri* from Paris. Their sons were sent to France for an education and came back pattering the lingo of the *boulevardier* and scoffing at the barbarism of their own country.

The clergy awoke from their long nightmare and discovered that religion and the liberal dictatorship of Don Porfirio were not necessarily incompatible. The ranks of the clergy were swelled by Spanish, French, and Italian priests, until by the end of the regime they numbered some five thousand, against the pitiful five hundred of the dark days of Juárez. Only the native clergy grumbled.

If the dictatorship of Don Porfirio meant the return of the Silver Age for the Creoles and the clergy, for the foreigner it was the Golden Age. Mexico became "the mother of foreigners and the stepmother of Mexicans." The foreigner soon learned that he could buy justice and favors from the swollen and underpaid bureaucracy, which grew to include a large percentage of the literate population of the country. *Empleomanía*, the government-job mania, infected the whole middle class of Mexico. But the foreigner was king, for the new paradise was made possible by his money and industry, and the sweat of Mexican workmen. His factories and mines were rarely disturbed by strikes or similar unpleasantnesses, and, when they were, the Rurales, the army, and the judiciary saw to it that the malcontents gave no more trouble. Strikers were slaughtered by the score and by the hundred at the Cananea mines and the textile mills of Río Blanco. "You can't make an omelet without breaking eggs." Díaz made Mexico a colony of foreign capitalism, principally American, although Mexican capitalists did not suffer. His amazing success was to a considerable extent a by-product of our post-Civil War prosperity; Mexican economy reflected our booms and panics, and began to show signs of weakness about 1907.

Beyond question the material and even the cultural advancement of Mexico during the dictatorship of Don Porfirio was very great: so many miles of railroads, so many millions of dollars invested in this and that, so many years of peace and order, eighty millions of pesos in the treasury. It may even be true that Díaz was a superior kind of benevolent despot. It may also be true that some sort of military dictatorship was inevitable after the frightful chaos of the mid-century, and that if Don Porfirio had not taken over, Mexico would have been torn to pieces by the rival caudillos whom he so effectively checkmated. Otherwise, the price of the *Pax Porfiriana* was too high. It threw Mexico back into the hands of an irresponsible autocracy, without the Laws of the Indies or the salutary fear of a royal visitor to curb it. There was no law but the will of Don Porfirio. The legislature became a mockery, kept to lend the color of legality to his acts. He cynically referred to his lawmakers as *mi caballada*, "my herd of tame horses."

Elections were such a farce that hardly anyone took the trouble to vote. All of the offices of the Republic were filled with Don Porfirio's men. Between 1883 and 1894, by a series of colonizing laws passed by his caballada, Díaz gave away, to foreign speculators and personal friends, 134,500,000 acres of the public domain, that is, *about one-fifth of the entire area of the Republic.*

Not satisfied with this colossal rape, the land sharks prevailed upon Díaz to throw open for seizure and settlement the remaining lands of the Indian communities—which he could legally do under the "Ley Lerdo." When the Indians objected, as did the Maya and the Yaqui, the army and the Rurales put down the "rebellions," and thousands of prisoners were sold into slave gangs to cultivate henequen in Yucatan and tobacco in the Valley Nacional of Oaxaca. By the end of the Díaz regime not ten per cent of the Indian communities had any land whatever. In short, the Díaz regime was the denial of elementary justice to a large part of the population. The price was blood.

The fall of Don Porfirio was as inevitable as it was unplanned. Up to 1908 all suggestions that the Golden Age might end were rigorously suppressed, and their authors expiated their temerity in exile, prison, or death. In 1908, however, the aging dictator granted an interview to an American newspaper man, James Creel-man, which was published in *Pearson's Magazine* under the heading "Thrilling Story of President Díaz, the Greatest Man on the Conti-nent."

The greatest man on the continent had told Creelman that the Mexican people were now ready for democracy and that he in-tended to retire in 1910. The story was probably meant for circula-tion north of the border, or perhaps it was a trial balloon. If the latter, it was soon bouncing wildly about among the politicians and intellectuals of Mexico. The news was too good to be true, for the truth was that the younger generation was bored with its dodder-ing dictator and his senile government. Not a few men were con-cerned with the fate of the country when Don Porfirio should retire, for no provision had been made for the succession, and several offered themselves as potential saviors of the fatherland.

The one who first capitalized on the situation was Francisco Madero. Madero was not a revolutionist. Indeed, a more unlikely leader of a revolution can hardly be imagined. He came from a large and rapacious family of landowners of Coahuila. He was a kindly man with no particular training for anything. Following the mores of his class, he had spent part of his youth in Paris, and had managed to complete a semester's residence at the University of California. His diminutive size (five feet two), squeaky voice, and lack of biceps he compensated for by going in for messianic oddi-ties: teetotalism, vegetarianism, and spiritualism. In one of his séances his Ouija board told him that he was to be president of Mexico, and the Creelman article told him that the time was at hand.

His first step was to publish his book, which had nothing remark-able about it, being a few mild suggestions, to the effect that it might be a good idea to restore the Constitution of 1857 and give the people a chance to elect a *vice-president.* That vice-president could easily be Panchito Madero, and Don Porfirio might die. Stranger things had happened.

Don Porfirio was good-natured about the competition of his puny antagonist and allowed him to travel about the country haranguing audiences; but to his astonishment Madero was every-where received by enthusiastic crowds. Madero invented a slogan that caught on: "Effective Suffrage—No Reelection!"

Madero's success was so sensational that Don Porfirio became alarmed and had him jailed in San Luis Potosí. Various other candidates were discouraged in one way or another, and Don Porfirio and his stooge, Ramón Corral, were duly elected president and vice-president on September 30, 1910.

Meanwhile, on Independence Day, September 16, the Great Centennial was inaugurated, with 20,000,000 pesos spent on fireworks, decorations, military parades, banquets, speeches, poems, and carloads of champagne, while Francisco Madero, in his cell at San Luis Potosí, was writing the "plan" which was to ignite the glorious bonfire of revolution.

Revolutionary with a Paintbox
by Diego Rivera

From the time that he was ten years old, perhaps even sooner, Diego Rivera knew that art was his destiny. At the age of thirteen, he was accepted as a student in the San Carlos School of Fine Arts in Mexico City. He left there at sixteen, when most students are first admitted. Later, he received a scholarship for four years' study in Europe, which he spent mostly in Spain and in Paris.

In October 1910, at the age of twenty-four, Rivera returned to Mexico in time to witness the beginning of the revolt against the Díaz regime. In July 1911 he went back to Europe where he remained until 1921. He took naturally to being a revolutionary in politics as in art. His brilliant frescoes, for which he was commissioned by the government, attest to this viewpoint.

During the four years I had been away from Mexico, the political situation had deteriorated, and unrest was reaching a revolutionary pitch. Díaz, sensing that the end of his thirty-year dictatorship was near, yet unwilling to relinquish absolute power, was resorting to open terrorism.

One day a friend of mine named Vargasrea and I had a lunch appointment with a third comrade, General Everaro Gonzáles Hernández, in a popular restaurant in Mexico City. Vargasrea and I were late, because I had been painting in a distant part of the city, and it took us longer to get to the restaurant than we had anticipated.

On our arrival at the restaurant, we found General Hernández rolling in agony on the floor. He had been poisoned, but no doctor had been summoned by the frightened waiters and customers.

Gasping his last breath, he told Vargasrea to sell his horse, his saddle, and his side arms and use the money to pay his debts. These possessions, he said, were all he had left in the world. And then he died. Thanks to our being delayed, Vargasrea and I almost certainly escaped being poisoned, too. Many other opponents of the dictatorship had died after eating an apparently harmless meal.

As a contribution to the revolution, I designed a huge poster, copies of which were distributed among the peasants throughout all Mexico. Its message to the poor, ignorant farmers was that divine law did not forbid them to repossess the land which rightfully belonged to them. The corrupt Church of the time had been preaching the converse.

The slogan, dominating the poster, read: THE DISTRIBUTION OF LAND TO THE POOR IS NOT CONTRARY TO THE TEACHINGS OF OUR LORD JESUS CHRIST AND THE HOLY MOTHER CHURCH.

Since the majority of the peasants could not read, the message was illustrated by a painting showing a family plowing their field behind a team of oxen. Above the oxen hovered a benevolent image of Christ fondly gazing upon his children, whom he blessed for preparing the field for growing.

My paintbox might symbolize my state of mind at this time. Underneath the tubes of color was live ammunition, which I carried to partisans behind the government lines. Many of these revolutionary fighters were friends of my childhood and early youth.

Every district of Mexico City had its network of underground cells. I was sometimes invited to speak to the members, usually about painting. I fulfilled my assignments to the letter, but I also seized upon every pretext to inspire my audience to greater revolutionary fervor.

But, the poster excepted, I did not do a single sketch expressing my revolutionary feelings. My eyes were, however, transmitting to my brain continuous, vivid images, which have never lost their distinctness. When I later painted scenes going back to this period, I seldom had any need of preliminary drawings.

From time to time, I continued working on landscapes. I also began to prepare an exhibition of the paintings I had brought back from Europe. I went about this task with inward repugnance because of my dissatisfaction with these works. However, I was badly in need of money. I wanted to return to Europe to resume my studies, and I had not forgotten Angeline.

I was helped in my preparations for the exhibition by my friend Francisco Urquidi, then Secretary of the School of Fine Arts, and its Director, Lebrija. My former teachers, José Velasco, Félix Parra, and José Posada also took part in arranging the show.

Perhaps because I was bored and disgusted, I hatched a plot with

Lebrija and the architect, Eduardo Hay, to give the exhibition a more worthwhile purpose. Our aim was nothing less than the assassination of Díaz, which we believed would save the lives of many brave Mexican freedom fighters.

The exhibition was to open at eleven o'clock in the morning on November 20, 1910. My part in the plot was to smuggle explosives into the school in my paintbox. My friends, the officials of the school, pulled wires to get Díaz to attend the opening. We were elated when we received word that Díaz had accepted their invitation.

I arrived at the school long before eleven and met Lebrija. A tall and gaunt Don Quixote, he was nervously wringing his hands in impatience.

He said, "All right, Diego, we are awaiting the command of the *pestilente,*" and his eyes shone with a bright unnatural fire.

As I climbed the stairway, paintbox in hand, I saw Urquidi staring down at me. He didn't say a word but practically pushed me into his office, took the box, opened the small steel safe which contained the school funds, and locked the paintbox inside it.

"It will stay there till the right moment," he declared, embracing me warmly and whispering in my ear, *"Viva la Revolución."*

But, unfortunately, the right moment to open the safe never came. A few minutes after the explosives had been stowed away, the Chief of Police arrived at the school, accompanied by plain-clothesmen, uniformed police, and soldiers of the regular army. Politely, he asked for Lebrija, the Director, who, I knew, was now too scared to come down. I told the Chief that he had not yet been seen.

At last, having screwed up his courage, Lebrija appeared, exchanged introductions with the visitors, and took them on a tour of the school as he was expected to do. Along the way, the police examined everything they came upon—except the safe. Which goes to show how their respect for property can be used against the police.

I was with Urquidi, near the door of his office, when the police approached. The Chief stepped forward to shake hands with Urquidi, who then introduced me. When the cops looked around, Urquidi made a gesture as if to open the drawers to show them that nothing was hidden there, but the Chief stopped him.

"What do you mean, architect?" he asked good-humoredly, and

then ordered his men to leave the building. Then, promising to return with the President to see my paintings, he bowed himself out.

But instead of Díaz, his wife, Doña Carmen Romero Rubio de Díaz, patroness of the arts and philanthropy, arrived as the President's representative. It was she who officially opened the exhibition. Señora Díaz asked permission to make the first purchase. She paid handsomely for "Pedro's Place," actually the most important canvas in the show. It pictured a group of Basque fishermen and their wives returning from work. This painting, as well as many others of my early and late years, is today in the collection of Solo Hale in Mexico.

Before leaving, Señora Díaz congratulated me with a fine aristocratic smile. But I was really disappointed; there had been no occasion to open the steel safe.

Perhaps the Chief of Police was cleverer than we were. I prefer to believe that Señora Díaz was cleverer than he and the men who had hoped to murder her husband.

Viva the Revolution!

by Anita Brenner

The Mexican Revolution of 1910 began with the revolt against Porfirio Díaz and the election of Francisco Madero. Fifteen months after Madero took office, he was overthrown and assassinated by followers of Victoriano Huerta and Félix Díaz. Huerta was a "strong man" who hoped for American recognition. Meanwhile, revolt against Huerta grew within Mexico, from guerrilla leaders who feared that the United States would send troops to "enforce peace" and who wanted nothing from their neighbor to the north except guns. The revolution was loosely organized behind four chief leaders who called themselves Constitutionalists: Carranza, Villa, Zapata, and Obregón. Carranza was a civilian, and Obregón a very talented general. Both Villa and Zapata were guerrillas.

First among them—but by courtesy only, and just because he had been the first to issue a formal call against Huerta in the name of the Constitution—was the white-bearded Venustiano Carranza of Coahuila. He controlled the northeast corner of Mexico, which included the most convenient gun-running territory, and was near the strategic junctions of the railroads to the capital and to the oil fields.

His leading brain truster was Luis Cabrera, who believed that American capital should be curbed by stiff competition from other sources and that all foreign capital should leave a sizable slice of the benefits in Mexico. He wanted the revolution to cut into monopoly, curb the church as Juárez had done, destroy the remains of feudalism, and back a new, strong middle class—businessmen, industrialists, professionals, and small farmers. Carranza had been a senator in the Díaz days. He was a cold-eyed, sensual, stubborn old patriot who believed himself to be the only possible savior of his country, a superman. He gave himself the title of First Chief and fought implacably to enforce it.

To the northwest, in Chihuahua and Durango, was Pancho Villa, the former cattle rustler and pack driver. Sometimes he obeyed

Carranza, sometimes he didn't. He had rolled up a phenomenal record of victories since the fight against Díaz had begun and by now had a little council building him up as the future Strong Man. He had a foreign affairs department in the person of George C. Carothers, President Wilson's agent. He had a financial advisor who, it was assumed, was in touch with the Terrazas clan and with Hearst and other interested Americans. As a counselor of policy, Villa had General Felipe Ángeles, who hoped that law and order might be established not too far to the left. General Ángeles had attachés of his own, including the artist Francisco Goitia, whose job was to paint, as he went along, the triumphs and agonies of the revolution. Above all, Villa had the feared and famous—it seemed invincible—Dorado cavalry.

To the southwest, in Morelos and Guerrero, was Emiliano Zapata, called "The Attila of the South" by the newspapers of Mexico City. He operated in complete independence of the other revolutionaries and his council had no middle grounders at all. With him were an eloquent lawyer, Antonio Díaz Soto y Gama, and the Magaña boys who had agitated the college students, and the village schoolteacher Otilio Montaño, who had written in grim clumsy rhetoric the first formal revolutionary program—Zapata's *Plan de Ayala,* preaching complete, immediate expropriation of lands and other productive holdings for the benefit of the poor. The slogan "Land and liberty" didn't mean the acquisition of these things gradually and in the future; it meant land and liberty by direct action right now.

The only military chief who was his own brain trust was a *ranchero* and ex-mechanic from Sonora in the northwest, the plump and agreeable Álvaro Obregón. His personal followers were the fiercest fighters in Mexico, Yaqui Indians. He considered himself a socialist and was unique among the guerrillas in the way he ran campaigns. Before each major move he talked things over with his staff, taking stock of details in his remarkable photographic memory. Political matters he worked out with friends such as the other "socialist" generals—Hill, Alvarado, and Calles—and civilians who were mostly labor organizers and a few intellectuals connected with unions in some way. What Obregón decided to do was always a combination of desirables with practicables, in terms of the circumstances and people involved—that is, a shrewd, immediate political adaptation of the boys' radical demands.

These four men, with their armies and retinues, were the great guerrilla chieftains. In addition there were scores of other chieftains who, with a few hundred followers, acknowledged bigger leaders only provisionally, and there were still others trooping independently who recognized no overlordship whatever.

The first and indispensable requirement of a chief was that he had proved himself without fear in battle. The second was that he be a winner, and the third, that he be generous with the proceeds. They campaigned like tribes, each chief with his bunch of boys, sometimes allied loosely with other chiefs, sometimes following super-chiefs, picked according to their successes and the material returns on these. The battle cry was *"¡Qué viva Villa!"* . . . *¡Qué viva!* whoever the chief might be, followed by a hoarse, growling, shrilling *"¡Qué viva la revolución!"*

There was no agreement binding the revolutionaries. There was only a common enemy—Huerta—and a common drive to get a satisfactory place in life. And as the revolutionary wave began to roll—"Death to Huerta, down with the foreigners, Mexico for the Mexicans"—there was revealed also an unarticulated set of common hates which could be seen operating when a revolutionary army came to town.

First the jails were opened and the prisoners invited to join. Next a loan was levied on the local rich, except in the rare case of a rich man who was also a sympathizer. Goods were taken from the stores too, and here the line drawn was between Mexicans and foreigners, but in exact reverse of the distinction made in Díaz days.

Some chiefs issued receipts for what was taken and conducted the disgorging of stores and warehouses in a formal, systematic way. Mostly, however, it was done with a yell—"That one's a Spaniard!"—and the stuff was taken by whichever soldiers were the first, enthusiastically helped by the store's former customers. Food and liquor went at once in long, hilarious parties with music: songs about love, hunger, jail, and exile, punctuated with shots at times, to decide impromptu who was brave and who wasn't.

You could sometimes tell whose soldiers they were by the songs. Villistas tore loose about *Adelita,* "green as the sea were her eyes . . ." Carrancistas strung bawdy rhymes about politics and women to the chorus of *La Cucaracha,* the cockroach who couldn't travel any more. Zapata's men sang in melting tenor to *Valentina,* breaking to sudden ear-piercing whoops with "If I am to die tomorrow, let them kill me right away . . ." The next day was a town fair: a bunch of ostrich plumes exchanged for a Christ Child out of a church, perhaps, or a good cursing parrot for a mother-of-pearl-incrusted gun.

The fighting style of the troops became a projection of each region's kind of daily life. Some were *ranchero* units, based on the farm owned by the chief, or perhaps on a captured ranch, or on a hideout in the sierra neighborhood. Each had started round a core of home-town or home-farm boys. In Guerrero, for instance, the Almazán brothers, medical students of *ranchero* family, led off a unit of the local farmhands. In the village of Jiquilpan in Michoacán, young Lázaro Cárdenas, who had a little job as some sort of court clerk, opened the village jail and took its single prisoner away with him to find or make the nearest guerrilla troop. In some of the most arid places a few parish priests, perhaps remembering that the revolutionary heroes of generations past had been such men as they, unfrocked themselves and joined their rebel congregations. As a rule the general staff of each segment or troop or division consisted of two kinds of people: *rancheros* or independent peasants, and professionals—the young doctors, lawyers, writers, artists, druggists, telegraphers, engineers—who had sat smoldering on the discounted plaza bench.

The Zapatistas were a revolving peasant army, based on their own homes. The soldiers went back from time to time to look after their corn and chili patches. A detachment could often, if in a bad military spot, simply evaporate, each man becoming again a soft-eyed, vague-talking peasant by just slipping off his cartridge belt and putting it with his gun in a cache. It was impossible to defeat them, difficult even to find them, as they materialized only when they were ready to attack; and knew, besides, all the shortcuts in their mountain country and the tunnels and caves used by runners, soldiers, and spies since before Montezuma.

They wore ordinary peasant white, except the chiefs, who dressed in *ranchero* clothes; in Zapata's case symbolic, theatrical dead-black, skintight and set off with startling silver. Under the great hat his face was small, Asiatic, sensuous. Mandarin mustaches drooped over his full red lips, and his soft cat eyes looked out, as in a mask of skin, from the death's head of his skull. The first act on raiding a hacienda or municipal center was sharp and symbolic; they got to the safe and destroyed all papers dealing with land titles, and then invited the neighborhood peasants to homestead on the hacienda lands.

The northern revolutionaries had a more military look. They wore uniforms, or parts of them—khaki bought in the United States, and broad-brimmed Texas hats—supplemented with job-lot accessories. One division wore magenta socks; there was a battalion with silk bandannas and a brigade in orchid shirts. The cavalrymen wore mostly tight *ranchero* pants and military tunics. There were some troops of sierra Indians, braves in loincloths with a hawk look on their faces, carrying six-foot bows.

The main battles were along the railroads, with advance attacks often carried out in combination with railroad men who had waived their payroll and pension rights and had come in as revolutionaries. A locomotive might be speeded ahead, heavily armed, moving fast into a town like a tank; or an old engine or a handcar might be turned into a torpedo by loading it with explosives and sending it crashing into a Federal train.

When these armies moved it was like a mass migration. They carried families, three layers deep: some inside the boxcars, some on top, and others, mostly the boys and young men, in hammocks slung between the wheels. Tortillas were ground and baked on fires in oil cans along the whole top of the train, and dogs and babies accommodated themselves in the warmest corners inside.

The age span for soldiering was from about seven to seventy. Boys under ten were usually buglers, drummers, or couriers, and did sentry duty too. Beyond twelve no one questioned their place as full-fledged soldiers.

The women, though their job was foraging, cooking, and looking after the wounded, pitched in and fought if they felt like it. If a woman's husband was killed, she could either attach herself to some other man or take over his uniform and gun herself. Almost every troop had a famous lady colonel or lady captain, a husky, earringed girl armed to the teeth, and among headlong, reckless fighters one of the first.

All these people, Zapatistas, followers of Obregón or Carranza, painters and buglers, Yaqui Indians and mule drivers, were known as Constitutionalists—opposed to the Federals whose reluctant bayonets upheld Huerta. Within a year, despite all international calculations to the contrary, they had wiped the Federals out in three-fourths of Mexico.

Flight from Cuernavaca
by Rosa E. King

It was the year of the Centenario, *1910, the hundredth anniversary of the Mexican Declaration of Independence, that Mrs. Rosa E. King opened her hotel, the Bella Vista, in Cuernavaca. The climate and scenery brought many visitors to Cuernavaca, from Mexico City only fifty miles away, and from abroad. It was a fashionable and beautiful town.*

Few people realized how close Mexico was to revolution at that time. Least of all did Señora King realize that Cuernavaca would become a battleground for fighting between the Federalist forces and the followers of Zapata. Mrs. King was an Englishwoman who had made Mexico her home. After her husband died, it seemed like a good idea to remodel the four-hundred-year-old former manor house of a great hacienda into a luxury hotel. She had a talent for hospitality and Bella Vista opened with a flourish in June, 1910. From that moment, she admitted later, "I cast in my fortunes with the town, and from that time on everything that happened to Mexico was bound to happen to me also."

The happenings did not take long in coming. There was always a Federalist general and his troops stationed in Cuernavaca. There was shooting in the streets, and in the hills, when the Zapatistas were on the move. "The Zapatistas were not an army; they were a people in arms."

Finally, in August, 1914, the order came for all civilians native and foreign to evacuate Cuernavaca. It was the middle of the rainy season. Mrs. King, an American friend Mrs. Mestrezat and her nine-year-old daughter Catherine, prepared to evacuate, under the protection of a young Mexican, Captain Federico Chacón, who had adopted Mrs. King as his "mother."

When the moment came to leave, Mrs. King opened the last bottles of wine in the hotel cantina, and passed them out to the other refugees: "men huddled in their serapes, their wide-brimmed straw hats pulled down to shelter them, women wrapped in thin shawls which cradled their babies, clutching little bundles—all they could carry with them in their flight." Mrs. King wrote: "They had lost their homes. I had lost mine. Death stared us in the face. . . . I no longer felt alone, apart. Distinctions of nationality, race, class, meant nothing now. I was with these people. I was one of them." The next three days were a nightmare.

81

It was a pitiful sight to see the deserted houses and pass through the silent streets; not a person to be seen—all fled or hidden for fear of the Zapatistas. Although we did not know it, the greater part of the troops and townspeople had started long before daybreak —about eight thousand in all. Our little party was among the last to leave, which proved nearly fatal for us. Before we were out of sight of Cuernavaca the Zapatistas closed in behind us and attacked the rear of our column.

Our mules were faithful, but far from fast. The enemy was pursuing and bullets whizzed and whined about us. We dismounted and pulled the mules by their bridles, to encourage them to a quicker gait. For five hours, exerting our utmost strength, we tugged them along, and so forced them to a faster pace than their stubborn little legs would have accorded us had we been on their backs.

Strain as we would to outdistance our pursuers, the enemy kept pace. The firing went on. Now and then our cannon, ten of them, replied with deafening roar to the crack of the rifles. When I saw our pursuers firing upon the Red Cross ambulance and heard the bullets strike, I fainted by a stone wall. A poor soldier's woman stopped to kneel beside me and put *tequila*, a strong native liquor, in my mouth and nose. This revived me. At that moment Chacón rode up and dragged me out of the path of those who rode after us.

All afternoon we plowed on, sometimes dragging our mules through mud and water, sometimes resting on their backs. The way was all uphill, now; we were climbing constantly, ascending the first ridges of the wide mountain barrier that separated us from Toluca, in the State of Mexico, the town we were heading for. The spicy tang of great pine trees was all about us. My breath came with stitches of pain because of the exertion in the high altitudes, for our climb had begun at the mile-high elevation of Cuernavaca. How we suffered from thirst! There was no clean drinking water on our route, and we dared not turn aside to look for springs. We did not feel hunger, although we had started without anything to eat. A woman had brought each of us a cup of weak tea, with sugar, at the last moment before starting, and that was all we had had all day.

To cap it all, we were caught in two ambuscades. We lost two cannon and many men, for we had no defense against ambush.

The mountain country we were passing through was gashed with gullies and gorges and walled with rock. It was sublimely beautiful country to look at—even in our flight, I marked that—but cruel to us. Our troops could not mass together for strength. As we fled over the narrow mountain trails we were a long thin file of fugitives. Our enemies, concealed in the depths of green forest, shot at us as we moved past.

At last we reached the little town of Xochi, where we were to spend the night.

The evening was cool, and Chacón built a little fire to warm us. We sat there on the ground, the three of us—Federico, Mrs. Mestrezat, and I—dirty and disheveled, stiff and sore, and so tired that we wanted never to get up again. Presently our good friend Lieutenant Colonel Zaldo joined us, carrying under his arm a mysterious bundle. How he smiled when he whipped off the coverings and showed us what he had. Somewhere he had stolen a chicken. He had cooked it and was going to share it with us! From the pockets of his coat he even brought out a few biscuits to go with it. "Not young biscuit," he cautioned engagingly as we began to break into pitiable exclamations of joy, "not young biscuit—but very respectable. Honestly come by!"

He was a little light-headed, like the rest of us, at the prospect of food and warmth and safety and friendship after what we had endured all day. We had had all the horror we could hold. We were like children on a picnic as we spread out the meal on the ground between us. Was it good! . . . For weeks we had eaten nothing but beans and rice, or tea and coffee with sugar. No milk or bread. No chicken! We tore every shred of meat from the bones and sucked them clean. We rolled the stale biscuit over and over in our mouths till the last crumbs slid down our throats. Good! . . . There are some things in life one always remembers with exhilaration.

Little Xochi had one more joy for us—security for the night. A kindly woman placed a room in her house at our disposal, and Mrs. Mestrezat and I lay down on a small straw mat in the middle of the floor—the bare earth was all the floor there was—with eleven men lying around us in a ring, their rifles close at hand, to defend us in case of danger.

The quiet stars of early morning saw us again on our perilous journey. The ground underfoot grew rougher and rougher. We were riding over the *pedregal*, the lava flow spewed out by the volcanoes long ago. Our mules stumbled over rolling boulders and stepped into depressions in the pitted and porous rock.

And then, ahead and high above us in the mountains, we saw the town of Chalma, perched as if for safety in the rugged arms of a rocky slope. Chalma—a part of ancient Mexico, where in the days of the Aztecs there was a *teocalli*, a pyramid where prisoners of war were sacrificed to Ozteocotl, the gloomy god of the caves. Then came the crucified Christ and the legend of mercy to drive Ozteocotl back into the windy fastnesses of the mountains. On the inner walls of the houses and in the patios of the town, the Augustinian monks painted frescoes telling the history of Chalma, and the triumph of mercy.

We toiled with bursting lungs, not daring to rest, up the steep and almost impassable road—the penitential road that the pilgrims climb every year to reach the shrine of the Crucified Christ of Chalma. I had seen the pilgrims to this holy place passing through Cuernavaca in the old days.

Little had I imagined that the day would come when I should be driven cruelly, like a hunted animal, to the place of the Crucified Christ of Chalma by thousands of men who had gone there to pray! . . .

The horrors of that afternoon seem impossible to believe. On the road from Chalma to Palpam my mule was shot dead. The German took little Catherine up behind him. (Her mother was separated from us in the confusion.) Federico Chacón put me on his own horse, and walked, leading the animal, a beautiful chestnut stallion that had been the pride of a great landowner long since fled.

Then came the terrible words. "All women and children together and the troops to the sides." We knew what was coming.

From a little rise, I saw that the trail ahead lay along the shoulder of the mountain that formed one side of the gorge: a trail so rough and narrow in places that the vanguard of our column had to lengthen to single file, with the rock wall rising sheer on one side, and on the other the abyss.

Suddenly the fusillade came—quietly at first, like the rising of the wind: a wave of bullets pouring from the green mountainside across the ravine, pattering against the rock and beating down our people as hail flattens the stalks of flowers. A kind of shuddering groan went through our column; and then there was the steady staccato of the Rexers and quick-firing guns our artillery turned on the mountain as they ran. But still death streamed from the bland hillside. The men around me lifted their rifles and fired at the puffs of smoke that rose across the gorge, hurling defiance at the hidden enemy as they fell. There was something monstrous in our help-lessness, our inability to strike back one effective blow, that stripped us of human dignity and turned our men to raging beasts. Their snarls and screams and the terrible animal sounds they made in their throats as they fired mingled with the moans of the wounded and the shrill cries of the *soldaderas*, like howling Furies as they snatched the guns from the falling and passed them to those still on their feet. The town women fell on their knees and prayed, pulling their scarves over their heads, making no effort to flee from the falling bullets.

The child and I lay there waiting, waiting for we knew not what fate, when suddenly we heard it coming, as we thought. There was a tearing, crashing sound above us. A dead mule came hurtling down the steep side of the ravine, a man, or ammunition, on its back—all bound without stop for the bottom. We cowered flat against the rock, but as it passed us in its gravitation rush the mule struck me a blow near the spine that left my lower limbs almost paralyzed. When Chacón was finally able to come for us I had been unconscious for nearly half an hour, though I was still gripping the child and the saplings. Federico thought I had been shot, and Catherine was frantic and could not say just what had happened. When I revived I told him of the blow I had received. I was utterly helpless and in such terrible pain that I begged him to put me out of my misery and save himself and the child.

"Go on!" I said, "go on!" I thought of myself as already dead and out of it, and it exasperated me that Chacón should not under-stand this, and should stand there risking his precious life and the child's by delaying.

He paid no attention whatever to what I said, but grabbed my arms and dragged me inch by inch out of the ravine, Catherine clinging to me as best she could. He lifted me on his horse and placed the little girl in the saddle in front of me.

How we went on from there I hardly know. In a dazed way I was aware that we were going forward, always forward. I knew that, though many had fallen, soldiers still fought all around us; knew that their courage was protecting us, and knew a kind Providence was watching over them, over the little American girl and me. And the torturing will to live awoke again in me.

Suddenly an Indian appeared, a white flag in his hand. He approached our general, whom we had overtaken, to say that General Carranza's men were in Tenango and would help us. There was no stopping to listen to what the messenger had to say, for the firing was incessant. He was made to walk in front of our general as he talked. Our men were desperate and said that if this was another trap set for us, we must all die—which no one seemed to dread, as we had already suffered so much that death instead of more treachery would have been a happy release.

General Carranza, we knew, was one of the strong leaders from the north who had come marching down to avenge the shameful murder of President Madero. He led a revolution to cast out Huerta for having usurped the highest post in Mexico by means of a crime.

The troops in our column were government men, owing allegiance to President Huerta. It was of a piece with the rest of their luck that they should have fled straight into the hands of the Carranzistas! But the Carranzistas met us with mercy. No bullets! They had an eye toward converting our men to their cause.

The firing behind us ceased. The Zapatistas had no desire to match their strength against that of the fresh, well-equipped Carranzistas. Not a word was spoken. We marched on in deadly silence, all women and children to the front. Out of the eight thousand who had started from Cuernavaca, only two thousand were left. All our artillery was lost, all provisions gone; we ourselves were torn, wounded, and hungry, not caring much what they did to us.

The Carranzistas stationed along the road, leaning on their rifles, looked at us curiously. I saw in their looks what a cruel, pitiable sight we were. I knew then that my hair was matted with dust and my eyes reddened and swollen from sleeplessness and the fierce sun. I saw my hand on the reins, dirty, the broken nails still holding the earth of the *barranca,* where I had dug my fingers into the wall of the gorge as I fell. I saw that we were smeared with mud, our garments stiff with blood and filth, our faces all set in the same stark lines. We were more like animals than people, foul-smelling, indistinguishable, all the niceties of breeding and sentiment, all the fastidious habits that made us ourselves, rubbed out. These things had been the protection of our ego; without them we were like wounded beasts crawling to cover. I shrank from the gaze of the men by the roadside like someone naked in a bad dream. I wanted to cry, "This is not I!"

About two o'clock we entered the main street of Tenango. Here everyone was stopped and searched, and all disarmed except the captain and myself. Chacón was leading the chestnut by the bridle and the little girl was clinging on behind me. The soldiers reached for my pistol and the rifle that lay across the saddle, but Chacón stopped them with a friendly gesture. "Don't take her pistol. She is a foreigner and suffering." I showed my little British flag to prove what he said was true, and the captain and I were allowed to pass without having anything taken from us.

In the little plaza of the town a band was playing. I felt I could hold up no longer; the reaction was setting in, overcoming me. Tears poured down my face. Three men who were standing on the street corner came to us and asked if I had been wounded. When they heard I was hurt and in pain, one of them said he would take me to his wife. We reached his home. . . . I was lifted off the horse and put on a bed of the same kind as before, a mat on boards. The man sent his little boy to fetch a doctor at once. His wife began, very gently, to undress me. She was Indian, young and pretty and radiant with pity. She looked to me like the Virgin of Guadalupe herself. I was weeping uncontrollably.

"It's all right, Mother," said Chacón. "You are safe now . . . you can rest. . . ."

Pancho Villa and the Prisoners
by Martin Luis Guzman

During the time that General Francisco (Pancho) Villa was Chief of the Division of the North, there were many battles between factions of the revolutionaries, as well as between the rebels and the government forces. When this happened, "it was a case of hurricane against hurricane. It was kill or be killed."

One of those mornings Llorente and I went to see Villa. It made our blood run cold to look at him. The glitter in his eyes made me realize suddenly that mankind is not of one species, but of many, and that these species are separated by limitless space, have no common denominator. An abyss cleaves them, and it may cause vertigo to look from one of these worlds to the other, which lies opposite. As fleeting as a ripple on water there passed over my soul that morning, face to face with Villa, the giddiness of fear and horror.

To our "Good morning, General," he replied in a sinister voice: "Not good, my friends. There are more hats around than we need."

I did not understand what he meant by the expression, nor do I think Llorente did, either. But whereas he selected the part of wisdom, keeping quiet, I asked with stupid, almost crime-provoking tactlessness: "More whats, General?"

He took one step towards me and answered with the deliberation of a person who can barely control his anger: "More hats, my learned friend. Since when don't you understand the language of real men? Or don't you know that on account of Long-Ears (the damned son of a bitch, if once I get hold of him!) my boys are killing one another? Now do you understand why there are too many hats? Do I talk plain?"

I didn't say a word. Villa paced up and down the car, as if keeping time to the internal rhythm of his wrath. Every three steps he would say between his clenched teeth: "The damned son of a bitch. The damned son of a bitch."

From time to time Llorente and I exchanged glances, and finally, not knowing what to do or say, we sat down, close to each other. Outdoors the morning shone bright, its perfect harmony broken only by the distant noises and shouts of the camp. In the car, aside from the palpitations of Villa's rage, nothing was heard but the ticking of the telegraph apparatus.

Bent over his table, facing us, the telegraph operator worked on. His movements were precise, and his face as expressionless as his instrument. Several minutes elapsed in this fashion. Then the telegraph operator, who had been transmitting before, said, turning to his chief: "I think they're here now, General."

Taking his pencil from behind his ear, he began to write slowly. Villa came over to the little table where the apparatus stood. His air was at once agitated and icy, impatient and calm, revengeful and indifferent.

He stood between us and the operator, in profile, leaning forward. On one side of the dark blotch of his silhouette against the wall the energetic line of his under jaw and of his arm folded across his breast stood out, and on the other, concluding the powerful angle that descended from his shoulder, the curved, dynamic outline of his pistol butt. This morning, instead of his slouch hat, he wore a gray sun helmet, with green facings on the brim. This head gear, always odd on him, seemed to me more absurd than ever that day. Strangely enough, instead of taking away from his height, it seemed to add to it. Seen close to, and against the light, his stature seemed to increase enormously; his body stopped all the light.

The operator tore off the pink pad the sheet on which he had been writing, and handed the message to Villa. He took it, but handed it back immediately, saying: "You read it to me, friend, but read it carefully, for I think this means business now."

There was a sinister inflection in his voice, so portentous and threatening that it was reflected in the voice of the operator. Separating the words carefully and pronouncing every syllable, he began in a low tone: "I have the honor to inform you. . . ."

As he read on, his voice grew stronger. The message, which was laconic, gave notice of the defeat that Maclovio Herrera had just suffered at the hands of the troops pursuing him.

Villa's face seemed to pass from the shadows into the light as he listened. But instantly, as he caught the final words, his eyes blazed again, and his face flamed with his most terrible rage, his uncontrollable, devastating wrath. The commander of the troops, after giving the list of his casualties, had ended by asking instructions as to what to do with the hundred and seventy of Herrera's men who had given themselves up.

"What to do with them?" shouted Villa. "What a question! What should he do except shoot them? I honestly believe every one of my men is going bad, even the best ones I absolutely relied on. And if they're not, what in hell do I want with these generals that get friendly even with the traitors that fall into their hands?"

He said all this without taking his eyes off the poor operator, through whose pupils, and then through the telegraph-wires, Villa perhaps hoped to make his anger reach the very battlefield where the corpses of his men lay.

Turning to us, he went on: "What do you think of that, gentlemen? Asking me what to do with the prisoners!"

But Llorente and I hardly returned his glance, and, without answering a word, looked off into space.

This did not disturb Villa in the least. Turning to the operator, he ordered him: "Come on, friend. You tell that damned fool I don't want him using up the wires on nonsense. He's to shoot the hundred and seventy prisoners immediately, and if he hasn't notified me in an hour that the order has been carried out, I'll come there myself and put a bullet through him so he'll know how to manage things better. You understand?"

"Yes, General."

And the operator began to write out the message.

At the first word Villa interrupted him:

"What are you doing, not obeying me?"

"I'm composing the message, General."

"What do you mean, 'composing'? You send that off the way I said it to you and that's all. Time wasn't made to be lost fooling with papers."

At this the operator put his right hand on the transmitter and, pressing the lever with his little finger, began to call: Tick-tick, tiqui; tick-tick, tiqui.

Between a pile of papers and Villa's arm I could see the knuckles of the operator's hand, tense and vibrant from the contraction of the tendons as they produced the homicidal sounds. Villa did not take his eyes off the movements that were transmitting his orders seven hundred miles to the north, nor did we. I kept wondering —with that stupid insistence we have in dreams—at exactly what moment the vibrations of the fingers were spelling out the words "Shoot immediately." For five minutes that was a horrible obsession that blotted out every other reality, every other sensation.

After the operator had sent off the message, Villa seemed to grow more calm and sat down in an armchair near the desk. He sat there quietly for a little while. Then he pushed back his sun helmet. Then he buried the fingers of his right hand in the reddish tangle of hair that hung over his forehead, and scratched his head as though he were trying to get at some inward itching of the brain, of the soul. Then he sat quietly again. Perhaps ten minutes had elapsed.

Suddenly he flung round towards me and said: "What do you think about all this, friend?"

I answered evasively: "Were you talking to me, General?"

"Yes, to you."

Hedged in like this, I tried to turn it off using the language of real men: "Well, there are going to be a lot of extra hats around, General."

"Maybe I don't know that. That wasn't what I asked you. What about the consequences? Do you think it's right or wrong, this business of the shooting?"

Llorente, braver than I, cut in ahead of me: "General," he said, "to be frank with you, I don't think that order is fair."

I shut my eyes. I was sure that Villa was going to get up—or, without even getting up—and whip out his pistol to punish this criticism of his conduct in a matter which had flicked him on the raw. But several seconds went by, and then I heard Villa ask, without getting up, and in a voice whose calm contrasted strangely with the storm that had so recently preceded it: "Well, let's see. Why don't you think my order was right?"

Llorente was so pale that it was hard to tell his skin from his collar. Nevertheless he answered firmly: "Because, General, the message says the men surrendered."

"Sure. What of it?"

"When they are taken that way, they shouldn't be killed."

"Why not?"

"That's why, General. Because they surrendered."

"You're a funny fellow. That's a good one. Where did you ever learn such things?"

My shameful silence had become unbearable. I broke in: "I feel the same way, General. It seems to me that Llorente is right."

Villa enveloped us both in one glance.

"And what makes you think that, friend?"

"Llorente explained why: because the men surrendered."

"And I say again, what of it?"

As he repeated it this last time, a certain uneasiness was apparent which made him open his eyes still wider to take us both in with his restless glances. From the outside I could feel the pressure of this look of his, cold and cruel, and from the inside, an irresistible impulse to talk, which was pricked on by the vision of the distant executions. I had to hit quickly on some convincing formula. "The person who surrenders, General, by doing so spares the life of others, since he renounces the possibility of dying fighting. And this being so, the one who accepts the surrender has no right to order the death sentence."

Villa looked at me steadily, and his eyeballs stopped rolling from one to the other of us. Jumping to his feet, he shouted to the operator: "Listen, friend, call them again, call them again."

The operator obeyed. Tick-tick, tiqui; tick-tick, tiqui.

A few seconds went by.

Villa inquired impatiently: "Do they answer?"

"I am calling them, General."

Llorente and I could not sit still, and we too came over to the instrument table.

Villa asked again: "Do they answer?"

"Not yet, General."

"Call louder."

The operator could not call louder or softer, but it was plain from the contractions of his fingers that he was trying to make the letters clearer and more exact. There was a short silence, and in a little while the receiving instrument began to tick.

"Now they're answering," said the operator.

"All right, friend, all right. Now you transmit as quickly as you can what I am going to say to you. Pay attention: 'Hold up shooting of prisoners until further orders. General Francisco Villa.' "

Tick, tiqui-tick, tiqui. . . .

"Finished?"

Tick-tiqui, tiqui-tick.

"All right, General."

"Now tell their operator that I'm right here beside the instrument waiting for the answer, and that I'll hold him responsible for any delay."

Tiqui, tiqui, tick-tick, tiqui-tick, tick. . . .

"Have you told him?"

"Yes, General."

The receiving instrument began to tick.

"What does he say?"

"He says he is going to deliver the message himself and bring the answer."

All three of us stood beside the telegraph table: Villa strangely restless; Llorente and I weak with anxiety.

Ten minutes went by. Tick-tiqui, tick, tiqui-tick.

"Are they answering?"

"It's not them, General. It's another station calling."

Villa took out his watch and asked: "How long ago did we send the first order?"

"About twenty-five minutes, General."

Turning to me, Villa asked: "Will the counterorder get there in time? What do you think?"

"I hope so, General."

Tick-tiqui, tick, tick. . . .

"Are they answering, friend?"

"No, General, it's somebody else."

Villa's voice was husky with an emotion I had never heard in it before, and it grew deeper each time he asked if the call was the answer to his counterorder. His eyes were riveted on the little lever of the receiving apparatus, and every time this made the slightest movement, he asked as though the electricity of the wires were reaching through to him: "Is it him?"

"No, General, it's somebody else."

It had been twenty minutes since telegraphing the counterorder when finally the operator said: "Now they're calling," and picking up his pencil, he began to write.

Tick, tick, tiqui. . . .

Villa bent farther over the table. Llorente, on the contrary, seemed to stiffen up. I walked over beside the operator to read what he was writing.

Tick-tiqui, tiqui, tiqui, tick-tick. . . .

After the third line Villa could not curb his impatience and asked me: "Did the counterorder get there on time?"

Without taking my eyes off the paper, I nodded my head.

Villa pulled out his handkerchief and mopped the sweat off his forehead.

We stayed and had dinner with him that afternoon, but he made no reference to what had happened that morning. Only as we were leaving, late that evening, Villa said, without any preamble: "And thanks, friends, for that thing this morning, that business of the prisoners."

Revolt of Youth, 1968
by Octavio Paz

The Olympic Games held in Mexico in 1968 were the occasion for a student revolt which touched off a political and philosophical controversy. The government maintained that "foreign elements" were involved. Many Mexicans were shocked at this outbreak of violence. The most outspoken critic of the government was Octavio Paz, poet and philosopher. As a protest against the attitude of the government, Paz resigned his post as ambassador to India. The following statement is part of a lecture he delivered at the University of Texas on October 30, 1969.

The student movement in Mexico was in some ways like those in other countries, both of the West and of Eastern Europe. It seems to me that the closest affinities were with those in the latter countries: nationalism, reacting not against Soviet intervention but against North American imperialism; aspirations for democratic reform; and protest, not against Communist bureaucracies but against the Institutional Revolutionary Party. But this revolt of Mexican youth was singular, as is the country itself.

There is not any dubious nationalism in this statement. Mexico is a country that occupies an eccentric position in Western civilization—it is "Castilian streaked with Aztec," as the Mexican poet López Velarde wrote—and within Latin America its historical situation is also unique: Mexico lives in a post-revolutionary period while the majority of the other Latin American countries are going through a pre-revolutionary stage. Finally, its economic development has been exceptional. After a prolonged and bloody period of violence, the Mexican Revolution was able to create original institutions and a new state. For the last forty years, and especially for the last two decades, the nation's economy has made such strides that economists and sociologists point to Mexico as an example for other underdeveloped countries. The statistics are indeed impressive, especially if one keeps in mind the condition of the nation when the Revolution broke out in 1910, as well as the material and human destruction it suffered during more than ten years of civil strife.

In order to gain international recognition of its transformation into a modern or semi-modern country, Mexico requested, and was granted, the designation of its capital as the site of the 1968 Olympic Games. The organizers of the Games not only passed the test successfully, they even added an original program to that of the sports events, a program underlining the pacific, noncompetitive nature of the Mexican Olympics: exhibits of international art; concerts, plays, and dance presentations by orchestras and companies from all over the world; an international meeting of poets; and other events of a similar nature. But, in the context of the student revolt and the repression that ensued, these celebrations seemed nothing but gaudy gestures designed to hide the realities of a country stirred and terrified by governmental violence. Thus, at the very moment in which the Mexican government was receiving international recognition for forty years of political stability and economic progress, a swash of blood dispelled the official optimism and caused every citizen to doubt the meaning of that progress.

The student movement began as a street brawl between rival groups of adolescents. Police brutality united them. Later, as the repression became more severe and the hostility of the press, radio, and television—almost all pro-government—increased, the movement strengthened, expanded, and grew aware of itself. In the course of a few weeks it became clear that the young students, without having expressly intended it, were the spokesmen of the people. Let me emphasize that they were not the spokesmen of this or that class but of the collective conscience.

From the very beginning an attempt was made to isolate the movement by placing it in quarantine, in order to prevent the spread of ideological infection. The leaders and officials of the labor unions hastened to condemn the students in menacing terms; so did the official political parties of the left and of the right, though with less vehemence. Despite the mobilization of all the means of propaganda and moral coercion, not to mention the physical violence of the police and the army, the people spontaneously joined the student demonstrations, and one of them, the famous "Silent Demonstration," brought together about 400,000 people, something never before seen in Mexico.

Unlike the French students in May of the same year, the Mexican students did not propose violent and revolutionary social changes, nor was their program as radical as those of many groups of German and North American youths. It also lacked the orgiastic and near-religious tone of the "hippies." The movement was democratic and reformist, even though some of its leaders were of the extreme left. Was this a tactical maneuver? I think it would be more sensible to attribute that moderation to the circumstances themselves and to the weight of objective reality: the temper of the Mexican people is not revolutionary and neither are the historical conditions of the country.

Nobody wants a revolution. What the people do want is reform: an end to the rule of privilege initiated by the National Revolutionary Party forty years ago. The students' demands were genuinely moderate: derogation of one article in the Penal Code, an article that is completely unconstitutional and that contains the affront to human rights called "crime of opinion"; the freeing of various political prisoners; the dismissal of the chief of police; et cetera. All of their petitions could be summed up in a single word that was both the crux of the movement and the key to its magnetic influence on the conscience of the people: *democratization.* Again and again the demonstrators asked for "a public dialogue between the government and the students" as a prelude to a dialogue between the people and the authorities. This demand was an echo of that which a group of us writers had made in 1958, during similar but less widespread disturbances that foretold much worse ones to come—as we warned the government at the time.

The attitude of the students gave the government an opportunity to correct its policies without losing face. It would have been enough to listen to what the people were saying through their student spokesmen. They were not expecting a radical change, but they did expect greater flexibility and a return to the tradition of the Mexican Revolution, a tradition that was never dogmatic and that was very sensitive to changes in popular feeling. In this way the government could have broken out of the prison of words and concepts in which it had enclosed and isolated itself, the prison of all those formulas that nobody believes in any longer and that are summed up in the grotesque expression with which the official family describes the only political party: the Institutional Revolution.

By freeing itself from its prison of words, the government could also have broken out of another prison—a realer one—that surrounded and paralyzed it: the prison of business and of the interests of bankers and financiers. A return to communicating with the people would have meant recovery of the authority and freedom to carry on a dialogue with the right, the left, and the United States. With great clarity and concision, Daniel Cosío Villegas, one of the keenest and most honest minds in Mexico, pointed out what in his opinion (and, I should add, in the opinion of most thinking Mexicans), was "the only remedy: to make public life truly public." The government preferred to resort, alternately, to physical force and institutional-revolutionary rhetoric. This oscillation probably reflected a struggle between the technocrats, desirous of saving what little was left of the revolutionary tradition, and the political bureaucracy, which favored a strong hand. But at no time did the government show any desire to "make public life truly public," and to begin a dialogue with the people. The authorities did propose negotiations, but behind the scenes, and the talks aborted because the students refused to accept this immoral procedure.

Near the end of September the army occupied the University and the Polytechnical Institute. This action was so widely criticized that the troops withdrew from both institutions. There was a breathing spell. The students, full of hope, gathered for a meeting —not a demonstration—in the Plaza of Tlatelolco on the second of October. At the end of the meeting, when those attending it were about to leave, the plaza was surrounded by the army and the killing began. A few hours later it was all over. How many died? No newspaper in Mexico dared to print the number of deaths. Here is the figure that the English newspaper *The Guardian,* after a careful investigation, considered the most probable: 325. Thousands must have been injured, thousands must have been arrested. The second of October, 1968, put an end to the student movement. It also ended an epoch in the history of Mexico.

PEOPLE OF MEXICO

The majority of Mexicans today are of mixed blood, Indian and Spanish. They are called *mestizos,* which means "mixed." Above all, the Mexican values himself as a person. Costumes and customs, as well as physical appearance, vary greatly from village to village, and region to region.

Above: A youth from the mountainous state of Chihuahua in the north. *(National Museum of Anthropology, Mexico City)*

Above left: This old man of Puebla is resting, possibly waiting for a bus. He wears the typical baggy white suit, large-brimmed sombrero, and carries a folded serape, or wool blanket, tossed over one shoulder. *(National Museum of Anthropology, Mexico City)*

Left: A girl from the seaport town of Vera Cruz twists colored yarn in her two braids. She wears beads and earrings and a simple white dress which is comfortable in the humid weather of the Gulf Coast. *(National Museum of Anthropology, Mexico City)*

This girl from the Lake Chapala area carries a tray of fresh bread gracefully. (*Beverly Johnson*)

Architecturally, Morelia's cathedral is considered to be one of the finest in Mexico. Here, as in all Mexican cities, the downtown area (*el centro*) is focused on the cathedral, where there is a constant flow of busy people. (*William H. Field*)

A young mother from Oaxaca, with the ever-present baby, wears an embroidered blouse and a woven shawl, or *rebozo*, over her head. (*National Museum of Anthropology, Mexico City*)

Another mother from Oaxaca proudly shows off her youngest baby. She may have several older children at home in the care of the grandmother or other relative. (*National Museum of Anthropology, Mexico City*)

Right: This laughing boy is typical of Mexican children.

The Park of Blue Water (*Parque de Agua Azul*) is Guadalajara's pride, with shady walks, a zoo, and a miniature railroad. Best of all for the children are the trampolines, cargo nets, and ladders which challenge their agility. (*William H. Field*)

North American students at the summer school in Guadalajara dance the Jarabe Tapatio, a national folk dance, which originated in the state of Jalisco. Their partners are local men, called *Tapatios*, and their music comes from a mariachi band which has sought shelter in an arcade. (*William H. Field*)

Giggling girls from Vera Cruz wear simple cotton dresses. *(National Museum of Anthropology, Mexico City)*

"Take our picture, too!" call these boys who have climbed the steep hill above Morelia to celebrate the Feast of the Assumption of the Virgin. On this day, August 15, all over Mexico, there are fireworks before dawn, bands playing in the streets, carnivals, Ferris wheels, and cotton candy. *(William H. Field)*

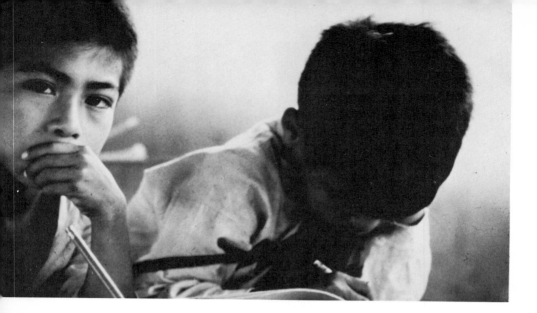

Above: Two schoolboys prepare for the future. The crusade for education is called "the greatest achievement of the Mexican Revolution" by Alfonso Reyes, a famous Mexican author. (*National Museum of Anthropology, Mexico City*)

Two women and a child in Puebla walk freely on bare feet, in comfortable white garments. The women's *rebozos*, or shawls, can be worn over the shoulders, draped over the head, or looped on one hip to hold a baby. (*National Museum of Anthropology, Mexico City*)

Top: These fishermen in the state of Sonora are catching fish for home use. *(National Museum of Anthropology, Mexico City)*

Bottom: This farmer, also in Sonora, uses a very simple plow. Nearly half the people in Mexico still depend on agriculture for a living. Corn, beans, and wheat are the three chief crops. They are mostly for home consumption. *(National Museum of Anthropology, Mexico City)*

The *charreada* is a neighborhood rodeo, usually held every Sunday. The gentlemen riders observe strict rules as they compete in roping, steer-wrestling, and horsemanship. The opening parade of this *charreada* in Guadalajara is led by a boy who expects to become a champion rider when he grows up. *(William H. Field)*

The spectators are the friends and families of the competitors. Beer, tequila, coke, and home-made tacos, sold by the daughters, are popular with the audience. *(William H. Field)*

PART 4
RICH MAN, POOR MAN

My Father, Jarano
by Ramón Beteta
translated by John Upton

This episode from the childhood of a well-known Mexican writer, economist, government official, and television personality reflects the customs of a middle-class Mexican family. Ramón Beteta's life spanned the first sixty-five years of the twentieth century, from the final days of the dictator Díaz to the development of modern Mexico. From his early youth he was an intelligent participant and observer.

We called our father by his first name—Carlos—which, far from offending him or striking him as lacking in respect, gratified him; he was confident that such intimacy in no way lessened our filial love. For him, such a mode of address was an objective proof of his "broad-minded attitude"—as he called it—toward his children.

Privately, however, my brother and I called him "Jarano." This nickname was used only by the two of us, unknown to anyone else, and there was an air of secrecy about it, and a special meaning. It expressed our father's aggressive Mexicanness; his liberality, excessive at times; our affection for him, not untinged by respect and even by fear; and, at the same time, his inability to understand certain things and his inconsistency, which often bordered on caprice.

In our hearts we knew very well that it was not proper for us to use such a nickname; but the word "Jarano" summed up so perfectly all that was, in our eyes, good and bad and above all peculiar about our father, that having once adopted it we were never able to give it up. We called him that until the day of his death.

The incident that gave rise to the name was so typical of his turn of mind that I cannot resist the temptation of relating it here.

Jarano was fascinated by horses and anything that had to do with the Mexican cowboy, which was odd in view of the fact that he was a city man who loved the capital and all it offered in the way of amusements, night life, and conveniences. He had never lived in the country nor owned a scrap of land, and it had never crossed his mind to raise anything, even a plant in his garden at home. But, as I say, he loved horses and instilled in his sons an enthusiasm for every aspect of the equestrian art. We rode almost as soon as we could walk.

One of my earliest childhood memories, in fact, is being astride a little, old, grizzled horse that must have been slow and gentle but seemed terribly tall and spirited to me. Jarano had probably borrowed it from one of his friends.

Jarano rode whenever he could. This was not very often, for he never could afford to keep even a miserable nag, let alone a stable. And yet on the slightest provocation he would don his charro costume, even when he was not going riding. He wore it to bullfights, for example, or to village fiestas. This disturbed us because it seemed incongruous. When we saw him in it we felt that peculiar kind of embarrassment we called "mu," which one experiences whenever someone makes a fool of himself. "Mu" is a feeling of misery characterized by the desire not to look at anyone—especially the subject—and is in direct proportion to the degree of kinship or intimacy that links us to the person who is making, or is about to make, a fool of himself.

As long as my father's enthusiasm for the Mexican cowboy costume did not affect us directly, our suffering was limited to the "mu"; but there came a day when he decided that we, too, must wear charro suits. Worse yet, not the complete outfit, but only the sombrero and serape. It was not merely a matter of wearing them on trips to the country—which we wouldn't have minded at all—but of donning them for social calls, and even for school. This dress seemed absurd to us, and from the moment we were told of his decision we lived in torment at the thought of how our cousins and fellow students would laugh at us. We tried in every way to get out of it, but our protestations were useless. From the subsequent arguments and our rebellion sprang the nickname "Jarano."

This is how it came about. We were getting ready to pay a call at my maternal grandmother's house, where we often spent the afternoon with the aristocratic old lady's numerous other grandchildren.

That day my father insisted that we wear the broad sombreros, like those used by real charros in the country, and the bright-colored serapes he had bought for us. The sombreros were rather cheap ones, without decoration. We had worn them for the first time on the previous Sunday on a trip to Tepexpan, where some of my father's clients—very modest country people —had invited us to spend the weekend. There, sombreros and serapes had been perfectly suitable, as they protected us from the sun and the rain; and we had made the mistake of saying so. But to put them on now, for a visit to the San Rafael district on a clear afternoon, struck us as out of place and absurdly ridiculous. We were afraid, and with good reason, that everybody would make fun of us.

We tried to explain this to our father, but in vain. Weren't we already humiliated enough whenever our elegant cousins greeted us with, "Here come the kids from Number Two," referring to the "inside" number of our apartment? But Jarano insisted, with the adult's lack of understanding of a child's fine sensitivity to ridicule, which makes him miserable if his clothing is in any way different from that of his friends. Why should we care if they called us "the kids from Number Two"? That was, after all, our number on the "private street"—which was surely quite respectable—where we lived. And if we didn't have a whole house to ourselves, it was through no disinclination on his part, and we should be thankful we didn't live in a tenement in the heart of the city, as he had when he was a child. As for the sombrero, we had to admit that it was comfortable and in good taste, and protected us from the weather; and if our silly cousins made fun of it, it was because they liked to think of themselves as aristocrats. We, however, his children, were lucky enough to be real Mexicans and had no reason to admire Porfirio Díaz and his dictatorship; nor was there any occasion to think of ourselves as foreigners or to be ashamed of wearing the typical sombrero of our Motherland, the hat of the charro and the men of the soil: the *jarano*.

Jarano! It was the first time we heard the word. My brother and I exchanged a knowing look; the name had etched itself in our minds.

There was nothing to be done. We left the house in our sombreros and gaudy serapes—mine was red and white, my brother's green and red—certain that everyone on the street would stare at us as a couple of queer specimens.

The truth is that no one paid any attention at all to those two children walking in front of their mother along the nearly deserted streets of the San Rafael district. But we searched the faces of the passers-by, waiting for some humorous remark about our outfits. Nobody said a word, however, until we reached the gate of the family mansion where my grandmother lived. The gate opened onto the garden, a veritable park, across the street from the then famous Mascarones School. There that afternoon, as every Saturday, some of our thirty-six cousins and their friends were gathered.

As soon as we came through the gate one of them called out: "Look at the kids from Number Two! They're all dressed up like charros!" Darío, the cousin we called "the General" because, in spite of being one of the youngest, he was always the leader in our games, deciding what we were going to play and who should take part, grinned at me and said, "What's doing, little cowboy? Did you come here on your dog?"

This struck the others as terribly funny, and there was a roar of laughter. I didn't say anything, of course; but I was angry at being made fun of and yet at the same time quite willing to admit that my cousin's remark was justified.

We took off our sombreros and serapes and began playing games, and my embarrassment passed. But all the rest of the afternoon I kept dreading the horrible moment when we would have to put them on again to go home.

Fortunately, it was dark by the time we left, and the serapes were not as conspicuous. It was a cool evening, as most evenings in Mexico City are, and the blankets felt warm and comfortable. But the sombreros, those damned *jaranos*, seemed even more incongruous at night; in the daytime they at least sheltered us from the sun.

There were other experiences like this, each more unbearable than the last; but we never forgot that day when we first heard the word *jarano*. The *jaranos*, the *jarano* hats! My brother and I didn't even have to discuss it: the word was so typical of my father that it suited him perfectly as a nickname. Besides, we felt that we had invented a term with a special meaning of its own to be added to our vocabulary. From that day on "Jarano" was our father's name and *jaranadas* were the peculiar things he did; *enjaranarse* became a verb meaning to behave as he would have done; a *jaranismo* was any way of expressing oneself that was similar to his. His strange sense of humor, for example, would lead him to say in jest something disagreeable that the person addressed could easily take quite seriously; this was a *jaranismo*. Also *jaranismos* were his peculiar ways of criticizing, correcting, or disagreeing with people by saying something that no one else would dare to put into words.

So this new word took out naturalization papers in our family; even after we were grown up and married, we still spoke of committing a *jaranada* or being a *jarano*. Even our children, who had never known him, used these expressions constantly.

Jarano heard of his nickname only shortly before he died. He found out about it, quite by chance, when he was already very ill; he merely smiled in an understanding way, without seeming to be offended, although it is most unlikely that he ever suspected the full meaning and flavor of the word. That secret name, for us, summed up his whole way of life.

Indian Market
by D. H. Lawrence

Market day has been an important occasion in Mexico since pre-Conquest times. Every village of more than a thousand people has its set market day, usually one day a week. At this market, local village products are supplemented by people from neighboring villages who bring in their baskets, their pots, and other handmade objects. There may be fifty or a hundred different vendors, mostly women, with their wares spread out artistically to catch the eye of the buyer. Fruit may be stacked like Aztec pyramids. Straw hats may be neatly fitted together. Rugs will be spread out or hung on racks to show their gay designs and vivid colors.

It is Saturday, and the white dots of men are threading down the trail over the bare humps to the plain, following the dark twinkle-movement of asses, the dark nodding of the woman's head as she rides between the baskets.

From the valley villages and from the mountains the peasants and the Indians are coming in with supplies, the road is like a pilgrimage, with the dust in greatest haste, dashing for town. Dark-eared asses and running men, running women, running girls, running lads, twinkling donkeys ambling on fine little feet, under twin great baskets with tomatoes and gourds, twin great nets of bubble-shaped jars, twin bundles of neat-cut faggots of wood, neat as bunches of cigarettes, and twin net-sacks of charcoal.

Onwards, on a strange current of haste. And slowly rowing among the foot travel, the ox wagons rolling solid wheels below the high net of the body. Slow oxen, with heads pressed down nosing to the earth, swaying, swaying their great horns as a snake sways itself, the shovel-shaped collar of solid wood pressing down on their necks like a scoop. On, on between the burnt-up turf and the solid, monumental green of the organ cactus.

They are mostly small people, of the Zapotec race: small men with lifted chests and quick, lifted knees, advancing with heavy energy in the midst of dust. And quiet, small, round-headed women running barefoot, tightening their blue rebozos round their shoulders, so often with a baby in the fold. The white cotton clothes of the men so white that their faces are invisible places of darkness under their big hats. Clothed darkness, faces of night, quickly, silently, with inexhaustible energy advancing to the town.

The market is a huge roofed-in place. Most extraordinary is the noise that comes out, as you pass along the adjacent street. It is a huge noise, yet you may never notice it. It sounds as if all the ghosts in the world were talking to one another, in ghost voices, within the darkness of the market structure. It is a noise something like rain, or banana leaves in a wind. The market, full of Indians, dark-faced, silent-footed, hush-spoken, but pressing in in countless numbers. The queer hissing murmurs of the Zapotec language, among the sounds of Spanish, the quiet, aside-voices of the Mixtecas.

To buy and to sell, but above all, to commingle. In the old world, men make themselves two great excuses for coming together to a center, and commingling freely in a mixed, unsuspicious host. Market and religion. These alone bring men, unarmed, together since time began. A little load of firewood, a woven blanket, a few eggs and tomatoes are excuse enough for men, women, and children to cross the foot-weary miles of valley and mountain. To buy, to sell, to barter, to exchange. To exchange, above all things, human contact.

That is why they like you to bargain, even if it's only the difference of a centavo. Round the center of the covered market, where there is a basin of water, are the flowers: red, white, pink roses in heaps, many-colored little carnations, poppies, bits of larkspur, lemon and orange marigolds, buds of madonna lilies, pansies, a few forget-me-nots. They don't bring the tropical flowers. Only the lilies come wild from the hills, and the mauve red orchids.

"How much this bunch of cherry-pie heliotrope?"

"Fifteen centavos."

"Ten."

"Fifteen."

You put back the cherry-pie, and depart. But the woman is quite content. The contact, so short even, brisked her up.

"Pinks?"

"The red ones, Señorita? Thirty centavos."

"No. I don't want red ones. The mixed."

"Ah!" The woman seizes a handful of little carnations of all colors, carefully puts them together. "Look, Señorita! No more?"

"No, no more. How much?"

"The same. Thirty centavos."

"It is much."

"No, Señorita, it is not much. Look at this little bunch. It is eight centavos."—Displays a scrappy little bunch. "Come then, twenty-five."

"No! Twenty-two."

"Look!" She gathers up three or four more flowers, and claps them to the bunch. "Two *reales*, Señorita."

It is a bargain. Off you go with multicolored pinks, and the woman has had one more moment of contact, with a stranger, a perfect stranger. An intermingling of voices, a threading together of different wills. It is life. The centavos are an excuse.

The stalls go off in straight lines, to the right, brilliant vegetables, to the left, bread and sweet buns. Away at the one end, cheese, butter, eggs, chickens, turkeys, meat. At the other, the native-woven blankets and rebozos, skirts, shirts, handkerchiefs. Down the far side, sandals and leather things.

The serape men spy you, and whistle to you like ferocious birds, and call "Señor! Señor! Look!" Then with violence one flings open a dazzling blanket, while another whistles more ear-piercingly still, to make you look at *his* blanket. It is the veritable den of lions and tigers, that spot where the serape men have their blankets piled on the ground. You shake your head, and flee.

To find yourself in the leather avenue.

"Señor! Señor! Look! Huaraches! Very fine, very finely made! Look Señor!"

The fat leather man jumps up and holds a pair of sandals at one's breast. They are of narrow woven strips of leather, in the newest Paris style, but a style ancient to these natives. You take them in your hand, and look at them quizzically, while the fat wife of the huarache man reiterates, "Very fine work. Very fine. Much work!"

Leather men usually seem to have their wives with them.

"How much?"

"Twenty *reales*."

"Twenty!"—in a voice of surprise and pained indignation.

"How much do you give?"

You refuse to answer. Instead you put the huaraches to your

nose. The huarache man looks at his wife, and they laugh aloud.

"They smell," you say.

"No, Señor, they don't smell!"—and the two go off into fits of laughter.

"Yes, they smell. It is not American leather."

"Yes, Señor, it is American leather. They don't smell, Señor. No, they don't smell." He coaxes you till you wouldn't believe your own nose.

"Yes, they smell."

"How much do you give?"

"Nothing, because they smell."

And you give another sniff, though it is painfully unnecessary. And in spite of your refusal to bid, the man and wife go into fits of laughter to see you painfully sniffing.

You lay down the sandals and shake your head.

"How much do you offer?" reiterates the man, gaily.

You shake your head mournfully, and move away. The leather man and his wife look at one another and go off into another fit of laughter, because you smelt the huaraches, and said they stank.

They did. The natives use human excrement for tanning leather. When Bernal Díaz came with Cortés to the great marketplace of Mexico City, in Montezuma's day, he saw the little pots of human excrement in rows for sale, and the leather-makers going round sniffing to see which was the best, before they paid for it. It staggered even a fifteenth-century Spaniard. Yet my leather man and his wife think it screamingly funny that I smell the huaraches before buying them. Everything has its own smell, and the natural smell of huaraches is what it is. You might as well quarrel with an onion for smelling like an onion.

The great press of the quiet natives, some of them bright and clean, many in old rags, the brown flesh showing through the rents in the dirty cotton. Many wild hillmen, in their little hats of conical black felt, with their wild, staring eyes. And as they cluster round the hat stall, in a long, long suspense of indecision before they can commit themselves, trying on a new hat, their black hair gleams blue-black, and falls thick and rich over their foreheads, like gleaming bluey-black feathers.

Market lasts all day. The native inns are great dreary yards with little sheds, and little rooms around. Some men and families who have come from far, will sleep in one or other of the little stall-like rooms. Many will sleep on the stones, on the earth, round the market, anywhere. But the asses are there by the hundred, crowded in the inn-yards, drooping their ears with the eternal patience of the beast that knows better than any other beast that every road curves round to the same center of rest, and hither and thither means nothing.

And towards nightfall the dusty road will be thronged with shadowy people and unladen asses and new-laden mules, urging silently into the country again, their backs to the town, glad to get away from the town, to see the cactus and the pleated hills, and the trees that mean a village. In some village they will lie under a tree, or under a wall, and sleep. Then the next day, home.

It is fulfilled, what they came to market for. They have sold and bought. But more than that, they have had their moment of contact and centripetal flow. They have been part of a great stream of men flowing to a center, to the vortex of the marketplace. And here they have felt life concentrate upon them, they have been jammed between the soft hot bodies of strange men come from afar, they have had the sound of strangers' voices in their ears, they have asked and been answered in unaccustomed ways.

There is no goal, and no abiding place, and nothing is fixed, not even the cathedral towers. The cathedral towers are slowly leaning, seeking the curve of return. As the natives curved in a strong swirl, towards the vortex of the market. Then on a strong swerve of repulsion, curved out and away again, into space.

Nothing but the touch, the spark of contact.

Courtship—Old Style
by Elizabeth Borton de Treviño

Elizabeth Borton, a young American journalist, entered Mexico with no thoughts of marriage, and remained to become the devoted wife of a handsome young Mexican engineer. She learned to admire and appreciate the old-fashioned courtesies and customs of a well-to-do Mexican family in the provinces. However, her brother-in-law Bob, who had spent some years studying and working in the United States, thought he preferred the American way of easy friendship between the sexes and informal dating.

In Monterrey the ancient Spanish custom of the *serenata* exists today, in all its pristine usefulness, though it has died out in many other provincial Mexican cities. While the band plays in the center of the square, and chaperones watch from the sidelines, the girls progress around the square clockwise, while the boys walk counterclockwise. It is almost the only way young people have a chance to meet each other, unless they are invited to the same parties.

Bob used to go to the *serenatas* in Monterrey and watch the boys and girls going around the plaza, making each other occult signals, with amused contempt. He was wont to smoke a cigar and take a seat on a bench usually reserved for a chaperone and do his best to keep a straight face as the girls paraded slowly past, pretending indifference when boys wielded a fabulous eyebrow technique in their direction.

In Mexico, the sexes are separated early, and they are not allowed to fraternize, even informally, until it is time for the mating dance to begin.

In Monterrey the *serenatas* are held in the Zaragoza Plaza on Sunday evenings, in the Purissima Plaza on Thursdays, on other evenings in the plaza of the Colegio Civil, Niño Artillero, and others. The boys and young men stroll carelessly round and round the plaza, while the girls, in little clutches of three or four, walk in the opposite direction. This brings them abreast of each other, so that looks may be exchanged.

109

The chaperones who load the benches on the outside edge of the square, and who seem to be knitting or indolently fanning themselves, never miss the twitch of a lip and are known to have ears worse than lie detectors. They keep a weather eye on the rising moon and the chimes from the church tower, so that their maidens may not stay too late.

Here in the *serenatas*, courtships begin, and the whole procedure is surrounded with such a terrifying set of rules and regulations that only the most desperately in love, the most patient, persistent, and impassioned, ever get to the altar.

When Bob had nothing better to do, he went to the *serenatas*, just for laughs.

One night, for the fun of it, he joined the boys going round and round, his cigar in his mouth, his hands in his pockets. And he came abreast of Beatriz. He has never been the same since.

Beatriz is the daughter of a doctor. She had just been graduated from the School of the Sacred Heart, and was now free to emerge into the world of men, courtship, and the *serenatas*. But she had older sisters; she was no greenhorn, and she knew all the ropes.

She was everything Bob had made fun of, she was all the things he thought he didn't like. He liked small plump girls, preferably blonde, agreeable, cuddly. Beatriz is tall and willowy and haughty, in the Spanish tradition. She had night-black hair and jet-black eyes, almond shaped, the preferred *almendrados* of the gypsies. When Bob removed the cigar from his mouth and tried to get out a pleasant word, a croaked "Nice evening, isn't it?" she swept past him all disdain.

"Waddya know?" said Bob to himself. He is no fool. He knew something had happened to him. Dispiritedly he went home to ask Mamacita about all the rules and bylaws. He was floored. "No, it's too tough," he decided. "I could never go through with it all."

But somehow, he found himself at the next *serenata*. He walked morosely in line with the boys, without his cigar, without hands in his pockets. He was correctly dressed, sedate and proper. He even wore a necktie, something he seldom bothered with. Beatriz moved toward him, wearing a dress of palest yellow. "Who wears yellow is certain of her beauty," goes the old Spanish saying. Roberto lifted his eyebrows at her. She dropped the longest blackest lashes he had ever seen but otherwise gave no sign that he was animal, vegetable, or mineral.

He stumbled round and round the plaza, absolutely bewitched, like all the others.

I was chatting in the patio with Mamacita when he came home.

"They got me, pal," confided Roberto to me. "They waited until they saw the whites of my eyes, and then they let me have it with both barrels. I'm a dead duck."

He lurched toward his room.

"He is in love," remarked Mamacita. *"Pobrecito* (Poor thing)."

So began that memorable courtship, which I watched breathlessly. If you think that life in the provinces is dull and quiet, you ought to be on one end of a Mexican courtship, or even an innocent bystander. Nothing is more dramatic, intense and formal, with absolute doom falling on either partner who takes a step out of line or does anything not strictly according to the numerous iron-clad rules. When we finally got Beatriz and Bob to the altar he had dwindled down twenty pounds, and she, a tall girl, was a wraith.

They had definitely been through the mill.

After the first *serenata* and the first eyebrow raising, the boy has to attend every *serenata* at which his beloved is likely to appear. Bob did this, doggedly. Week after week went by without her having noticed that he was alive and he was about to give up. Then one evening, as he came abreast of her, hopeful brows elevated pleadingly, Beatriz looked him straight in the eye and said distinctly " 'Allo!"

Bob was then permitted by the rules to break out of line and walk beside her. Like well-trained troops the girls walking with her fell back two paces to the rear.

"Say," began Bob joyfully, "I didn't know you speak English!"

"Do not spik," said Beatriz, and that was all she said to him for another couple of weeks, though they walked round and round for miles. Then she began, shyly, to chatter to him in Spanish and about a month later he had what might be construed as encouragement.

"I learned to say that word in order to interest you," she confided in Spanish.

"What word?"

" 'Allo."

"Dawg nab!" crowed Bob (his favorite oath) and she repeated wonderingly, "Dok naab?"

At this point the suitor had taken an irrevocable step. He had committed himself. This walking in the *serenata*, Roberto beside Beatriz, is no mere gesture of friendship. It is the first step in the dance of courtship. Everybody notices, everybody comments. "Roberto is courting Beatriz" the word goes around. This is important. The girls have a strong and perfectly disciplined union. If, after publicly walking with Beatriz in several *serenatas*, Roberto does not in due course take the next prescribed step, all the girls write him off as a *vacillón* . . . a playboy, a flirt; "*nada serio*" (not a bit serious) . . . and he will have a very hard job indeed getting another girl to respond to his lifted brow in the *serenata*. He may have to work *months* before a single self-respecting card-carrying member of the *señorita*'s union will even say good evening.

Next the swain will have to contrive introductions to some member of the girl's family, preferably a brother. If there are no brothers, then some dragon aunt. This takes some detective work and scurrying around, and commerce being in the blood stream of the male there is occasionally a passing of bills. But the formal introduction must be achieved somehow, for the young lady alone is not permitted to invite him to call.

However, long before the invitation to call has been nailed down, the lover must do certain other things. First, he must find out where his lady goes to church and to which mass. He must contrive to be seen at this mass if it kills him. (Even if she goes to five-o'clock mass, and there are stern *señoritas* who do this, in order to test their suitor's devotion.) He must be observed standing with folded arms at the back of the church, presumably possessed by pious thoughts. The girl, of course, knows that these are diluted by amorous agitation.

Thus Roberto, long a heathen and a relapsed heretic, became an ardent attendant at mass at La Purissima every Sunday morning at six.

All this has its meaning. First, the suitor gives the girl a chance. If she never speaks to him, he cannot even begin to court. Then the introduction, to make his intentions clear, and to allow the family to check on him. No hole and corner business. Last, and very important, he must indicate that he is a decent Christian young man, and no stranger to church.

Now he is permitted to accompany her home after mass, and to carry her prayer book.

In due course, he may invite her to a movie.

The *cine,* however, must be an *afternoon* movie. Mexicans well know the pernicious effects on the young of a full moon or of any moon at all. As for a dark moonless night . . . *"Qué horror!"* Having been invited to an afternoon *cine,* the girl must ask permission to attend. Until she is married, no young Mexican girl of good family may do anything whatsoever outside her home without express permission from her parents.

This permission is not tossed off indiscriminately. The whole matter has to be taken up with Mamacita, who ponders the young man's family and prospects, and thinks over his record (as supplied by the underground). There is still time to cut this thing off root and branch. An invitation to an afternoon movie in a sleepy Mexican provincial town is fraught with a good deal more drama and significance than might be assumed.

But if Mamacita, after consultation with Papacito, has been prevailed upon to grant permission to go to the movie with Roberto, it is with the stipulation that Beatriz must be accompanied by a couple of sisters and possibly an aunt or a cousin. Under no circumstances is she to go alone. Unheard of. And *not* in a car. Riding in a car unless it is overflowing with other people, in broad daylight, and with several flinty-eyed adults in the group, is considered definitely dangerous, and perhaps the Mexicans have something there. Any Mexican chaperone worth her salt is capable of producing a quart bottle of gasoline from her reticule, in case of any suspicious stalling of the motor, for every trick and falsity of the male is known to these ladies, and nobody gets up early enough in the morning to get ahead of them.

After a few afternoon movies, well spaced, it becomes known that Beatriz and Roberto are *novios.* This means they are "going steady." It is a sort of rehearsal for being official *novios* or really engaged. But in Mexico it is almost as confining a relationship as marriage.

As soon as Beatriz admits that she is Roberto's *novia,* she is subject to his orders, to his tastes, preferences, and indications. This is customary. He may tell her not to use any rouge or lipstick, on pain of his displeasure, or he may say "Let your hair grow, I do not care for bobbed hair," or "Never let me see that red dress again, I prefer you in pale blue." The girl is bound to obey him in everything, and furthermore, she now has to ask *his* permission, as well as Mamacita's and Papacito's, to do anything outside her home.

The following telephone conversation is typical. The young man is called to the telephone. It is his *novia*. She wants to ask permission to have her hair dressed.

"At what time?" asks the *novio* sternly. "Which beauty shop? Who will accompany you? Mind you go straight home afterward. I do not want you to associate with Nena González, she has had three *novios* in the past year and is too frivolous. And do not have those side curls done; I like your hair loosely waved. Let's see, it is now four thirty. I will allow you one hour at the beauty shop and at five thirty exactly I will come to your balcony. Very well. Goodbye, *mi vida*."

And so on. If the girl gets recalcitrant anywhere along the line, the word will go out along the underground to other young men of marriageable age that they had better not have anything to do with Beatriz. She is a Tartar, you can't get her to do anything for you. She won't obey, she is a bad risk.

Now since Roberto is a *novio* he may visit Beatriz at her balcony whenever he wishes. Houses in the old part of Monterrey are built flush to the street with great windows open all the way down to the street. Inside are strong wooden shutters that may be closed at night and outside there are iron bars. These bars keep the lovers far enough apart to take care of morals, though some bold ones may kiss through the bars. (Better not let Mamacita catch them, however.)

Now the *novio* may bring serenades to his love, hiring groups of musicians to play the guitar, violin, and bass viol and he may sing with their accompaniment if he has a good voice. Usually the serenades occur after midnight, and the young lady may not show herself at the window in her night dress, so the lover takes a chance that she notices and listens. Sometimes the unfortunate girl notices too well. One young friend of mine rang up her *novio* one morning to thank him for the lovely *gallo* or serenade and he answered unpleasantly, "What serenade?"

"Why, the one you brought to my window last night!" cried my friend.

If she had been quick-witted, she might have scented trouble and have turned aside from danger by pretending that she was twitting him.

But my feeble-minded friend plunged on, "The musicians played 'Pity, Pity On Me Who Suffer' three times! You know it is my favorite song."

The *novio* had not sent the *gallo;* indeed a rival had brought it to the window of his hopeless love. The *novio* suspected this, he accused the girl of flirting. She said he should have thought of serenading her at least. One word led to another, and the awful consequence was that they proceeded to *terminar,* or terminate relations.

To *terminar* means literally "to finish." This is a serious, a heart-rending business. In the provinces, the idea that you can be *novios* one day and simple friends the next is incomprehensible. No such wishy-washy relationships are allowed. You are in love or you hate each other.

He has done something horrible to you; he has caused you to lose your time. Now you have to begin all over. Of course, it is well within the bounds of possibility, that if the *novio* goes through enough humble eating of crow or if he is seen with a gun at his temple by a reliable witness, you may accept him back as a *novio* again. The point is, emotions have to be at white heat or none of it is any fun.

The moment comes when Roberto must take the final step. He must ask to call. Permission is granted. The date and the hour for the call are arranged. The moment the doors of the *zaguán* of Beatriz's house clang shut behind him, he is an engaged man. He is now what is called the "official" or accepted *novio.*

At each step of the courtship the *novio* must go one pace further or he stands to be blacklisted for years. And all the while he is subjected to a fanatical and constant spy system. All the friends and relatives of the girl render her regular daily reports on the *novio*'s movements. Woe if he has been seen walking home from mass with some other *señorita!* Woe if he has been caught near the balcony of some rival charmer. Woe if he has made a trip out of the city without the express permission of his *novia!* Woe if he has been observed in swimming without wearing around his neck on a chain the holy medal of his sweetheart! Woe if he has been seen to pat the head of some small child of unknown parentage . . . perhaps it is his! *Anathema!*

After he became the *novio* official, Roberto was able to invite Beatriz to an evening dance, accompanied by other *parejas* of his brother and wife, or her brothers. Naturally Beatriz danced only with Roberto and Roberto only with Beatriz. They would both be thought libidinous were they to stand and gyrate in the embrace of any other person!

On a certain day, therefore, Mamacita made Papacito put on his best suit, and she arrayed herself in her best black crepe and her formal hat with plumes. They were to accompany Roberto (nervous and muttering Dog-nab every few minutes) to the home of Beatriz to *pedir* her. To formally ask for her hand in marriage.

In the doctor's formal *sala* the four parents sat in dignified conclave. Mamacita and Papacito indicated Roberto's solvency and nobility of character. Beatriz's parents took these matters into careful consideration. Vermouth and sweet cakes went round. At last a formal date was set for the wedding. It was to be six months' distant. Beatriz needed a tonic, her doctor father thought. Roberto had to save up for the expenses of the wedding.

It is customary for the *novio* to give the *novia* a sum of money to cover the purchase of her wedding gown, slippers, veil, underwear and flowers, and all the clothes she will need for her trousseau, as well as the traveling expenses of herself and a chaperone, while she goes to the nearest large city to buy her things. This dates from the old tradition of the Mexican gentleman bringing his bride a coffer in which are her wedding garments.

Meanwhile, he gets busy finding a house and furnishing it. Some of the trouble and expense of furnishing the home is taken care of by a canvass of possible wedding gifts. Thus maybe the girl's parents intend to give her a rug and a sofa for the *sala,* while his will give the bedroom. An uncle is touched for the stove and some kitchen furniture. A group of the *novio*'s friends chip in to purchase a dining-room set. And so on. But whatever he lacks, the bridegroom must provide himself.

The maiden brings to her marriage her linens, some gifts, and her lovely self. Nothing more. The bridegroom even pays for the wedding reception and banquet.

All the girl's family is obligated to pay for is the "civil" wedding, which, according to Mexican law, is the only one establishing legal rights. This must be performed by a judge, and duly registered. However, only a small percentage of citizens consider that this civil wedding is the real one. The real wedding takes place before the altar in church. Thus it often happens that due to churches being booked full for weddings, and due to tradition itself which counsels a lag between the civil and the religious ceremonies, the young married woman, who has been legally united to her husband by a judge, remains in her father's home another month or so, and then is married in church. Only then may the wedding journey take place; only then are the young people really considered man and wife by all their Catholic families and feelings.

Roberto's courtship was spangled with dramatic quarrels and reconciliations. Once they terminated. Beatriz threw the book at him, as the saying goes. After all, he had been away from Monterrey a long time, and a girl can't be too careful. He might have got some of those strange foreign ideas in the United States. Several times the *novia* exercised one of her privileges, which is to impose a *castigo* or chastisement. To punish the *novio* for some offense, she tells him that she will not see him or answer his phone calls for a fixed period of time.

If he is seen at a dance or a *serenata* or even a movie, he is done for. Roberto took to his cigar.

Their wedding was charming. The old Mexican custom indicates that the couple are met by the priest at the door of the church and there married. The bridegroom passes the bride moneys of gold and silver, to indicate that he endows her with all his worldly goods. Then, when mass begins, they hear mass together as man and wife on their knees. Tall candles burn in front of them, for fertility. During the mass, the bridegroom is enveloped in the bride's veil, at one point, to show that she will protect and care for his comfort and at another point, they are bound together with a chain of flowers.

Some weeks after his marriage, when they had returned from their honeymoon, Roberto came to see us. He was a happy young bridegroom. But he had spent ten thousand pesos and the purpose of his visit was to congratulate Luis on having had the good sense to marry a foreign woman who didn't know all about these expensive customs.

"I can tell you it will take me *years* to save up that much money again," declared Roberto, "and you can bet I'll never get a divorce! Dog-nab!"

The Miners of Guanajuato
by Dana Catharine de Ruiz

Tuso—a small, burrowing, underground animal—is the special nickname given to the miners of Guanajuato, who have been burrowing into the rich, brown, muscular foothills of the surrounding Sierra Madre Occidental for over four hundred years. Searching for gold and silver, the tusos have found it in great quantities. They have also developed interesting traditions and customs which set them apart from people who work in other trades.

One night in 1548, near the little Indian village of Guanajuato, two men met on their way from Mexico City to Zacatecas, hoping to make their fortune. Glad to have company on the long trip, they made their camp together, building a small fireplace over which to cook what little food they had. In the middle of their stories of the riches they would find in the North, legend has it that the two travelers realized that the stones they had gathered to build their fireplace were shining very brightly, too brightly to be anything else but gold. They quickly registered their claim to what is said to be the first mine in Guanajuato under the name of San Bernabe, in honor of the saint whose feast it had been when they made their discovery. This mine is still being worked, now under the name of La Luz—evocative of the firelight which led to its discovery.

After the Spanish Conquest, hordes of Spaniards flowed into Guanajuato making the unlikely little village built up and down the sides of canyons the center of incredible wealth for the next several hundred years. It is said that three-fifths of the world's silver and gold were poured out of the mines of Guanajuato into the crown of Spain, for which the city was given a title by Carlos V—*Muy Noble y Leal Ciudad de Santa Fe y Real de Minas de Guanajuato.* The miners of this very noble and loyal, royal mining city of Guanajuato wore silver in their hats and on their jackets and spilled gold dust from their pockets.

Besides the obvious vices their money was responsible for, the miners also contributed greatly to the building of many of the

118

magnificent Churrigueresque churches to be found in each *Mineral* —the small, and at that time, very rich mining centers of the city. These churches with their towering altarpieces covered in gold leaf, magnificent German pipe organs, and walls decorated with amethyst and quartz crystal from the mines themselves, are among the few reminders of those fabulous days of the past.

Today the miners walk down the dusty roads to Cata, Valenciana, El Cubo and La Luz, wearing denim overalls and jackets. Perhaps the only gold they'll ever wear is that which they sport in their front teeth to give their smiles character, as they say.

Another leftover from Guanajuato's rich mining past and even farther back in time than that, is the spring ritual "Viernes de Dolores," celebrating the miners' patron, the Virgin of Sorrows, a week before Good Friday. The mines are gay colorful places on this day. Altars are erected for the special Mass celebrated at each mine. A painting of the Virgin with a sword piercing her heart which depicts the grief of the week to come, is shaded by a canopy of silvery poplar leaves from which dangle oranges, bananas, and coconuts. Copal—Aztec incense—is burned among the little pots of new wheat, and the two worlds of Mexico blend with its smoke.

The miners invite everyone to come drink *agua fresca*—a fresh fruit drink made of crushed strawberry, lemon or orange juice topped with *chía* seeds. According to the custom, one can knock at any door in Guanajuato and be served *agua fresca*. This day and this day only, the miners will allow their wives and sweethearts to enter the vertical shaft mines. On any other day, a woman in a mine is bad luck. The mines are dangerous enough as it is!

The rest of the city celebrates this spring "Friday of Sorrows" by rising at 6 A.M. The girls dress in long colorful skirts, blouses embroidered with flowers, and rebozos to warm their shoulders in the cool of the early morning. All of Guanajuato, young and old, goes to the Union Garden to promenade to the waltzes played by the Municipal band. The flower vendors have arrived before anyone else and have filled the surrounding streets with carnations and roses and *nubes*—a small white flower called "clouds" which are brought to hand out to friends. Altars in each home are decorated with branches of poplar, little pots of new wheat, copal, and beautiful cut tissue-paper flags depicting religious scenes.

There are vendors of paper flowers too, who have come from far away to be at the Union Garden in Guanajuato on this day. They stand with their wooden staves blooming with tissue-paper flowers, their faces as blooming with smiles. The little garden is overflowing with people and flowers, it is hard to tell which is which! And soon the tiled floor is carpeted with the green leaves and petals of the flowers which have been crushed underfoot. By 10 or 11 A.M. that is all that remains of the fiesta.

But the Fiesta of the Virgin of Sorrows is only one day in the year. Most of the time, to be a miner is not such pleasant business. Why do men choose to become miners and to burrow underground? It is hard, dangerous work. Every day holds the possibility of being hit by flying stones from the blasts.

It is said that a young man who begins to work in the mines at the age of 18 becomes "*cascado*"—literally, broken—by silicosis, or tuberculosis—by the time he is 28.

Why then? Mining is not just another job. The miners love their work, and speak of it as they would of a woman. It has the same mysterious hold on them, and their eyes light up with something perhaps no one but a Tuso can understand.

Pito, the Wanderer
by José Rubén Romero
translated by William O. Cord

Pito Perez, the wanderer, is the leading character in a best-selling Mexican novel, which has appeared in twenty-two Spanish-language editions and has been made into two movies. The hero, or non-hero, is a philosopher and poet who has become a popular folk-hero.

The dark silhouette of a man was plainly outlined in the luminous arch of the bell tower. It was Pito Perez, intently absorbed in his contemplation of the surrounding countryside.

His bulky, ill-fitting shoes had come apart and they seemed to grimace as if in pain. His pants appeared to have been made of cobwebs and his jacket, fastened in front with a safety pin, cried out for help through all its open seams. But its pleas did not stir the pity of the people. An old, broad-rimmed straw hat formed a golden halo around his head.

Beneath these miserable rags was seen an even more wretched body with its rough, colorless skin. The face, pale and lean, seemed to be that of an ascetic wasted away by fasting and religious vigils.

"What are you doing here in the tower, Pito Perez?"

"I came to fish for memories, with the view as my bait."

"Well, I came to hammer out poetic imagery in the forge of twilight."

"Am I bothering you?"

"Good Heavens no, man. Am I in your way?"

"Not in the least. We came up into this tower with different goals in mind and each of us, in his own way, will achieve his end: you, the poet withdrawing from the world long enough to search for rhymes for your sonnets, those fourteen trembling, little birds; I drawing close to my village, to see it, to feel it once again before leaving, perhaps for good; to take with me the memory of all its little nooks and corners, its streets and roads and byways, its gardens, its hills. Perhaps, perhaps never again will I see them!"

121

"Once again the wanderlust, Pito Perez?"

"What else? I am a restless Pito, a restless dingus who will never strike it rich. Believe me, I don't want to go. I swear it. I'm trying not to leave this land which after all is very much mine, very much a part of me. Ah! Canuto's tasty tidbits! And Aunt Susa's stew! And the coconut tortes that Lino the baker makes! But, I have just come off a long and fateful drunken binge and my relatives want to get rid of me, as does everyone else. Everything around me proves it to me: the stores won't give me credit any more; my friends don't invite me to their get-togethers; and the Mayor treats me as if I were the world's worst criminal. Why do you think he doubled this last jail term I just finished serving? Well, only because I made an innocent comment at the moment I was being sentenced to the tank. He gave out with his solemn sentence: 'Pito Perez, for being drunk and outraging the public decency, ten dollars fine, or thirty days.' To which I answered with all due civility: 'But, sir, what are you going to do with your dingus holed up so long?' The Mayor blasted me with the artillery of his authority, sentencing me to clean the prisoners' latrines for three nights in a row. Haven't you ever noticed that the profession of being a tyrant is much easier than being a physician or a lawyer? First year: an endless cycle of promises, smiles, and courteous words to those who elected him; second year: ending old friendships or paying off old friends to avoid being reminded of the past by their presence—creating a Supreme Council of Brown Nosers; third year: complete courses in self-worship and delusions of grandeur; fourth and final year: complete predominance of personal opinions and abuses of all kinds. After four years the Degree of Tyrant begins to become quite repulsive to everyone and no university would dare revalidate it."

"You are quite intelligent, Pito Perez. One can scarcely find reasons as to why you waste your life away drinking, carousing, and censuring others."

"I'm a friend of Truth. And, if I get loaded, it is for no other reason than to bolster my courage to speak it out. But as you know, from the mouths of babes and drunks. . . . Add to all this the fact that I really do hate and despise the privileged classes."

"Come on over. Sit down. Let's talk as if we were old friends."

"Suits me. Our conversation could be titled: *Dialogue between a Poet and a Madman.*"

We sat down on the outside edge of the tower with our legs dangling down. My new shoes, next to Pito's, were well polished and they shone with that foolish pride of the rich. In fact, they had such a shine that Pito looked at them very scornfully and I felt the full impact of his stare. Our feet epitomized our entire social world filled with its injustices and inequalities.

"Why did you say that our conversation would be a dialogue between a poet and a madman?"

"Because you boast of being a poet and everybody here in town thinks of me as a plain old incurable idiot. They swear that there's a screw loose in my whole family. That's a good one! They are sure that my sisters, Herlinda and María, suffer from some religious disease and because of it they never leave the church. The people swear that Concha is off her rocker because she spends all her time teaching street dogs to sit on their hind paws, and her brown and white cat to eat at the table with all the grace of a real gentleman. They say that Josefa threw herself down a well, head first, because she was crazy. And Dolores fell in love with a circus performer for the same reason, according to the infallible conclusions of those Holy Fathers who run loose around here. My brother, Joaquín, the priest, won't hear confessions from the zealous females because he's wacky, and I get crocked and I sing and I cry and I walk through the streets with my clothes torn to shreds because I'm nuts! What idiotic logic! Those who live without the will to live, those who live only because they are afraid to die, they are the crazy ones! Those who try to hide their true feelings, they are the crazy ones! And those who would like to run off with a circus performer but don't dare because of what others might say, they are the crazy ones! And those who torture harmless animals instead of teaching them to love man, they are the crazy ones! Isn't that so, Brother Francis Assisi? Those who kneel before some joker who is really their equal, some wiseacre who mumbles Latin and wears a cassock, just to tell him obscenities—like those washerwomen who go down to the creek every Saturday to wash their blouses, knowing full well that next week they will be back to do the same thing because they have only one blouse—they are the crazy ones! And even crazier than I are those people who do not laugh, or cry, or drink, because they are slaves to useless social customs! I prefer my mixed-up family and not that flock of hypocrites who see me as a black sheep simply because I don't sleep on their dunghill or bah in unison with all the others."

"But, it is one thing for some to think you mad and quite another for you to live so oddly—and please excuse me for speaking to you so frankly—without your honorable family reputation meaning anything to you. For what end does your intelligence serve you?"

"Intelligence! The hell you say! The only thing that is certain, and you won't believe this, is that I am a real wretch. My bad luck has followed me since the day I was born and everything I try comes out just the reverse from what I wanted. But, don't think that I drink because of that! I get drunk because I like to—and for no other reason. If I have any talents, I use them to find a means to get my drinks free. That way, I get double pleasure. Oh, how I enjoyed that time when I drank a whole barrel of grain alcohol in Flores' tavern. And without anyone realizing how crafty I really was! I'll tell you how I did it just in case some day you want to make use of my trick.

"In Flores' tavern, the barrels of wine serve as backs for the customers' chairs. Knowing this, I used go to there every night and, completely sober, I would sit down near one of the barrels. After some time of idle chitchat, I would get to my feet, always with some difficulty and always talking with a thick tongue. And, night after night, the owners would say: 'That Pito Perez! He really gets soused! He comes in stone sober and crawls out on all fours!' And it was true. I had to go down the street on all fours so I wouldn't lose my way home, sometimes meowing like a cat and other times barking like a dog—and so lifelike, that the real animals followed me and tried to fool around with me. The real secret of my binges was this: With a corkscrew I was able to make a hole in the cork of the barrel and in it I put a piece of thin tubing which, hidden beneath my coat, brought to my mouth the comfort of that tasty liquid which, from so much drinking, was quickly liquidated forever. With a blob of sap from a logwood tree, I disguised the hole. (It's a pity that others can't plug up their own holes the same way.) The vice of wine is terrible, my friend, for as a starting point, a sot must lose all sense of decency. It takes a lot to lose it, but when one is freed of it how relaxed, how unworried he is. As they say, one of the best known shameless bastards of Mexico has preached."

"Tell me something about your life, Pito Perez."

"I can't now because I have to keep a date with a friend who has offered to buy me a few drinks. It would be sacrilegious not to take advantage of such a great opportunity."

"Then, let's make a deal: Come here every afternoon and then, when we climb back down the tower, I'll pay for your conversation with a bottle."

"Anything I want? Cognac? Champagne? But, don't get frightened. Those drinks are for the wealthy immigrants who really don't love our country. I imagine that those who drink these things are like those Mexicans who went to Europe to bring back an emperor as fair as champagne.

"It is necessary to make use of what a country produces: To govern us: a dark-skinned man, like Juárez; to drink: from Puruaran, tequila or charanda or aguardiente, the offspring of the sugar cane, which indeed is as noble as the grape. I assure you that if Mass were consecrated with aguardiente, the priests would be more humble and more kindly with their flocks."

"OK. Since you are such a unique character, I will pay you, for each hour of conversation, with a bottle of that Puruaran aguardiente which you praise so highly. We human beings are cruel in this respect: we offer a drink to a hungry man, but never a piece of bread."

"And do you think you're going to have a good time listening to me, and that my life is a mosaic of witty remarks? Or a little music box that plays only happy tunes? My life is a sad one, like that of all cheats. But, I have seen people laugh so often at my sorrow that I have ended up laughing at it myself, thinking that my pain will not be so bitter since it affords some pleasure to others. I'm on my way now to find my benefactor because I never renege on a deal to drink at someone else's expense. Tomorrow it's your turn, as we have agreed."

And Pito Perez disappeared down the spiral stairway of the tower, like a dirty penny disappears into the slot of the collection box.

Black Gold
by Carleton Beals

Prospecting for oil, the black gold of modern Mexico, was developed during the twentieth century by foreign capital, much of it North American. When Lazaro Cárdenas was president in the late 1930s, the government expropriated all foreign-owned oil properties, paying for them a price set by the government. The following incident belongs to the period before government control.

Come the seekers for oil, sniffing along the "golden lane" of Tamaulipas for hidden black treasure. On that lane lives a humble family, Señor Ignacio Ramírez and his sweet young bride. Dark of skin, she wears beautiful red and gold embroidered *huipiles* and flowers in her black hair. Their cornfield whispers songs at the caress of the breeze from the Gulf; their orchards shed blossoms in the early spring. They are happy, little knowing that under their feet flows the black tide of power, which turns turbines and flings battleships across far seas.

The oil seekers try to buy Ramírez' property. He is happy as he is; he refuses. So they try to lease merely the oil rights. Ramírez ponders. Money after all is good. Why should he give over his wealth cheaply. He has heard tales: Cerro Azul, making hundreds of millions; wells that gush tens of thousands of barrels of the precious black liquid in a day.

He demands a million dollars for his property.

Two nights later he is murdered. The culprits are arrested by the police, but the military commandant snatches them away to the island prison fortress of San Juan de Ulua. Later they are poisoned.

Sadly Concha walks through the whispering cornfield; its songs are different now.

Some days later, she notices a foreigner in a wide Texas hat, riding past her gate. He is young and handsome, probably an American. Every day he rides by. One morning he asks her for a drink of water. They talk.

126

He claims to be a rancher, further up in the Sierra. He is very nice and courteous; and he seems to like her. She looks after him a bit wistfully.

She does not know that he is a lawyer for one of the most powerful foreign petroleum companies, that he is a southern gentleman with violent color prejudices.

Now he stops at her gate every day. He makes love to her and ere long she responds to his simulated passion. There are long walks under the swollen tropic moon; junkets by the rippling shore. At first she was afraid, thinking he wished merely to possess her. But he offers marriage. The day is set. Her former husband is a remote dream now.

One day, he suggests a marriage contract should be signed. Such a course is always customary among his people. This seems foolish to Concha, but she acquiesces. He is a sun god to her; anything he says must be wholly right.

They journey to an elegant office in Tampico. There are numbers of men, some Mexican, some foreigners. They have hard wolfish faces, or soft cunning feline faces—but simple Concha does not perceive this. There is champagne and congratulations; and then papers. Long typewritten sheets. She is to sign here.

She takes up the pen, hesitates a moment.

Breathless suspense. Is she going to refuse to sign? No, she is merely looking for the proper line. She affixes her signature.

She has signed away all of her oil rights. She is dispossessed. The blond foreigner rides by no longer.

The Children of Sánchez
by Oscar Lewis

Jesús Sánchez, born in Vera Cruz in 1910, the year of the Revolution, tried to support his family by working in a restaurant, playing the lottery, and doing occasional odd jobs. He was hardworking, authoritarian. He had four children by his first wife, Lenore: Manuel, Roberto, Consuelo, and Marta. These children, born after the Revolution, put great emphasis on freedom and social mobility. But when they were out of a job or sick, they knew that their father would never refuse to help them.

The Sánchez family lived in the Casa Grande *vecindad*, a large one-story tenement in the heart of Mexico City. Within the *vecindad* stretch four long, concrete-paved patios or courtyards, about fifteen feet wide. Opening onto the courtyards at regular intervals of about twelve feet, are 157 one-room windowless apartments, each with a barn-red door. In the daytime, beside most of the doors, stand rough wooden ladders leading to low flat roofs over the kitchen portion of each apartment. These roofs serve many purposes and are crowded with lines of laundry, chicken coops, dovecotes, pots of flowers or medicinal herbs, tanks of gas for cooking, and occasional TV antennas.

In the daytime, the courtyards are crowded with people and animals, dogs, turkeys, chickens, and a few pigs. Children play here because it is safer than the streets. Women queue up for water or shout to each other as they hang up clothes, and street vendors come in to sell their wares. Every morning a garbage man wheels a large can through the courtyards to collect each family's refuse. In the afternoon, gangs of older boys often take over a courtyard to play a rough game of soccer. On Sunday nights there is usually an outdoor dance. Within the west entrance is the public bath house and a small garden whose few trees and patch of grass serve as a meeting place for young people.

I, ROBERTO

When we moved to the Casa Grande I was still quite small. Our first room there was very tiny and in terrible condition. The floor was full of holes, out of which came large rats. We would lose lots of things down those holes, money, marbles, combs. There was no electricity there then, until my father paid them to connect it up. I liked being in it, but neighbors kept moving in and I had to test them, to make them come into our circle. If they didn't, they were led a miserable life.

I began to like fighting. I didn't go complaining when they hit me, but would tangle with anybody immediately. Thus, I relieved my brother of the responsibility of having to fight for me. Actually, I never wanted to fight with anybody, but they kept looking for it. I had to defend myself and continued to do so all my life.

The top *gallos,* the ones who fought best, became part of the group of leaders. They were ranked like the army: Wilfredo, Captain; Ignacio, Lieutenant; Hermilio, Second-lieutenant; Manuel, Sergeant; I, Roberto, Second Sergeant; and so on. When we measured our strength with the captain, we were the ones who decided what we would do when we played. One after another of us began to dominate.

There is a game, "follow the leader," in which ten or fifteen of the gang would get together and follow "the hand," the leader. If he jumps over a sewer, all the others have to do it. If they don't, we gang up on them. When I was "the hand," there were quite a number of complaints brought to my *papá.* I got into trouble because I jumped the fence around the little garden here in the *vecindad.* I could jump it easily, but there were boys who couldn't and they began to destroy it. Also, there were my escapades with the water and sewer pipes. They were all the way up at the top and I used to climb to the roof that way. As a result, I pulled down or loosened a few pipes.

I liked to walk around the rooftops, too, and fell more than once. Most of the time, I fell feet first, standing up, and that's why the boys called me the "Orang-outang." When we played soccer and would lose the ball on the roof, the "Orang-outang," to make a good impression, would climb up to look for it. The neighbors would tell Elena, or complain to my father and he would send Manuel to look for me. He was always sensitive about the neighbors' complaints. Later, when I got home, I relaxed my body and waited to receive the blows.

When Elena asked my father for permission to visit her mother, who lived in a village in Jalisco, I begged her to take me. Consuelo, whom Elena loved the most, thought she should be the one to go but my *papá* sent me along, to look after Elena, or perhaps to spy on her. Anyway, the two of us left on the train. It was my first long trip and my memories of it are pleasant.

To me, to recall is to live again! I liked the way of life there. The village was picturesque, with unpaved streets and adobe houses. I liked the village church the most. I got to know Elena's family, her mother, Santitos, her brothers, Raimundo and Arturo, her two sisters, Soledad and Concha, who later died. Señora Santitos was a fine person, very decent. Like Elena, she had no schooling and didn't know how to read and write. I liked them all.

They taught me how to milk the cows, and I even drank the milk straight from the teats. I would push aside the calves or the baby goats and lie down and drink! We spent about a month there, a happy month for me.

Consuelo and Fermín

Fermín came to live in the tenement six or seven months before I celebrated my fifteenth birhday. He was a relative of my stepmother, Elena. This young man was a shoe finisher, and was very handsome, even though his hair and face were usually covered with the dust of the shoe shop, and he wore old overalls without a shirt. He would follow me when he saw me on the street and say, "Consuelo, Consuelo, don't be so proud. Just turn around and look at me. Don't be mean. Look at me, or else I'll throw myself under a bus—while it's parked." I wouldn't say a word but I would smile and, with him behind me, walk faster, frightened to death that we might meet Roberto. If my brother were to see me, he would knock me down.

When I paid no attention to him, Fermín tried to win Antonia's confidence. One night my father sent Tonia and me for the bread. I don't know whether they were in cahoots or not, but I saw Fermín standing in the entrance to the tenement, very clean and his hair combed. Antonia said to me, "You stay here while I go for the bread," and walked on. I felt as though a bucket of ice water had been poured over me. I was afraid because of all the insults I had given him, like, "Take a bath first," "*Pachuco*," "You're *loco*." I also thought of the gossip if I were to be seen in the street with a man at this hour.

But he said, "Consuelo, I love you, honest to God, I want to marry you. But don't call me *Pachuco* just because I work." He seemed so ridiculous talking to me like that, looking at me so sadly. I felt like laughing. He went on, "When I see you pass by, I feel like yelling, you are so pretty. Tell me when I can see you and you'll make me the happiest man on earth. Tell me what you want me to do. I'll do the impossible for you. Tell me!" I noticed that he had very nice features. To be talking in this way seemed stupid but on seeing how tender his eyes were, I stopped smiling. Tonia was coming back with the bread, so I hurriedly told him. "Yes, yes, wait for me in a little while in the corner of my courtyard."

On the way back Antonia asked me what he had said. Disinterested outside but very excited inside, I said, "Nothing, he just wants me to be his girl." Tonia said, "Do what he says. He's very handsome. You see how he keeps after you." But I didn't get out that night. At supper time my father was right opposite me. When I heard a whistle that seemed to say my name, I almost spilled my coffee. Tonia made signals to me with her eyes. I finished my coffee quickly and asked my father for permission to show Señora Yolanda my sewing. It didn't work.

A few days later I met Fermín as I was coming home from work. I explained that my father was very strict and didn't let me go out alone at night. He accepted my explanation on the condition that I come out that night; if I didn't, he was going to knock on my door. Holy Virgin! Knock on the door! The house would fall in on me! "Yes, this time I'll come out. Honest, Fermín. Wait for me."

At eight sharp I heard the first whistle, and it made me jump. "What's wrong with you, clown?" my father immediately yelled at me. "Nothing, *papá*, I think I was falling asleep." That was very good, because then he didn't let us go to sleep immediately. I took advantage of the opportunity to ask him to let me go out for a little walk. He agreed.

I went to Irela's house—a friend of Marta's. I remember the advice she gave me: "Go on, don't be a fool. Now that they've let you go out, give them something to hit you for."

"All right, but tell me if anyone comes, eh, Irela?"

I shot across the courtyard like a skyrocket and was still trembling when I got there. Fermín greeted me. "Good evening, my love, I've been waiting for you and at last you're here." Then he kissed me. I held my breath and felt as though I was smothering. I pressed my lips together and with my eyes wide open looked at his eyes, which were closed. It lasted only a moment. When Fermín felt that I wasn't kissing him back, he moved away and said he knew I didn't love him but that later on I would. Meanwhile he thanked me for having given him that kiss. "I gave him a kiss!" I sighed with relief. Now I knew what a kiss was.

But then I remembered how dirty he looked during work and it disgusted me. I said good-bye to him and went back to Irela's house. "You're terrific," she said, and kept laughing to see me scrubbing at my mouth with my hand and making faces. I felt like throwing up. She asked me, "And you didn't like it?" I told her I didn't thinking that would set her a good example. But as she kept talking I realized that she could teach me things.

The next night at eight sharp, there was Fermín's whistle. I managed to get out. As soon as he saw me, he kissed me. There was another kiss on leaving. Meanwhile he talked to me, "When I get the money together, we'll get married, little one. You'll just see what a pretty house I'll fix up for you. Or I'll take you to my homeland, my village in Jalisco." I listened to all of this leaning on his shoulder or watching his eyes, which was what I liked best about him. But to manage to be with him was a triumph, as I would hardly ever get permission from my father. Fermín trusted me and waited hours for me to come out, sometimes with luck, other times not. Even if it rained, he was there. My father didn't suspect me.

The Wonder Kids of Monterrey
by Michael Scully

Mexico has produced international champions in many sports: including golf, baseball, and horsemanship. The Mexicans have a growing interest in Little League tournament teams. Baseball, or béisbol, *is a top sport among the younger generation.*

The kids from Monterrey, Mexico, on the northbound bus, were the smallest of the 3,000 teams entering the Little League baseball tournament of 1957. They were also the poorest, and in a way the least experienced. Some had never before ridden a bus, had a barbershop haircut, or even seen downtown Monterrey. This 150-mile trip to McAllen, a Texas border town, was the bright peak of their twelve-year-old lives.

But they were realistic kids. Had anyone told them they were off on the greatest small-boy adventure since Jack climbed the Beanstalk, he would have got fourteen skeptical grins. And if he'd added that they would wind up as the guests of presidents and great cities, he might have heard a murmured *"¡Qué locura!"*—"What a craziness!" They knew their money would barely take them to McAllen. If they could beat Mexico City, the only other team from Mexico in the competition, they could call themselves champions of Mexico and that would be glory enough.

To save bus fare the kids and their coaches walked across the border bridge, lugging playing gear and clothes. At three to a room, they got a low rate in a McAllen motel. Harold Haskins, manager of the team, induced a café to cut prices on two meals a day. By lunching on hamburgers and walking to the park, he hoped they might afford to stay three days.

On the field next afternoon, the Monterrey boys looked like little brothers of the Mexico City team, but their attitude was king-size. When a fan asked, "Don't those big boys scare you?" tiny "Pini" (Pee-wee) González smiled up at him. "We don't have to *carry* them," he explained calmly, "—just play them."

133

And so they did. While his infield moved with the timing of a pony ballet and outfielders stood idle, whip-thin Enrique Suárez held Mexico City hitless until his team piled up nine runs. Score: 9–2. Next day, with the same cheerful insouciance, Monterrey beat McAllen's own team 7 to 1.

On the third day Monterrey introduced one of the most versatile ballplayers of any age: Ángel Macías, a right-handed shortstop and left-handed first baseman, who also plays the outfield, and pitches —with either hand! Right-handed, he held Mission to one hit. Monterrey, winning 14–1, found itself scheduled for the district playoffs. And Haskins found only three dollars in his pockets with which to feed fourteen ravenous appetites.

That was Chapter I of the great sport story of 1957.

When Mexico City's Little League was founded in 1952, its teams were made up of fine, vitamin-packed boys from prosperous homes. But a few years later when an American Legion post formed the Monterrey League, organizer "Lucky" Haskins gave a chance also to the barefoot small fry from the factory zone, and struck a rare vein of spirit. To kids from homes where wages barely bought corn, beans and occasional meat, a chance to play *béisbol* in real uniforms was a miracle. Mentally alert and fast afoot, they quit practicing only for darkness. Analyzing their zest, Haskins, once a U.S. college star, concluded, "They have the secret ingredient of winners—they *want*."

The team also had César Faz, Haskins' head coach and field manager. A Texan by birth, Faz had been the proud bat boy of the San Antonio Missions and the St. Louis Browns. He had studied the ways of such crafty veterans as Rogers Hornsby, Hank Severeid and Gabby Street. Now a Monterrey metalwork expert, his mind was a crossfile of baseball lore. He drilled his players in fundamentals—signals, swings, pick-ups and throws—until the team had the deftness that saves fractions of seconds and inches. Equally important, he made himself a big brother to the boys, and so was able to exercise the kindly but effective discipline which is characteristic of their homes.

The result was a pint-size anomaly. McAllen fans at first glance felt sympathy for these shyly smiling kids with the built-in sun tan. But from the moment they took the field and began to warm up —with an assured air, carefully rehearsed to disconcert their opponents—the boys commanded respect.

Faz, who insisted that all take a pre-game nap, faced rebellion when the kids saw their first swimming pool—and their scheduled opponents splashing happily in it. Gazing at the swimmers, he observed, "Huh! Knocking themselves out, aren't they?" Then he turned. "Okay, those who want to win today's game will go to bed. The others may go swimming." His athletes considered that, smiled, and meekly filed to their rooms.

After three straight victories the kids were eagerly asking, "What next?" The coaches, with funds near zero, were in a quandary. But help came from new-found friends. Two Texas ranchers, declaring, "These boys are too good to quit for want of a few dollars," took over the motel bill. The café cut its prices again; fans invited the team to meals. And back in Monterrey, as the newspapers extolled the *chamacos maravilla*—wonder kids—there was a scurrying to raise new funds.

Meanwhile, the kids, oblivious to financial crisis, eliminated Weslaco, 13–1, in the district tourney. Then in the decisive game with Brownsville, Ángel Macías had a brief first-inning lapse; two hits and a walk filled the bases. But the ambidextrous youngster smiled reassurance at the bench, hitched up his pants and struck out the side. Permitting no more hits, he won 6 to 1. With the final out, he trotted eagerly in to the jubilant coaches. *"Now* may we go swimming?" he demanded.

Next came the sectional playoffs at Corpus Christi, where carloads of McAllen fans followed to cheer Monterrey on to two more victories. Then, sweeping through another pair of games at Fort Worth, they emerged with the Texas championship. Now their travels were financed by tournament receipts. At the Fort Worth airport, boys who had never been higher than they could climb gaped unbelieving at the airliner waiting to take them to Louisville and the southern regional playoffs.

The press, newsreel men, even autograph seekers met them in Louisville. Life was becoming a bit bewildering. All that zooming through the sky had left them wondering whether they were still in the same world with Mexico. Even the crowd, cheering them in unintelligible English, emphasized their distance from home.

As they started against Biloxi, Miss., the kids had clearly lost their sharp edge. For three innings they played uncertainly. Then Haskins produced his homesickness antidote, a phonograph record. As loud speakers blared the valiant, challenging *"Corrido de*

Monterrey," the dugout became a row of tear-streaked grins. There was still a Mexico! In five minutes the *chamacos* filled the bases, and slender "Pepe" Maiz cleared them with a four-run homer. Final score: Monterrey 13, Biloxi 0. Then the indomitable Macías, with a one-hit game, beat Owensboro, Ky., 3 to 0.

On August 19 the kids who had left home for a bus ride to the border reached the mecca of sub-teenage baseball, Williamsport, Pa., where each year the Little League World Series brings together champions of east, west, north, and south.

The western team, sun-ripened boys from La Mesa, Calif., averaged 5 feet 4 inches tall, and 127 pounds. Those from Escanaba, Mich., and Bridgeport, Conn., were slightly smaller. The Monterrey squad averaged 4 feet 11 inches, and 92 pounds. When special Series uniforms—cut to U.S. small-boy dimensions—were passed out, "Pini" González (4 feet 4, and 70 pounds) pulled his pants up to his shoulders and grinned over the waistband. "Look, I'll need a necklace for a belt." The *chamacos* elected to use their old uniforms.

But their spirits were soaring now; Mexico had caught up with them. Before the game with Bridgeport, the Mexican flag went up while a band played their national anthem. Monterrey's mayor and city treasurer, Mexican diplomats from Washington, D.C., and a delegation from New York were in the stands. Even the English-speaking crowd was mixing *"Vivas!"* and *"Olés!"* with its "Attaboys!" Fresh from their nap, the kids caught a good Bridgeport team napping. A daring steal of home by Fidel Ruiz led them to a 2–1 victory.

What happened next day should happen once to every twelve-year-old, to convince him that dreams can come true. A Monterrey newspaper used four pages to tell of it. Even the restrained *New York Times* called it "almost unbelievable." The smallest team met the biggest team, La Mesa, in the climax game. With his mates overmatched by five inches and thirty-five pounds each, Ángel Macías mowed down eleven Californians on strikes, and forced the rest to ground out. There were no walks, no errors. It was a perfect no-hit game, and the *chamacos*, with four runs in the fifth, had parlayed their bus ride to McAllen into the world championship.

As the cheers of ten thousand swept Memorial Park, Ángel, possibly the only switch-pitcher in baseball, climbed into César Faz' arms for the happiest sport photo of the year. Then, quickly regaining his native dignity, he told a microphone, *"Estoy muy contento."* ("I'm very happy.")

But that was not the end. The kids flew to New York as guests of American Metal Climax, Inc., whose Mexican subsidiary is a sponsor of the Monterrey league. At Ebbetts Field in Brooklyn they met the Dodgers and Cardinals, to whom Macías explained how to become a switch-pitcher ("You just grow up that way"). In Washington, D.C., President Eisenhower gave them each a pen inscribed with his name, and Vice President Nixon took them to lunch with Mexican Ambassador Manuel Tello. Then, flying to Mexico City, they received trophies from President Ruiz Cortines and solemnly conveyed the regards of a mutual friend, Dwight Eisenhower.

And there was still Monterrey.

There is a vivid Spanish phrase: *echar la casa por la ventana*—to throw the house out of the window. Monterry had done that a week before, after the final out at Williamsport, with factory whistles blowing, bells ringing, fire sirens shrieking, skyrockets bursting. Now the city did it again. The plane bringing the kids home was engulfed by a crowd of fifteen thousand, and half the city surged along their route to the state capitol. There were speeches, music, the dedication of a Roll of Honor of seventeen names to be fixed forever on the capitol walls—and peaks of such crowd fervor that the boys had to be rushed indoors for safety.

But when all that had subsided, there were left some results worth appraising. In their 13-game sweep through the homeland of baseball, the *chamacos* had scored 99 runs, their opponents 13. Macías, in six games, had pitched two one-hitters plus his no-hitter, and struck out 73. Such figures were enough to give U.S. boys, and some of their elders, a new evaluation of the nation to the south.

The kids did something else, too. Everywhere, their infectious grins and innate good manners, as well as their size and precision play, won the U.S. crowds. Some Texas fans even went to Mexico for the triumphal homecoming.

In the factory zone of Monterrey, the small houses crowding the rutted streets are flimsy and sparsely furnished. "You might call these boys poor, but *not* underprivileged," says César Faz. In their homes there are usually family unity, order and contentment—and mothers who work hard at their primary job of being mothers.

"Some of these kids," says Haskins, "never saw TV or a movie, never owned a bicycle. But, reared with old-fashioned discipline, they have learned to work for what they want, and what they wanted on that trip last year was to win."

The tiny Macías home is typical. Along with the glittering momentos of their conquest, Angel and eleven other boys received something more substantial: scholarships to Monterrey's best private schools. Today in the Macías front room there stands a home-made cabinet filled with the souvenirs of fleeting glory—cups, medals, pictures, presents from the presidents of two countries, a ball signed by Stan Musial, a rabbit's foot from the boys of La Mesa, Calif. But squarely in the middle of all these glamorous memories, Angel's mother keeps the one most important thing, her son's report card. It says that the only switch-pitcher in baseball is near the top of his seventh-grade classes—learning English, too.

Women Who Led the Way
by J. W. F. Stoppelman

"These women," says a friend of the author, "have proved by their actions that the women of this country can equal any man in leadership." Through education and improvement of social services, both María Lavalla Urbina and Amalia de Castille Ledón have devoted their lives to the emancipation of Mexican women.

The dense crowds in the narrow Calle Argentina, in the center of Mexico City, overflow into the patios and wide corridors of an old palace containing the offices of Prevención Social, a branch of the Ministry of Justice. People walk up and down talking together, or stand around waiting in front of closed doors. Many sit silently upon benches along the walls. At the end of one of the passages a young man in slacks and turtleneck sweater is enthroned behind a worm-eaten desk. He is the Cerberus guarding María Lavalla Urbina, head of the Prevención Social, against unnecessary disturbances. He studies my visiting card long and seriously, carries it into the office and returns at once. "Well—you can go inside!" he says jovially.

The room I enter is bright and large, with gray walls. Between two high windows sits Señora Urbina at a metal desk. She gives me a nod, and a signal to sit down at a conference table.

For more than half an hour I watch the coming and going of visitors, mostly officials bringing documents for perusal or signature. They carry on a hurried conversation with their chief, or greet her with the traditional Spanish double embrace, as a long-lost friend. And finally Señora Urbina is ready for me.

Yes, confirms the señora, she was indeed the first woman lawyer in Mexico's southwest. To be exact, at Campeche, near the edge of the jungle where once the culture of the Mayans flourished. "My fellow citizens were greatly annoyed with me for claiming a place in a profession that so far had rigorously excluded women!"

But soon they had more reason for anger. María Urbina distin-

guished herself to such a degree that she was elected a judge in
Mexico City. Three times in succession she served the full term for
which a judge is nominated in Mexico. She took decisions without
the assistance of a jury in cases of the most diverse nature: robbery,
assault, murder, rape and holdups. Then, some years ago, she was
granted temporary leave of absence to organize the newest branch
of the Ministry of Justice, the Prevención Social.

Under her guidance more than seven hundred men and women
now work throughout Mexico on the problem of juvenile delin-
quency and, as elsewhere in the world, special attention is given
to transforming young offenders into decent citizens. A number of
institutions cooperate: Social Assistance, Social Security and several youth associations. A Court for Minors has been established,
and in the more remote sections of the country thirty teams, con-
sisting of doctors, nurses, social workers and anthropologists, en-
deavor to change, slowly but surely, the often incredibly primitive
conditions under which the Indians and their children live.

"Have you in all these years of public service ever felt that you
are obstructed because of being a woman?"

Señora Urbina smiles significantly. "I have not often been given
the chance to forget that I *am* a woman!" she exclaims. "Most
Mexican men still firmly believe that a woman's place is in her
home, and that all her life should be exclusively devoted to her
family. True—they have by now become more or less reconciled
to the idea of having female lawyers, doctors, nurses around. But
a woman in a high Government post? Ah—that's a different story!"

"You have been a leading figure in the Mexican feminist movement for a long time. Where does it find the bulk of its followers?
What has the movement so far done for the women of Mexico?"

"The real interest in the emancipation of our women does not
come from our well-to-do, from our laboring class or from the
millions of Indian women in the backwoods. The middle classes
are our strongest supporters—teachers, office workers, shop assistants, doctors. And what have we achieved? Well, we have
gained ground, though not without much trouble. You see for
yourself: I am an example. And there are many other females in
leading positions. We try to persuade our women to use their
comparatively recently acquired rights—to go to the polls, for
instance, whenever there is an election. We mean to build a community in which our men have lost their fear of female competi-

tion. No country can truly thrive if its women are not allowed to contribute their share in its development."

"And what about the millions in the hinterland you mentioned? What does your movement do for them? It seems to me that at present they get little more out of life than hard labor, and families that are much too large."

Señora Urbina hesitates.

"Yes," she admits, "that is a great problem. The only solution lies in general education—and that requires a lot of time. If we talked now to the average peasant woman about her rights, she just wouldn't understand us. Education—well, something is being done in that direction. Though I shall not contradict you if you say that it isn't enough by far."

"And meanwhile the children of those large families have little chance to get on to a higher social plane; right? Don't you believe then that much smaller families are a first necessity? That birth control might well be the best solution of all? And has your movement done anything to further it?"

Señora Urbina looks at me in surprise.

"No, certainly not!" she says decidedly. "We would not dream of defending the introduction of birth control as a government measure. You must not think that this is due to religious influences. It is simply that it clashes with our feelings. *Mexicans love their children,*" she adds in English, and smiles.

"And where will you find work in the years to come for a population increasing from year to year by more than three per cent?"

"We mustn't despair," Señora Urbina concludes, but in her eyes I read resignation. "As the population grows industries will doubtlessly expand. There will be new industries besides. Other sources of subsistence will also be found. I am sure of it."

Amalia González Cabellero de Castille Ledón is a tall, blond woman with purely Spanish features. She is cautious in her answers to even the most innocuous questions. It is easy to recognize in her the prudent diplomat; and, indeed, she has been Plenipotentiary Extraordinary of the Mexican Government to Sweden, and its ambassador in Switzerland.

Those two nominations crowned a quarter of a century of hard, devoted labor in the service of Mexican feminism. As far back as 1945 she represented Mexico at the World Conference for Equal

Rights for Women at San Francisco. Repeatedly she has served on the Mexican delegation to the United Nations' General Assemblies in New York. She also organized the first regional conference for the discussion of women's problems in North and Central America. At present she is Assistant Minister for Education and Cultural Affairs. Her immediate superior is the well-known former Director-General of the Social and Economic Council of the United Nations, Jaime Torres Bodet.

Discussing with her the subjects that are now closest to her heart, I ask whether she thinks sufficient progress is being made in the struggle against illiteracy.

"Since 1944 we have had obligatory schooling for all children," she says, "but I admit that for too many years that law had little practical significance. Now, under Torres Bodet, we work hard for its enforcement. New schools are being built everywhere, and more training schools have been opened to combat the great shortage of teachers. But the problems we have to cope with, especially in the rural areas, are colossal. Very often the children speak only the ancient Indian language of their region, or at best just a few words of Spanish. What we need there, first of all, are bilingual teachers, and that in itself is a big enough problem. The polyglot nature of the hinterland, together with the enormous differences between the tribes in their outlook on life, are our greatest obstacles. Nonetheless, there is no reason for pessimism. We see good progress being made across the length and breadth of Mexico. Even the older people begin to display an interest in knowledge, no matter how fundamental, especially in the big cities and the industrial parts of the country."

Señora Ledón does not see anything extraordinary in having attained one of the highest government posts. "I am by no means the only woman fit for this kind of work!" she says modestly. "Nowadays there are many university-trained women available, but often they have been too shy to compete with men. That picture is changing very rapidly; there are plenty of women ready to take responsibility for important executive posts. Public opinion is still not completely in their favor. Our men are still inclined to see ambitious graduate women as dangerous competitors. Also, they continue spreading the slander that women can never do things as well as men, especially when it comes to intellectual work and political leadership. In commercial circles things are a little better. I know a few female directors of commercial enterprises."

She agrees with Señora Urbina that the well-to-do show little interest in the feminist movement. They go on giving their card parties and organizing their bazaars and charity balls. Real interest comes exclusively from the middle classes. "That *clase media*," Señora Ledón prophesies, "will grow enormously during the next twenty-five years. From it Mexico will get the impetus and the strong drive towards quicker and greater development."

"Which, even so, will still be slow progress."

She nods.

"Unfortunately that is right. There's so much left to be done. Enormous sums of money will be needed to do it." She pauses a moment. "Our taxes are too low, especially for those who could well afford to pay a great deal more. Maybe an entirely new taxation system should be introduced. Also, we are in dire need of more generous tax regulations for new enterprises, both from North America and elsewhere. At present those regulations are not sufficiently attractive."

There is a moment's silence. Then Señora Ledón says: "The women of Mexico have too little contact with the European women. That should change; we can learn much from one another. And I do believe that together the women of the world can do a great deal to protect mankind against the horrors of a possible nuclear war. I often think," she concludes, "that world peace might be achieved sooner if women played a greater part in the efforts to attain it."

PART 5
FOLK ARTS
AND FINE ARTS

Maya Art
by Miguel Covarrubias

Of all the indigenous people who lived in Middle America during the pre-Columbian period, none reached a higher culture than the Maya. The Aztecs were more powerful politically; they had a genius for administration. They had fine arts, too, but they excelled more in architecture and the dance than in painting and drawing. The Olmecs and the Zapotecs produced sculpture and art objects of exquisite design and artistry, but none compare with the Maya. Covarrubias also compares the Maya favorably with the best of the Old World civilizations. "Maya art combines the precise hieraticism of the Egyptians, the decorative flamboyancy of China, and the sensuous exuberance of the art of India."

The ancient Maya developed the arts of architecture, sculpture, painting, and decoration to a degree of complexity without precedent in America. Maya art is perhaps the most realistic in the sense of representing the human form literally, with its true anatomical proportions. The Maya tackled the representations of group composition with personages in naturalistic poses, often foreshort-

Abridged from *Indian Art of Mexico and Central America*, by Miguel Covarrubias. Copyright © 1957 by Alfred A. Knopf, Inc. Reprinted by permission of the publisher.

ened, and with emphasis on movement—ideas that never concerned the artists of other, more formalistic cultures. However, the Maya area was always relatively isolated, and Maya art was rigidly restricted to the representation of ceremonial and religious ideas. Consequently, it is only natural that it grew into a symbolic, highly decorative art at the service of an urban priestly aristocracy. To the common people of the time, the official art—the stelae, the reliefs, the glyphs—was probably as strange and incomprehensible as it is to the Maya peasant of today. The sumptuous palaces and lofty temples must have seemed as exotic and theatrical as the mystery of the Catholic cathedrals seems to a modern peasant.

Despite their complex mentality, the Maya made a restricted use of themes in their art; they limited themselves to the glorification of the priestly aristocracy and the representation of religious ideas —the gods, certain mythical monsters and dragons, astronomical concepts, and ordinary animals and plant forms when they had some symbolical or glyphic connotation, never scenes of daily life or representations of ordinary people unless they were show slaves or victims.

The ever present subject matter is not a god, as in Buddhist or Hindu art, but the apotheosis of an important priest or chief, either performing some rite or in the act of vanquishing an enemy. They are shown standing, seated cross-legged, or reclining on a throne, richly dressed and holding some sort of weapon of rank. Great care was always lavished on the minute and deliberate representation of the details of dress or personal adornment, often to the extent of almost concealing the figure, with only the face, arms, and legs clearly discernible.

The wealth of information of the ceremonial dress of the Maya has been thoroughly studied and analyzed, and I shall list here only what seem the most important of these elements. They deformed the skull into an exaggerated tall and narrow head, and they tattooed or, rather, scarified their faces with delicate rows of small welts around their mouths. They remodeled their noses, perhaps with some sort of putty, raising the bridge up to the middle of the forehead to conform with a concept of beauty involving long, high noses. They wore their hair long, cut into locks of different lengths, which they twisted and built up into complex hairdresses adorned with flowers and jade spangles and tubes.

On their ears they wore great jade earplug flares with a central ornament of jade tubes ending in a small jade blossom. They used jade rings, and on their wrists and ankles wore cuffs and leggings of row upon row of emerald-green jade beads. They wore short skirts and decorative loincloths, capes, and belts with elaborate jade buckles. Of jade also were the wide collars of beads, either strung in rows or forming a sort of net that covered the shoulders, and the necklaces with gorgets, often in sets of three, made of jade masks.

They also wore very elaborate sandals of jaguar skin with fringes and complicated buckles. But the most spectacular part of Maya dress was the helmet, often in the shape of a fantastic animal, topped with monumental swirling fans of long quetzal feathers. As accessories they carried feathered spears, shields, scepters, and a ceremonial bar in the shape of a two-headed snake. The spectacle of one of these Maya lords dressed in garments of golden jaguar skins lined with blood-red cloth and covered with green jade and iridescent feathers must have been magnificent.

Ever present in all aspects of Maya art is the mask, in front or profile, of the rain god Chac, in all degrees of stylization; it is derived from an "Olmec" jaguar mask. The mask of Chac, like its "Olmec" ancestor, appears everywhere like an obsession—on the bases of monuments, in headdresses, and apparently to fill any empty space. Other masks of deities are used in the same manner —the mask of the sun god with its strabismic, large, deep-set eyes, and the mask of the death god with its fleshless jaws. Equally important is the endless variety of dragons and serpents, complete or represented just by heads, which crawls through the intricacy of Maya symbolic decoration. There are celestial dragons, dragons with human faces emerging from the monster's jaws, two-headed serpents, feathered serpents, fire serpents, and so forth.

Many animals are represented in Maya art—jaguars, bats, monkeys, tapirs, deer, dogs, armadillos, quetzals, and the mythological *Moan* bird, half quetzal, half Chac, as well as frogs, turtles, fish, and snails from which little human beings emerge. Of great importance also is the representation of a sacred tree, the Tree of Life, shown on the great slabs of Palenque, such as the "Slab of the Cross," on the "Foliated Cross," and on the slab that covered the sarcophagus found in the Temple of the Inscriptions. Common also is the representation of a water lily, which often emerges from the mouth and eye, or grows from the head, ear, nose, or neck of mythical beings such as the Moan bird, the long-nosed god, or, more rarely, the jaguar.

There are further representations of the moon and the planet Venus, skulls, crossbones, and so forth, and, last but not least, glyphs and numerals used for their decorativè value, with human and monster faces, hands, and other more or less abstract motifs that often make an inscription a veritable artistic masterpiece of design and a clever juggling of related forms.

Poet Nun of the New World
by Carlos González Peña

translated by Gusta Barfield Nance
and Florene Johnson Dunstan

The colony of New Spain did not produce many original literary voices. So it was all the more remarkable when a woman, and a nun, wrote poetry far superior to that of her century and her peers. She wrote carols, and poems of religious and worldly love. She had something to say and the genius to say it with honesty and a delicate perception of human values. At the age of eighteen, she entered the Convent of San Jerónimo, took the veil as Sor Juana Inés de la Cruz, and remained there the rest of her life.

J uana Inés de Asbaje—such was the name the blessed nun bore in worldly life—was born in a farmhouse in San Miguel Nepantla, in the territory of Amecameca, on November 12, 1651.

Her precocity presaged the robust strength of her genius. At three years of age, without the knowledge of her mother, she began her studies. "My mother having sent my sister, older than I, to one of those so-called 'friends' to be taught to read, I followed her as a prank; and, on hearing the lesson given to her, I became fired with the desire to learn to read; deceiving the teacher, I said that my mother wished me to receive a lesson also."

Whatever the lesson was, it must have been easy for a pupil of such ability. In two years, says her biographer Father Calleja, she had learned "to read, write, count, and perform all the quaint intricacies of pretty needlework."

She had been born with the natural gift of expressing herself in verse. Before she was eight years old, she had composed a *loa* (a commendatory introduction) for the Corpus Christi festival. In the meantime, her intellectual curiosity continued to grow. She heard that in Mexico City there were a university and schools in which the sciences were studied. "And as soon as I heard this, I began to beseech my mother with urgent and persistent entreaties to allow me to change my manner of dress [the future nun proposed to disguise herself as a man] and go to Mexico City in order to study and to attend the University while living in the home of some relatives. She did not permit me to do so—and quite rightly—but I satisfied my desire by reading many different kinds of books belonging to my grandfather, without letting punishments or reprimands stop me."

Juana Inés was eight years old when she moved with her parents to the capital of New Spain. Here all wondered, as she said, "not so much at my talent as at the memory and information I had at the age when it seemed that I hardly had time to learn to talk." Twenty lessons from the bachelor Martín de Olivas were sufficient for her to acquire a mastery of Latin. She had not only ability, but the will to work. When she wished to acquire new knowledge, she adopted the harsh practice of setting a time limit for herself by cutting her hair; if her hair grew out before she accomplished her purpose, she cut it again, since she did not think it appropriate "that a head so devoid of knowledge should be covered with hair, which is a most desirable adornment."

She was beautiful with spiritual and profound beauty, which is quite evident and unforgettable in the portrait Cabrera made of her when she was a nun. Since she was intelligent as well as beautiful, her fame spread and soon she became prominent at court as a lady-in-waiting to the wife of the viceroy. The latter was quite flattered by the many poems that the poet dedicated to her. A little later, astonished at the intelligence Juana Inés seemed to possess and desiring to test her, Viceroy Marqués de Mancera called to his palace all the professors at the university and also all scholars in Mexico City who were learned in the arts and sciences.

The young girl appeared before an assembly of about forty theologians, scripturists, philosophers, mathematicians, historians, humanists, and poets. And "just as"—in the words of the viceroy—"a royal galleon would defend itself from smaller sloops which were attacking it, so did Juana Inés extricate herself from the questions, arguments, and rejoinders that all, each in his field, propounded."

While living in the palace of the viceroy, she was not only admired for her rare intellectual gifts, but courted for her beauty. Strangely enough, however, at this time she suddenly determined to embrace a monastic existence.

Considering the spirit and customs of her age, such a resolution was not extraordinary, but for those who are acquainted with one element of her lyrics—perhaps the best part of her poetry: the love element—there is concealed in that important and possibly dramatic moment of her life a mystery that perhaps will never be solved. Was a hidden passion, perhaps a disappointment in love, the motive that impelled her to enter a cloister?

She offered an explanation, certainly, of the motive which caused her to take that step, by saying: "I became a nun, recognizing that the profession had aspects (I am speaking of the accessory, not the essential things) repugnant to my intellect; but withal, in view of my complete distaste for marriage, taking the vows seemed the least undesirable and most reasonable choice I could make. For the sake of the assurance of salvation, that being of the first and greatest importance, I yielded up all the foolish desires of my being: the wish to live alone, to have no obligatory duties that would deprive me of freedom to study, and no community gossip to disturb the restful silence of my books."

But the heat of the flame which burns in some of the poet's verses is sufficient to indicate that she made the foregoing statements after she became a nun, with the purpose of keeping her real reason secret, and not while she was contemplating taking the vows.

In the shadow of the cloister, she lived among her books, maps, and musical and scientific instruments, consecrated to study. But such consecration could not always be constant or tranquil. Once her Mother Superior, "very saintly and candid," ordered her to abstain from study as a sinful thing. In view of her health, physicians, on another occasion, made the same recommendation. But since she had a strong will and since her consuming love of books and her desire for knowledge constituted her reason for living, she devoted nearly all of her time in the convent to study.

Toward the close of her life, events forced her to depart from the path she had been obstinately following. It happened that she challenged some statements made by Father Vieyra, a famous preacher, thereby giving an opportunity to Don Manuel Fernández de Santa Cruz, Bishop of Puebla—who assumed the pseudonym of "Sor Filotea"—to address to her a stupid letter in which, after flattering her for the above-mentioned challenge, he exhorted her to lift her eyes to heaven and give up secular learning in order to consecrate herself entirely to religion. "You have wasted much time," concluded the bishop, "in the study of philosophers and poets; now it is right that you should give up books and devote your time to perfecting yourself."

Literary history owes much to the impertinence of "Sor Filotea"; if his letter had not been written, the best document on the life and psychology of the poet would be lacking. This document is the valuable letter which Sor Juana sent in reply to the Bishop of Puebla, a letter in which she gave the most complete data now available on her life, her character, her literary inclinations, and the difficulties arising from these, and in which, further, with the most noble integrity, she declared herself in favor of the education of women and maintained her right to question the sermon with which she had disagreed.

Very deep, however, must have been the effect produced on the mind of the illustrious nun by the bishop's warning that she should consecrate herself entirely to religious matters and completely separate herself from secular things. For, shortly thereafter, she ordered sold, for the benefit of the poor, the four thousand volumes in her library, as well as her musical and scientific instruments and her maps. She made a general confession and signed with her blood two protestations of her faith. In the solitude of her cell, there remained only devotional books, the reading of which she interrupted frequently with the rigors of cruel penances. In the fervor of such mystic ardor, Sor Juana had spent two years when an epidemic of malignant fever desolated Mexico City and invaded the convent. Impelled by a great love, the poet then nursed her sick sisters, and, being stricken in turn, she fathomed the secret of death on April 17, 1695, at the age of forty-four years.

Even if Sor Juana's poetry is not always devoid of affectation, her best poems reveal the influence of no school, portray her own unique personality, and have "enduring and absolute poetic value," as Menéndez y Pelayo says. These are the works that make her the major poet of her epoch and place her among the greatest poets in the Spanish language.

"Sor Juana's poems of worldly love," in the judgment of Menéndez y Pelayo, "are the most gentle and delicate that have ever come from the pen of a woman." There is such eloquence in them —Sor Juana succeeds so easily in using the right word at the right time (the true touchstone of sincerity in love poetry)—that the suspicion, well founded, indeed, has been voiced that a passion, as fervent as it was mysterious, must have filled the life of the match-less poet. The amorous demands, the soft cooing, the painful complaints, the jealous raptures, the grief broken with sobs are not, and could not be, artificial and feigned experiences: they have the incontestable accent of truth.

LOVE LYRICS BY SOR JUANA INÉS DE LA CRUZ
translated by Peter H. Goldsmith

> *Who thankless flees me, I with love pursue*

> Who thankless flees me, I with love pursue,
> Who loving follows me, I thankless flee;
> To him who spurns my love I bend the knee,
> His love who seeks me, cold I bid him rue;
>
> I find as diamond him I yearning woo,
> Myself a diamond when he yearns for me;
> Who slays my love I would victorious see,
> While slaying him who wills me blisses true.
>
> To favor this one is to lose desire.
> To crave that one, my virgin pride to tame;
> On either hand I face a prospect dire,
>
> Whatever path I tread, the goal the same:
> To be adored by him of whom I tire,
> Or else by him who scorns me brought to shame.

Males perverse, schooled to condemn

Males perverse, schooled to condemn
  Women by your witless laws,
  Though forsooth you are prime cause
Of that which you blame in them. . . .

Their resistance you impugn,
  Then maintain with gravity
  That it was mere levity
Made you dare to importune.

What more elevating sight
  Than of man with logic crass,
  Who with hot breath fogs the glass,
Then laments it is not bright!

Scorn and favor, favor, scorn,
  What you will, result the same,
  Treat you ill, and earn your blame,
Love you well, be left forlorn. . . .

Whose the guilt, where to begin,
  Though both yield to passion's sway
  She who weakly sins for pay,
He who, strong, yet pays for sin?

Then why stare ye, if we prove
  That the guilt lies at your gate?
  Either love those you create,
Or create those you can love.

Made in Mexico
by Patricia Fent Ross

The Mexicans are a creative people. This is true for the fine arts of architecture, painting, jewelry-making, music, dance, and literature. It is equally true for such popular arts as pottery, basket-making, glass, leatherwork, feather-work, and woodworking. When you see something marked "made in Mexico," it is more likely to have been made by hand than in a factory. Mexican folk art is strong and beautiful. The individual craftsman expresses himself continually in articles for everyday use, beautifully designed and decorated. This was true among the Indians of pre-Conquest days, and it is true today.

Most of the handicrafts of Mexico are ordinary things for daily use, and they are arts because the craftsmen take the time and the trouble to make them beautiful as well as useful. They are the sort of things everyone used to make by hand, but nowadays, in most countries, people have forgotten how to make things because they have long since grown accustomed to buying what they want ready-made.

The Indian and mestizo villagers of Mexico still make by hand most of the things they use, even though it does take lots of time. Every blanket, every dish, and every chair they make is a separate piece of work, an individual creation just a little different from all other things of its kind. But they are so used to having only hand-made things that it is the factory-made goods that seem rare and strange to them. They charge very little for their work—much less than it is worth, in fact. Usually they count up the cost of the materials they have used and add a little for their time, unless they forget it, but they never think of adding anything for the imagination and skill they must have to do their work. North Americans think and talk a great deal about their "know-how" in technical processes and administrative methods in industry. But the Mexican craftsman takes his "know-how" in the handicrafts for granted. No one thinks any more of his knowledge than one does of the farmer's knowing how to plant his fields.

Long ago, in the days when Mexico was an Indian country, many years before Columbus discovered America, the people of the more advanced nations had adopted the habit of specialization. One man might be a very good potter but a poor weaver. So the potter made pots and dishes for the weaver's family, and the weaver made cloth for the potter's family. And both of them traded their goods to the farmer for grain and vegetables to eat.

It is not just the individual craftsman that specializes in a certain kind of handicraft. Whole villages will work at pottery-making, or weaving or lacquerwork. And each village has its traditions, handed down by its ancestors. All the pottery of a village is likely to be the same color and texture, because all the potters use the same kind of clay. But they also all use a certain style of decoration, because that is what their ancestors did. Each piece is individual and just a little different from every other piece, but they are all of the same general type of design, and all are painted in the same colors.

Such a village is known all over the country as making a certain thing in a certain way. So that when one looks at a bowl or a vase, or a lacquered tray, one knows at once where it was made. When one wants to buy a certain kind of pottery or blanket, he goes to the village that makes it, on that village's regular market day.

The people of a weaving village will buy their dishes and cooking utensils from a nearby pottery-making village, and the potters will go to another town for their hats and serapes, but the country people never use things made outside their own region. That is so strong a custom that they would feel disloyal to their own *tierra* if they wore or used things from another region.

The Mexican people love their country very much and are proud of both their Indian and Spanish heritages. But almost more than his country as a nation, the Mexican loves his own *tierra*, that is, his own "land," the village where he was born. A Mexican born in one of the large cities feels the same way about his native city, but in the rural towns and villages, and especially in the Indian communities, that love of the home soil is especially strong. Most of the *campesinos*, the "country people," never leave their own *tierra*. But if one does leave and make a new life in the city or another town, he never quite rejects home. When a Mexican says *"mi tierra,"* there is love in the very sound of the words. And so as the *campesino* or the Indian loves his *tierra,* his own customs and traditions, so too he loves best the dress, the serapes, and the pottery of his region.

After Mexico was conquered by Spain, mural painting died out because the Spaniards were then the rulers and they did not like Indian painting. Catholic churches replaced the old Indian temples, and the churches were decorated with the work of the new colonial artists. There was no place for the religious murals of the Indians. But they still loved colors and liked to paint. So the succeeding generations of Indians and near-Indian mestizos found new ways of using their art.

The most important work of these amateur painters is the making of *retablos* or "miracle paintings," which have a very special place in the lives of all *campesinos,* in both Indian and mestizo villages. In fine art, the *retablo* is the big carved or painted altarpiece in a church, but in popular art it is the name people have given to the miracle paintings.

When someone is very ill, is hurt in an accident, or is in great danger, the family always prays to the Virgin or one of the saints for special help. If the patient lives and gets well, or escapes the danger, they believe that it is because the Virgin or the saint intervened to save him. Or if one has an accident that might well have killed him, but he escapes serious injury—as by a miracle—that, too, is because some favorite saint was taking care of him. So when he is well, or when he has escaped injury, he has one of the village artists make a picture that tells the story of his accident or illness; and in the upper corner of the painting there is the figure of the Virgin or of the saint who saved him. Then the picture is hung in the church as a thank-offering.

In many village churches the rear walls are completely covered with miracle paintings, many of which have hung there for two or three hundred years. Every village has at least one *retablo* painter. There are always men who work at other jobs, planting their fields, making pottery, or weaving. And in their spare time they paint pictures of miracles. They are very serious about their work. If one of them is asked to make a *retablo,* he will insist on knowing the whole story, and just why the person who wants the *retablo* thinks the Virgin or the saint had anything to do with his getting well. Unless he is convinced that the client really believes it was a true miracle, he will not paint the *retablo* for him. Once the painter is convinced of the miracle, he works with great care, reverence, and imagination to paint the story, taking special pains with the figure of the saint.

During the colonial period, and for a long time after Mexico became an independent country, the old Indian style of painting lived only in this folk art. But with the series of revolutions that began in 1910 and continued at intervals for the next ten years, many things changed in Mexico. With the revolution in government, there was also a revolution in art. A new group of young painters began attracting attention. These young intellectuals wanted to paint as Mexicans, not as Europeans. They were tired of borrowed traditions, and felt that too much stress had been placed on Mexico's Spanish heritage, and not enough on her Indian heritage. Their work has much the same quality—strong lines and brilliant colors—as the painting of their Indian ancestors. Also they revived the art of mural painting, and have done more than anyone else to make it popular again.

Folklore in Wax
by Carmen C. de Antúnez

Using wax as her medium, the Mexican sculptress Carmen C. de Antúnez adapted her art to the portrayal of scenes of traditional Indian life—their crafts, costumes, and dances. She chose for her dioramas, which have been exhibited in many sections of Mexico, such subjects as the Dance of the Old Men of Lake Pátzcuaro, the Plume Dance of the Zapotecs, and the Deer Dance of the Yaquis.

Interpreting in wax the works of nature, especially the human figure, is a highly realistic technique. In wax we found the ideal medium for reproducing anthropological types and for capturing minute details of the vegetation and landscape in different sections of the country.

Our purpose in this work is simply to perpetuate the ancient traditions and ancestral customs that advancing civilization has been gradually obliterating. We try to record faithfully vivid village scenes, proud and humble native types, and fantastic costumes.

The dioramas of native Mexican dances required long years of preparation. Careful study of many dances was essential, as well as absolute mastery of the different elements that make up the groups. From the time a given dance is selected to its final portrayal in small wax figures, we have to cope with an incredible number of details, manual tasks, and difficulties.

We start by going to the place where the dance originated. Often it takes some rugged traveling to reach remote villages, like those in the state of Nayarit, which even today are populated by pure-blooded Indian groups governed by their own laws. But geographic and climatic hardships are unimportant. We want to see the dance, which is usually performed most elaborately on the feast day of the village patron saint, or on other special occasions—when the crops are planted, at the beginning of the rainy season, or at harvest time. We arrive a few days early to make friends, distribute gifts, attend the market, familiarize ourselves with the customs, and pay friendly visits to the mayor, municipal president, or tribal chief.

At last the day of the fiesta arrives. By now we know the dancers and talk freely with them. They let us take photographs. They begin to give us facilities for our work, and our enthusiasm grows. They dance solemnly, liturgically.

This is where the Indian really lets go. His dancing expresses passion, rebellion, religion, tradition, creative genius. The fervent language of profound and secret religious impulses is spoken in the movements of the dance. The Indians appeal to both pagan idols and the Christian God, to the rains, the sun, the flowers. They dance with their hands, arms, legs, feet, their whole bodies responding to the rhythms. Happiness, exorcism and prophecy, ecstasy, magic, even a primitive sense of medical art, are apparent in their dances.

We observe feverishly, taking pictures and many notes. The next day we take advantage of their fiesta mood and the costumes and decorations they have prepared. They dance for us alone. By a previous arrangement, they repeat certain steps and turns several times, and at last we select a scene we will interpret in wax.

Meantime, we have also made friends with the musicians who play for the dances; this is important. We interview musicians and dancers individually; we faithfully copy the costumes, the ornaments, the musical instruments, and so on. We take more photographs and notes, and make colored sketches of the countryside. If only the atmosphere were something concrete that we could grasp intact!

We get out our working tools and make rough models, especially of the heads, in mud, clay, or directly in wax. During the dance, the facial expression is transfigured: the Indian at work is one thing; the Indian dancing is another. There are interesting sidelights in making the arrangements—the Indians attach considerable importance to the situation; they grow sorrowful; they impose conditions. People gather round, touch our tools; children surround us. We must consent to everything, drink what they offer us, eat what they give us, and return their invitations generously and promptly.

Meanwhile, the work progresses. We have precise information, and we have rough models. Now it is necessary to persuade one or two Indians to come with us to Mexico City to pose in the various positions of the dance, and to answer any questions that may arise. But they persistently refuse to leave their village. We beg them, we argue with them, and finally they give in if they can bring along their wives, two or three children, and their close friends.

Sometimes they change their minds after climbing on the truck or even after hours of travel on horseback or on foot. Then we must wait one or two days more and convince them all over again. When the vehicle finally pulls out we feel as though we are carrying a treasure inside, and hope we won't have to delay another moment on the road.

It is impossible to record all the emotions of the journey and the first days back in the capital. The Indians do not adapt easily. Since they cannot accustom themselves to a new diet, we must provide them with the food they are used to. We put them up in our own home so that we can constantly observe them for our work. Then we make life-size models of them in order to complete the groups with examples of individual anthropological types.

We like to have something very much their own on the figures; generally we use the hairs from their mustaches and beards, inserting them in the wax one by one. It takes a lot of persuasion to get them to a barbershop. But the barber, who is an enthusiastic admirer of the Indians and the wax figures, helps us by waiting for the opportune moment and removing the precious hairs skillfully so that he can deliver them to us intact.

We work all day, or, when an assistant has been showing the Indians the city during the day, all evening. We take them to the Shrine of Guadalupe and to the movies. They are usually wide-eyed and happy, but sometimes, still mistrustful, they try to escape. We keep a close eye on them lest, being strangers in the city, they come to some harm.

Almost always they stay in our house one or two months, and during this period our patience is sorely tried. They nearly always feel ill (actually, it is homesickness for their people), but they refuse doctors and medicines, being full of superstitions we cannot combat. We live through harried days, for if anything happened in our house, especially to the children, the whole village would hold us responsible. Months and even years after they return, they feel there is a tie between us.

We work intensely and enthusiastically, without any set hours.

Each figure is modeled in its proper position in beeswax that has been treated to help it withstand changes of temperature. First we melt the wax and tint it the color of the Indian's skin; then, while it is still warm, we gradually shape it. Once the proper pose is achieved, the figure is reinforced with wire.

The eyes, a vital part of the facial expression, are of enamel or glass. It is hard to get the figures in just the right place; sometimes the individual ones look all right, but displease us when placed in a group. We adjust them, change the poses, remove the eyes and try to make them correspond better to the over-all rhythm of the models. We touch up the faces, the hands, the skin, with colored wax; and last of all we dress them.

Miniature headdresses of vividly dyed feathers are prepared with Indian techniques. There are little palm hats and small serapes, woven especially by hand; necklaces and other jewelry; tiny wooden violins and guitars. We take great pains with the folds of the fabrics and the position of the instruments in the musicians' hands. We place the figures on the diorama or stage, which is about eight feet wide, six and a half feet high, and six and a half feet deep (the diorama figures are from twenty to twenty-three inches tall).

The platform is shaped like a half dome, with a landscape of the region painted on the inside—the same landscape that served as a backdrop for the original dance. As there are no corners, an excellent feeling of perspective is achieved. To both foreground and background we add bits of earth, little stones, artificial plants and cactus, and powdered pigments to indicate green or dry pastures.

In the end we have produced a diorama of a native Mexican dance, which is like a live document that surprised the dancers in action, caught their poses, their rhythms, the atmosphere, the very essence of their purpose. It is full of color and truth, because in making it we did not have to invent or falsify; we simply captured with affection the genuine beauty of the scene.

Alias Dr. Atl
by Alice Raine

The artist who calls himself Dr. Atl was born Gerardo Murillo in Guadalajara, the son of a doctor of chemistry. In his early days he was familiar with the vials and test tubes in his father's laboratory, which may have helped him in his later experiments with colors. When his family moved to San Luis Potosí, the boy attended the Jesuit College there.

D r. Atl of Mexico smiled and leaned back against the wall behind the serape-covered bed in his studio. The venerable painter par excellence of Mexico's valleys, mountains, and volcanoes likes to tell stories about himself. Perhaps more than anyone else, he has deliberately contributed to the legend that surrounds him. Even the Aztec name by which he is known was assumed, to emphasize his kinship with the Indians.

Though slight and frail, Dr. Atl somehow gives the impression of enormous vitality. The leathery toughness of his skin is a reminder of the days and nights he has spent in Mexico's rough mountain climes. Most of his hair has been burned away by age, sun, and lava dust, but his finely chiseled face is framed by a magnificent beard, almost white now, brushed and curried to a silkiness that contrasts sharply with the dark tweeds he usually wears. His large, dark eyes burn with a fierce flame that belies these signs of age and startles even the casual observer. In Mexico it is trite to say that Dr. Atl has become one with his volcanoes, but for those who do not know this extraordinary man it is still the most accurate comparison.

Recently this beloved painter endeared himself even more to his compatriots by giving all his work on the Paricutin volcano to the nation. Paricutin broke through the earth on February 20, 1943; it grew rapidly, burying the nearby villages of Paricutin and San Juan. Now quite a respectable volcano, it thrills thousands of visitors with its sudden growlings and explosions. Midwife, nurse, and companion of this phenomenon was Dr. Atl. His work on

Paricutin alone consists of 130 drawings and eleven paintings. Apart from its artistic merit, it is a unique contribution to vol- canology; here for the first time one man, combining poetry with technical and scientific knowledge, presents the birth and growth of a volcano. Dr. Atl has also kept a careful diary of three hundred pages that describes the year-by-year, day-by-day, sometimes even hour-by-hour development of Paricutin.

Though he paints with the understanding and devotion of a Turner or a Monet, Dr. Atl did not take up painting until compara- tively late in life. Like most young men of fairly well-to-do families, he went to Europe to study—Paris first, then Rome. There, besides working on his doctorate, he painted two murals and made head- lines on the day of his arrival by bathing in one of Rome's lovely fountains, carried away by his enthusiasm for their classic beauty. As soon as he heard of the Revolution brewing in Mexico, he hurried home. A friend of Jaurès and other European socialists, he was ready to rouse his countrymen with passionate phrases and helped form as he says, "regiments of workers, women, dogs, and parrots."

About this time he developed an eye disease that could be cured only by his living in the cleanest, coldest atmosphere outside a test tube. It was then that he moved to the last hamlet high on the slopes of Popocatépetl, a tiny conglomeration of huts called Tlamacas. In this limpid, sun-drenched atmosphere he developed an absorbing interest in mountains and volcanoes.

In 1943, Dr. Atl rushed to Michoacán, fascinated by the news of the volcano a-borning. Two Indian friends helped him build a sort of breastwork of branches and tree trunks beyond his little hut, as close as possible to the volcano. Then they returned to their vil- lage, leaving him alone. He stayed, off and on, for most of the next eight years, sometimes for a whole year at a time. Once he had to be carried back to Mexico, so weak had he become from constant exposure and lack of food. Had he returned immediately when gangrene set in, he might have saved his leg, but he never took time to think about himself.

Dr. Atl's diary describes his experience.

"As the sun began to set, the wind blew strongly from the north and the column of smoke, pushed toward where I was standing, began its rain of projectiles, quickly covering the barricade of tree trunks with great smoking stones. Since it was very cloudy and sand poured down abundantly, the landscape became invisible; so I went to sleep early in my refuge. . . .

Splendid sunrise. The sun illuminates the tragedy of the landscape. From this southern side the volcano seems more somber, more gloomy, but there is no cemetery of tree trunks around it. The winds, constantly changing, whirl the column of smoke. As it crosses my camp it covers everything with sand and pieces of rock, many the size of footballs. . . .

It began to grow dark. The sky clouded over and standing behind the sheltering fence, I waited for something to happen. Suddenly a violent wave of air knocked me to the ground. An enormous piece of slag passed over my head and buried itself nearby, with a shock that made the earth shake violently. The lava slag, when it falls, has a temperature of approximately 900 degrees on the outer surface. . . . As I returned step by step to my little camp, very slowly, admiring the volcano . . . the earth shook again and suddenly from the base of the cone there exploded a cluster of fire-flowers, wrapped in clouds of dust. A river of lava came rushing toward me. The heat suffocated me. I wanted to flee, but my legs refused to move. I grabbed the small trunk of an oak, but it burned my hands. There was nothing to do but see all I could before I died. The wide river of lava dashed down in a cascade, while from the fiery fountain rose an enormous whirlwind of flame, thick and red, and other whirlwinds of dust accompanied it in a fantastic dance. . . ."

Dr. Atl has specialized in Mexican panoramas, and in his work the mountains, valleys, and volcanoes attain an almost cosmic force. The earth's curvature, so often shown in his large canvases, adds to this impression. Painting Paricutin seems to have given him a new release and a more forceful style.

The Atl-colors he invented are now used by many painters, but most fail to bring out the luminosity and depth of landscapes that one finds in his work. The formula for Atl-colors contains resin, wax, and pigments; since they do not mix, the dry colors are super-imposed on each other. Petro resina, an Atl mixture of petroleum and resin, adds, according to the painter, "transparency and richness and guarantees the permanence of the colors."

MARKETS

Markets have been important in Mexico since pre-Conquest times. Families bring their products to the market in San Felipe de Santiago. (*National Museum of Anthropology, Mexico City*)

In the town of Santa Cruz Tepexpan, the market stalls are set up in the shadow of the cathedral. Every village of more than a thousand people has its set market day, usually once a week. (*National Museum of Anthropology, Mexico City*)

Left: Although mass-produced articles are spreading through Mexico, each region is still known for its particular color and design in *rebozos*, serapes, and rugs. There was no wool in Mexico until after the Conquest. In this photo, a woman from Puebla winds wool dyed with native dyes. *(National Museum of Anthropology, Mexico City)*

Above: This twelve-year-old boy first learned to weave on an ancient waist-loom four years ago. He is proud of the beautiful woolen *rebozos* he makes for tourists who stop at his family's home on their way from Oaxaca to visit the famous ruins at Mitla. *(William H. Field)*

Below: This woman of Oaxaca is also using the waist-loom, the only kind known in Mexico until the Spanish introduced the upright loom. *(National Museum of Anthropology, Mexico City)*

Left: On Sundays, families gather to picnic, gossip, and sell their wares in the patio of Uruapán's museum, once a church dating from the early sixteenth century. This busy little Michoacán city is noted for its delicate lacquer work. *(Margaret T. Field)*

Lower left: A woman sells fruit on a street corner in Paracho, a town of Michoacán famous for its handcrafted wood products. Young people come to this town for their first guitars; accomplished musicians for their finest instruments. *(Margaret T. Field)*

Right: This girl in Oaxaca is selling tortillas, the staple food of Mexico, made of ground corn, and baked on a griddle. *(National Museum of Anthropology, Mexico City)*

Left: This basketmaker is a skilled craftsman. The best baskets in Mexico come from Toluca, which has one of the largest straw markets in the world. Toluca baskets are made of heavy smooth reeds and fine marsh grasses from the nearby river swamps. *(National Museum of Anthropology, Mexico City)*

Top: This old woman selling peppers and other fresh garden produce lives in Patzcuaro, Michoacán. *(National Museum of Anthropology, Mexico City)*

Bottom: In this straw market in Oaxaca, vendors display not only baskets, but toys, mats called *petates*, hats, and many other items. Hats come in many styles. Sometimes, you can tell where a man lives and how he makes his living by his hat. *(National Museum of Anthropology, Mexico City)*

Left: Pottery and weaving are the oldest handicrafts in the world. In this photo a woman of Oaxaca offers her pots for sale along the highway. Each region has its distinctive pottery, using the type of clay available in that region and the colors and designs of the native people. (*National Museum of Anthropology, Mexico City*)

Below: These painted trays come from Morelia, in the state of Michoacán, famous for its fine lacquer work. In the sixteenth century, Bishop Vasco de Quiroga started the many folk arts for which Michoacán is well known.(*National Museum of Anthropology, Mexico City*)

The Folklore Ballad
by Lysander Kemp

Wherever you go in Mexico, you will hear música folklórica, *the popular music of Mexico. It differs from one region to another. Most of the time, it is accompanied by a* mariachi *band of six or more, playing stringed instruments, sometimes with a trumpet or two. Of all folk music, the most typical are the ballads, or* corridos, *which may be played and sung by a group, or by a single voice, the voice of Mexico, a man playing a guitar and singing a sad song.*

It was the first night of the fiesta for the Lord of the Mountain, the annual fiesta to celebrate the blessings of the great wooden crucifix in the Jocotepec church. The village plaza was crowded with games and rides and BB-gun shooting-galleries and tent cantinas; there were little stands down the first block of the main street and along the block by the school. January nights are cold here in the high country of Mexico, and after the *castillo*, the fireworks "castle," was burned in the plaza, I wandered to the street by the school, hoping to warm myself with a cup of *café con piquete*, which is black coffee with a "bite," with a shot of straight alcohol.

When I came near, I heard a guitar from among the stands. Hunting it out, I found the musician hunched on the curb, beside a table and bench where a woman was selling cups of what looked like tea. The musician was almost blind, and squinted strangely from behind the shield of his guitar; the woman was large and dark, wrapped in a black rebozo, listening, turning now and then to poke at the charcoal fire; the one customer at the table was an old man, indio-dark, in a black serape. The scene was lighted in brooding chiaroscuro by the smoking flame of a globeless oil lamp.

I stood back in the Rembrandt shadows, waiting for the musician to sing, and in a moment he struck different chords and sang, in his harsh expressive voice, the *corrido* or folk-ballad of *The Shooting of Cirilo Arenas*.

165

> *Fly away, fly away, little dove,*
> *Fly away, if you know how to fly,*
> *And tell my poor mother*
> *That they are going to shoot me.*

When Cirilo had finally met his "sad end," I asked the singer for *Rosita Alvírez*. He sang it for me, and after that I stood listening to other songs, until at last the woman gestured to me that I should sit down. I sat down at the low table and asked her what she was selling in the cups. *"Canelitas,"* she said—hot cinnamon tea, not the black coffee I wanted, but each cup with its "bite." For the next hour, till the police came by to close up the stand, I sat there in the flickering light, sipping *canelita*, talking with the vendor and the old man between songs, and hearing the music of Mexico, the true music of the people with its folk heroes, its calamities, its themes of love and bravery and violent death.

The Mexican *corrido* is an authentic folk-ballad, descended from the Spanish romances which first came to Mexico with the soldiers of Cortés. It has never achieved the beauty and power of the great *romances* or of the great English and Scottish ballads. But it has a crude vigor—and sometimes poetry—of its own, and although it is probably doomed to be lost in Mexico's headlong pursuit of the twentieth century, it has the present fascination of a living folk art.

The word *corrido* is most often said to derive from the verb *correr*, "to run," because many of the *corridos* run on and on. I prefer the less popular theory that the word is a slight corruption of *ocurrido*, "happening," for most *corridos* are just that, a recital of what happened to Cirilo Arenas, to Delgadina, to Francisco Villa. The music of the *corridos* is as simple as the texts, a brief melody repeated over and over till the end of the story.

The *corrido* once served to spread the news of battles, murders, catastrophes, and the like, and still serves that purpose in remote villages, where the singer arrives with his guitar to sing the news in the plaza or a cantina. But now that the radio and the newspaper have penetrated to all but the most isolated parts of Mexico, the *corrido* serves more to commemorate events already known than to bring fresh news. When I heard the *corrido* of *The Suicide of Julián Ramírez* sung in the Jocotepec plaza, and saw the singer's wife selling copies of the verses, printed on single sheets of "gray paper with blunt type," I thought that here was the *corrido* performing its traditional function.

> *Gentlemen I will sing*
> *Of what happened in Zacoalco*
> *Señor Julián Ramírez*
> *Died from taking poison.*

> *In order to leave this world*
> *He took poison for sure,*
> *He put an end to his life*
> *With a strong dose of cyanide.*

> *He loved all the women*
> *On the ranches and in the towns*
> *He liked to have a good time*
> *And to frequent the cantinas.*

And on, to his death in the sixteenth stanza:

> *It was exactly half past four*
> *When this tragedy took place.*
> *His agony lasted an hour,*
> *He died at half past five.*

Somewhat as the traditional *corrido* has never rivaled the great ballads of England and Spain, there are no literary *corridos* to rival *The Rime of the Ancient Mariner, La Belle Dame sans Merci,* the romances of Lope de Vega and Luis de Góngora, the great *Romancero gitano* of Federico García Lorca. But at least one Mexican poet, the contemporary Miguel Lira, has succeeded in using the *corrido* for literary purposes. He often confines himself to the narrow forms and feelings of the tradition, but in *El corrido de Domingo Arenas,* he has written a poem, not a set of verses.

> *The baker was making bread,*
> *Sweet bread,*
> *Salt bread,*
> *Little ring rolls for the children*
> *Watching him make the bread.*

The whole village watched him
Making the day's bread,
Sweet bread,
Salt bread,
Little white clouds with sugar,
Little half-moons with salt.

The whole village asked him,
"Don Domingo, what about the bread?"
"I am putting it in the oven,"
Don Domingo said.

Don Domingo had only one hand,
He made the bread with one hand;
He decked a little shrine to the other
With flowers and a candle.

On Sundays he went to mass,
Nobody in the village prayed better.
"Holy Mother of Heaven,
How could I ever forget you?"

Don Domingo had a sweetheart
Dark as the woods and the skies,
The rich darkness of midnight
Looked out of her eyes,
And her arms were as cool and calm
As beads on a string
Or the mirror of the water
In a spring.

First she teased and tormented him,
Later she screamed, "Leave me alone!"
Architecture of playing-cards,
Falling by its own!

Don Domingo forged the hatred
Of his dagger on an anvil,
The anvil was fierce red;
He put the dagger to bake
In the oven with the bread.

He roamed the mountain singing
"La cucaracha" and other ditties,
The moon rose over the mountain
On a platter of white lilies.
Domingo Arenas shouted,
"Sweet bread, salt bread!"
And his cries pecked at the white
Quiet of the city.

A hailstorm of red bullets
Filled the streets with poppies;
The trees bloomed and the blossoms
Were birds in their own blood.

"Look out, Domingo Arenas
Is coming up from the river.
Hide your daughters in the well,
Never mind how they shiver."

"I know. They are all hidden.
The water is full
Of fallen stars. I can hear him
Coming up the hill."

Arenas buried his hook-hand
In tobacco-colored flesh:
There was a blood-red clover
On his sweetheart's breast.

It was the last night of the two-week fiesta. The last *castillo*, a gigantic work of art, was burned at midnight, flashing its Catherine wheels and fountains, whistling and hissing and banging, and ending with a wheel of fire that whirled high into the night. There was a barrage of rockets then, some of them exploding like bombs, some of them bursting into a rain of colored lights, green and white and red, the colors of Mexico. The last rocket drenched the black sky and died, and the fiesta was over.

Modern Mural Painters
by John A. Crow

Mural painting is one of the oldest, as well as the youngest, of Mexican fine arts. The oldest temples and palaces found by archaeologists in Mexico were often decorated with extraordinarily beautiful wall paintings. During the Colonial period, the Indians found expression chiefly in the folk arts. When the time was right, after the Revolution of 1910, there was a renaissance among Mexican mural painters.

The great mural painting of Mexico today did not spring full grown from a vacuum, nor from any mind of Zeus. During the latter years of the Díaz regime its main features were already beginning to emerge timidly from the academic chains that enthralled it. The fine landscape painter Joaquín Clausell, that master of poignant oils Francisco Goitia, and the superlative engraver José Guadalupe Posada, all contributed their fair share to the renaissance in Mexican art which the Revolution set free with its explosion.

With this beginning, twentieth-century Mexican painting was off to a solid start. In 1909, when Rivera and Atl returned from Europe, the necessary push was given. Rivera had studied in France, Atl had seen the marvelous frescoes of Italy, and José Clemente Orozco, who was to develop into perhaps the finest painter of his country, had spent many hours standing beside the engraver Posada. Rivera exhibited his best pictures, and Dr. Atl spoke enthusiastically of the magnificent murals of da Vinci and other Italian Renaissance artists, whose technique, he said, had been lost for four centuries. Atl's eyes flashed fire and he began to preach nationalism in art. He experimented with colors, invented new and more durable tones suitable for painting on paper, canvas, or plaster. Orozco and the other young painters at the Academy caught Atl's enthusiasm and began to paint with strong, brisk, rapid strokes. Sometimes they even sketched models in motion. Before very long each one had found his own personal style. Gone forever was the photographic immobility of academic art.

In 1910 the Mexican government set up a huge exhibit of Spanish art in order to commemorate the 100th anniversary of Hidalgo's famous "Cry from Dolores." Many thousands of dollars were appropriated to bring from Spain some of the largest canvases of Sorolla, Zuloaga, and many other peninsular artists. The young Mexican painters, with Dr. Atl as their spokesman, protested their exclusion from the exhibit. Finally, the ridiculous sum of 3,000 pesos was given to defray the expenses of an exhibit of Mexican art.

Never before or since has there been such an exhibit in Mexico. Paintings and pieces of sculpture flooded every available hall and gallery, and in spite of the fact that most of these young artists were exhibiting for the first time, the Mexican pieces were more varied, more dynamic, and more inspired than those from Spain. They were acclaimed with enthusiasm. The young artists organized themselves into a Centro Artístico with the central purpose of painting the walls of the public buildings. Dr. Atl got permission for them to start on the newly constructed Preparatory School, but the Revolution broke out and the project was abandoned in panic. A dozen years passed before fresco painting actually made its start.

The Revolution was now in full swing, and the whole country smelled of blood and the smoke of battle. Orozco himself took no part in the Revolution and was never in any danger. The whole sorry spectacle passed before his eyes like a savage carnival scene. At last, sickened by the chaos and the killing, he left Mexico and came to the United States. He was always the "lone wolf" among the Mexican painters of our times.

In 1919 the Revolution was almost over. In the state of Jalisco a government of revolutionary artists was set up. Alfaro-Siqueiros was sent abroad and met Rivera in Paris. They fired each other with new ideas. In 1921 Siqueiros issued a manifesto in Barcelona in which he called for a return to the indigenous base of Mexican art and the abandoning of outworn European patterns. This new revolutionary art would, he said, express the hopes and sufferings of the masses. Both Siqueiros and Rivera became Communists and added frequent Marxist slogans to their violent outpourings of what art should and should not be.

Orozco kept himself apart from politics. In fact, he states in his autobiography that, "Artists do not have and never have had political convictions of any kind, and those who believe they do, are not artists." This was putting it a little too strongly, but it was his way of denouncing the loud certainties of Rivera and Alfaro-Siqueiros. Orozco, of course, could not possibly keep himself cut off from the social realities of Mexican life and never attempted to do so. But what he did try to do was to portray that reality as a spiritual rather than a political quality, and by so doing he made himself into a more universal artist.

Diego Rivera now returned to Mexico from Europe by way of Italy, where he was deeply impressed by the frescoes of the Italian Renaissance and the Byzantine mural mosaics. In the early 1920's José Vasconcelos, the new Minister of Education, turned the walls of many public buildings over to the young artists, and Mexican mural painting was born. Rivera, Orozco, and Alfaro-Siqueiros are the three best-known fresco artists, but there are many others. At first both Rivera and Orozco followed the Renaissance tradition, using limited, transparent colors, and fine, close brush strokes. Later on, the strokes became bolder, the colors more varied.

Miguel Covarrubias, himself one of the finest Mexican artists, explains that "the true fresco is painted with earth colors and water on a surface of wet plaster. Only an area that can be completed in a day's work is plastered, the next being prepared the following day and the two joined as inconspicuously as possible. The palette of the fresco painter is limited; Rivera uses only ten colors: six natural earths (oxides of iron), emerald green, two blues, and black. Orozco uses even fewer, resorting freely to an opaque white. Fresco painting requires great technical knowledge, speed and complete sureness of hand and intent, since no alteration is possible once the plaster dries."

Rivera and Orozco are very different kinds of men, and very different artists. Rivera is the out-and-out propagandist, politically sure of himself, and rather insistent on defiantly shouting out his opinions. His pictures are always strongly pro-Indian, pro-masses, and even more strongly anticapitalistic. This political propagandism has given to many of Rivera's best-known murals a cluttered effect which is certainly not the best art. The artist is so intent on getting in every bit of evidence which supports his preconceived point of view that the perspective of the work of art is often destroyed. Great crowds often flood Rivera's pictures and resemble a May Day parade rather than a distilled essence of artistic feeling. However, Rivera has at times painted the human face and form with profound emotion and a marvelous mastery of artistic technique. Often, too, his colors have a shining quality which is like that of the Mexican landscape itself, suggesting the colors of tropical birds and flowers.

Orozco is a man of torment who sees human suffering as inevitable in life and strives to capture that tortured feeling in his forms and colors. He is obsessed with fire, and flames of orange, red, and blood contort many of his most magnificent figures. Fire is man's conscience, fire purifies and cleanses while man struggles to move forward and to be free. Orozco admires dignity and justice. He detests pretense, debasement, corruption, and deceit. He believes that man is here for a purpose, and that purpose is to improve himself.

Alfaro-Siqueiros, who uses duco and other new paints, sometimes applied with a spray gun, has tried to create "a monumental and heroic art, a human art, a public art, with the direct and living example of our great pre-hispanic cultures in America." He believes that the mural art of Mexico today "is moving toward the accumulation and fusion of every plastic value of worth that history has left us. And it is the only movement in the whole world which is realizing such a purpose." The frescoes of this artist, with their monstrous figures and vivid forms and colors, are unique in modern art. They have a cumulative grotesque effect that is overwhelming.

Mural painting, now welded to modern architecture, is the great art of Mexico today. The Mexican frescoes are not paintings on a wall; they are paintings which are a wall. Together with the magnificent buildings which house them they have caught the surge of history, the suffering, growth, and aspiration which make up the spirit of Mexico in our time. Better than any other expression they link the present with the indigenous past, and in this fusion reach toward an even more powerful future.

PART 6
LEGENDS THAT LIVE TODAY

The Four Hundred Young Men
from the *Popol Vuh*
**English version by Delia Goetz & Sylvanus G. Morley
from the Spanish translation of Adrián Recinos**

The Popol Vuh *is a literary epic, the sacred book of the Maya Indians, the most civilized nation of Middle America before the Spanish Conquest. As important in its way as the Old Testament, the* Popol Vuh *tells the story of creation and other myths, traditions, and legends of the Quiché Maya who lived in Guatemala and the peninsula of Yucatán.*

These Maya Indians flourished during the period between the fifth and the ninth centuries. They built great cities of stone connected by stone roads, twenty-five to thirty feet wide, with causeways over marshlands, and bridges over streams. They were a great trading nation, on sea and on land, who built temples and pyramids in the tropical jungle. They used only hand labor and stone hammers and chisels. They decorated their architecture with mural paintings and massive sculpture. They provided ball courts and theaters for games and entertainments.

The early Spanish explorers who visited some of these cities compared them with the great cities of Spain. They passed them by because the empire of Montezuma offered greater plunder. Later, Alvarado and other Spanish captains traveled over Maya roads into the jungles of Guatemala. In the name of Christianity and the King of Spain, they razed many cities to the ground and destroyed tribal books and documents wherever possible.

In the last 150 years, scholars and archaeologists have begun to discover the true marvels of Maya culture. In this search, the Popol Vuh, *the Book of the People, plays an important part. There are stories of gods and heroes, of good magic and bad, of serpents, jaguars, turtles, eagles, and mosquitoes.*

   The following is both a hero story and a nature myth, about Zipacná, elder son of Vucub-Caquix, a chieftain who survived the flood but was killed for his arrogance.

Here now are the deeds of Zipacná, the elder son of Vucub-Caquix.

"I am the creator of the mountains," said Zipacná.

Zipacná was bathing at the edge of a river when four hundred youths passed dragging a log to support their house. The four hundred were walking, after having cut down a large tree to make the ridgepole of their house.

Then Zipacná came up, and going toward the four hundred youths, said to them: "What are you doing, boys?"

"It is only this log," they answered, "which we cannot lift and carry on our shoulders."

"I will carry it. Where does it have to go? What do you want it for?"

"For a ridgepole for our house."

"All right," he answered, and lifting it up, he put it on his shoulders and carried it to the entrance of the house of the four hundred boys.

"Now stay with us, boy," they said. "Have you a mother or father?"

"I have neither," he answered.

"Then we shall hire you tomorrow to prepare another log to support our house."

"Good," he answered.

The four hundred boys talked together then, and said: "How shall we kill this boy? Because it is not good what he has done lifting the log alone. Let us make a big hole and push him so that he will fall into it. 'Go down and take out the earth and carry it from the pit,' we shall tell him, and when he stoops down, to go down

From *Popol Vuh: The Sacred Book of the Ancient Quiché Maya*, From the Spanish Translation of Adrián Recinos. Copyright 1950 by the University of Oklahoma Press.

into the pit, we shall let the large log fall on him and he will die there in the pit."

So said the four hundred boys, and then they dug a large, very deep pit. Then they called Zipacná.

"We like you very much. Go, go and dig dirt, for we cannot reach [the bottom of the pit]," they said.

"All right," he answered. He went at once into the pit. And calling to him as he was digging the dirt, they said: "Have you gone down very deep yet?"

"Yes," he answered, beginning to dig the pit. But the pit which he was making was to save him from danger. He knew that they wanted to kill him; so when he dug the pit, he made a second hole at one side in order to free himself.

"How far [have you gone]?" the four hundred boys called down.

"I am still digging; I will call up to you when I have finished the digging," said Zipacná from the bottom of the pit. But he was not digging his grave; instead he was opening another pit in order to save himself.

At last Zipacná called to them. But when he called, he was already safe in the second pit.

"Come and take out and carry away the dirt which I have dug and which is in the bottom of the pit," he said, "because in truth I have made it very deep. Do you not hear my call? Nevertheless, your calls, your words repeat themselves like an echo once, twice, and so I hear well where you are." So Zipacná called from the pit where he was hidden, shouting from the depths.

Then the boys hurled the great log violently, and it fell quickly with a thud to the bottom of the pit.

"Let no one speak! Let us wait until we hear his dying screams," they said to each other, whispering, and each one covered his face as the log fell noisily. He [Zipacná] spoke then, crying out, but he called only once when the log fell to the bottom.

"How well we have succeeded in this! Now he is dead," said the boys. "If, unfortunately, he had continued what he had begun to do, we would have been lost, because he already had interfered with us, the four hundred boys."

And filled with joy they said: "Now we must make our *chicha* within the next three days. When the three days are passed, we shall drink to the construction of our new house, we, the four hundred boys." Then they said: "Tomorrow we shall look, and day after tomorrow, we shall also look to see if the ants do not come out of the earth when the body smells and begins to rot. Presently we shall become calm and drink our *chicha*," they said.

But from his pit Zipacná listened to everything the boys said. And later, on the second day, multitudes of ants came, going and coming and gathering under the log. Some carried Zipacná's hair in their mouths, and others carried his fingernails.

When the boys saw this, they said, "That devil has now perished. Look how the ants have gathered, how they have come by hordes, some bringing his hair and others his fingernails. Look what we have done!" So they spoke to each other.

Nevertheless, Zipacná was very much alive. He had cut his hair and gnawed off his fingernails to give them to the ants.

And so the four hundred boys believed that he was dead, and on the third day they began the orgy and all of the boys got drunk. And the four hundred being drunk knew nothing any more. And then Zipacná let the house fall on their heads and killed all of them.

Not even one or two among the four hundred were saved; they were killed by Zipacná, son of Vucub-Caquix.

In this way the four hundred boys died, and it is said that they became the group of stars which because of them are called Motz [a mass known also as the Pleiades], but it may not be true.

The Eagle and the Serpent
by William H. Prescott

Omens played as important a part in the life of the ancient Aztecs as they did in the life of ancient Greeks. There were omens of sacrifice, of earthquakes, of fire and disaster. No war could be waged, no feast celebrated without consultation with the priests and the interpretation of the omens for good or evil. So it is not surprising to find that the Aztecs founded their capital city of Tenochtitlán, following a message to the priest from their god, Quetzalcoatl, or "plumed serpent," according to a chronicle written in Náhuatl soon after the Conquest:

"Therefore go at once and seek out the tenochtli *cactus upon which an eagle stands with joy. It is there we shall fix ourselves; it is there we shall rule, that we shall wait, that we shall meet the various nations and that with our arrow and our shield we shall overthrow them. Our city of Mexico-Tenochtitlán shall be there, where the eagle cries and spreads his wings and eats, there where swims the fish and there where the serpent is devoured: Mexico-Tenochtitlán; and there shall many things be brought about."*

The Mexicans, with whom our history is principally concerned, came also, as we have seen, from the remote regions of the North —the populous hive of nations in the New World, as it has been in the Old. They arrived on the borders of Anahuac, toward the beginning of the thirteenth century, some time after the occupation of the land by the kindred races. For a long time they did not establish themselves in any permanent residence, but continued shifting their quarters to different parts of the Mexican Valley, enduring all the casualties and hardships of a migratory life.

On one occasion they were enslaved by a more powerful tribe; but their ferocity soon made them formidable to their masters. After a series of wanderings and adventures, which need not shrink from comparison with the most extravagant legends of the heroic ages of antiquity, they at length halted on the southwestern borders of the principal lake, in the year 1325.

They there beheld, perched on the stem of a prickly pear, which shot out from the crevice of a rock that was washed by the waves, a royal eagle of extraordinary size and beauty, with a serpent in his talons, and his broad wings opened to the rising sun. They hailed the auspicious omen, announced by the oracle as indicating the site of their future city, and laid its foundations by sinking piles into the shallows; for the low marshes were half buried under water. On these they erected their light fabrics of reeds and rushes, and they sought a precarious subsistence from fishing, and from the wild fowl which frequented the waters, as well as from the cultivation of such simple vegetables as they could raise on their floating gardens.

The place was called Tenochtitlán, in token of their miraculous origin, though only known to Europeans by its other name of Mexico, derived from their war-god, Mexitli. The legend of its foundation is still further commemorated by the device of the eagle and the cactus which form the arms of the modern Mexican Republic. Such were the humble beginnings of the Venice of the Western World.

The World and Other Folktales
by Américo Paredes

The oral tradition is strong in Mexican folklore, and the tales one hears are often a mixture of Spanish, Indian, and church lore. In Mexico, as in other countries, the folktale is one of the most reliable indices of social life and customs, often revealing more than the longest social treatise, or the most popular novel.

"The World" is basically an indigenous folktale from the Puebla region. It was told to the author by an Otomí Indian who remembers hearing it in his childhood from the "old people," his grandparents, who spoke Náhuatl. Yet it has characters and episodes clearly borrowed from Christianity.

The two short anecdotes which follow emphasize the triumph of the little fellow, the country person who uses his wits to achieve success.

THE WORLD

Once a man said, "I will go and plow the land." So he began to clear away the brush from the land. When he finished he planted beans, and after he was through with that he went home. Next day, when he went back, he found that the place was all brush again. He thought it was very strange, and he took his machete and cut down the trees once more. But next day he came upon the same thing.

So he says, "Who the devil is doing this to me!"

He did the work once more, but he did not go away. Instead he hid himself in the bushes. There he was, stooped down, watching, when he sees an animal with a little wand tapping on the trees and saying, "Get up! Get up, all of you! Up!" And the trees would get up.

"Ah, so you are the one!" the man said to himself. "Now you'll see!"

The little animal was the rabbit. The man let him get close to where he was, and then he said to him, "Why are you making me lose my time? Why won't you let me work?"

And the rabbit said, "Don't work any more, because the world is coming to an end."

The man did not believe him, and he answered, "If you don't tell me the truth, I'm going to kill you."

And the rabbit said, "I know what I'm saying; you listen to me. Look," he said, "I will go with you. Build a wooden box about the size of a room and put your family in there. And have them make all the tortillas they can. All I can eat is beans and herbs. I'll let you know when it is to happen."

Still the man thought about it for a while. Then he said, "All right; I'll do it."

Once he had finished, the rabbit got inside with him and his family, and they put a padlock on the door. Then it began to rain very hard, and the box went up and up until it reached the sky. All the animals and people were left way down at the bottom. They could see how the weather was, and how high they were, through a little hole in the roof. The box was all closed up, but it had its breathing hole. So they could see that the sky was very close to them, but little by little they came down until they reached the ground, which was dry by now. But it was full of the corpses of animals and men. Then the man opened up and said he was hungry, but the rabbit told him, "You still have some tortillas there, and I can't eat them." So the rabbit went out and found some herbs, which he ate.

The man said to his daughter, "Look, daughter, I'm hungry. Let's cook one of those dead cattle." They dragged it in, they skinned it, and they began to cut it up. They built a fire, and they started cooking it.

Then Our Lord God said to his little angels, "Go see what is happening, who is making all that smoke. But watch out, see that you don't eat anything."

The little angels came straight down and said, "What happened? What are you doing?"

The man answered, "Nothing. I'm eating meat."

The little angels said, "All right."

The man offered some to the rabbit, but he wouldn't eat any. That is why he stayed a rabbit, and the same size he is now. He also said to the little angels, "Don't you want a little piece?"

The little angels took it, and afterward they cleaned themselves well so God would not smell them. But the smell would not go away, no matter how hard they rubbed. They came before God, and he said to them, "What happened? What did you eat?"

And they said, "Nothing."

But you know how it is when you drink liquor or chew gum, or when you have a beer or a peppermint drop, how it smells from a distance. Well, God could smell them just like that. The little angels kept wiping and rubbing, and they would beat their wings. So God said to them, "Well, since you ate of that meat, from now on you will eat nothing but that."

They are the vultures!

And there it ends.

ALL's FOR THE BEST

This was a man who went to ask for work. To a town. And he came to a place and asked for work, and they told him, "Do you want work as a street-sweeper?"

"Yes, of course." The poor man didn't know how to do any kind of work.

They said, "Let's see. What's your name?"

"Well, so-and-so."

"Sign your name here."

"Well, I don't know how to write."

"If you can't write your name, we can't hire you. Not even as a street-sweeper."

"I can make an X."

"No, it isn't enough. You must know how to read and write."

The man went away very sad, and since he had to make some kind of a living, he began to sell a few little tomatoes on the street. And he did very well. He bought himself a flivver and kept on selling vegetables. And he kept doing well. And after that he opened a little stand and went up in the world with his tomatoes, those little tomatoes that he sold. And with the passing of the years he got to be rich.

One day he went to the bank, and he was carrying a lot of money. He went and put it in the bank. When they made him the slip— "Sign here, if you please"—he made an X.

He said, "Listen, señor. Please put down your name."

"I don't know how to write."

He said, "Just think, señor. You don't know how to write, and you are so rich. Imagine how rich you would be if you knew how to write."

"If I knew how to write, I would be sweeping the streets out there."

GOD GIVES A HUNDRED FOR ONE

This was a little Indian who owned a cow. The priest of the village took a fancy to the animal; he wanted to breed it to his bulls. So one day he said to his parishioners during the sermon, "We must give alms to the church and help our neighbors, for God gives a hundredfold for one."

A few days later he asked the Indian for his cow, but the Indian said he couldn't give it to the church, because that was the only one he had. But the priest insisted. Then the Indian's wife said, "All right, let him have her."

But before giving up the cow, she bathed it in saltwater and dusted it with powdered salt. Then she said to her husband, "The little cow is ready. Let them take her away."

The Indian did so, and he left his cow at the priest's. But the other animals smelled all the salt on it, and they crowded around and began to lick it. The cow was used to its own corral, so it jumped the fence that night and went off. And all the bulls followed it.

Next day the priest sent some men for his livestock. But the Indian told them, "No, this livestock is mine. God has given me a hundred for one. So I'm going to count the cattle, and if there aren't a hundred of them, the priest will have to make up the difference."

After this lesson the priest never again asked for tithes.

The Smoking Mountain
by Maurice Boyd

The twin volcanoes which may be seen on a clear day from Mexico City are as old as the land itself, and the tales about their origin are told by many Indian tribes who live within sight of their majestic heights. This tale combines natural history with the social customs of the Tarascan Indians who, at the time of the Conquest, ruled a kingdom nearly as large and powerful as that of the Aztecs. Their subjects were spread over what is now the state of Michoacán, parts of Querétaro, Colima, Jalisco, and Guerrero.

Many years before the coming of the white man there lived a beautiful princess in the land of the Toltecs. Her father, a Toltec king, was troubled because his eighteen-year-old daughter had never seen a Toltec youth capable of winning her heart. Since Toltec law declared that only Toltec youths of the highest nobility dared gaze upon the princess, the king feared she might never marry.

One day a handsome Tarascan prince of the dog-Chichimec tribe came over the mountains and descended into the land of the Toltecs. The foreign prince entered the Toltec capital of Teotihuacán in a golden litter borne by slaves. The Toltecs derisively called him Prince Atapaneo, which meant "he who is mounted." They had instantly recognized the newcomer as a Tarascan, for he wore no *maxtlatl*. The *maxtlatl* was a cloth wrapped around the waist, passed between the legs and tied in front, with its two ends hanging in front and in back. All the peoples known to the Toltecs except the Tarascans in the northwest and the Huastecas to the northeast, wore the *maxtlatl*. The Toltecs regarded both of these people as scandalous primitives.

Although not dressed in the Toltec fashion the Tarascan prince was richly clothed in regal garments bearing the symbol of the dog-totem of his people. An impressive Tarascan retinue followed him, carrying products for trade.

The Toltec princess, with her maids in attendance, was by

chance en route to the market in search of fine embroidery work for her white robe. On a narrow street she came face to face with the litter which bore the prince. At first sight she and the prince felt a mutual attraction although neither dared to speak for fear of betraying dangerous emotions.

The maids attending the princess sensed the excitement that caused the cheeks of the royal maiden suddenly to bloom and her heart to flutter so violently that it pounded audibly. Whispering among themselves at this reaction of the princess, the maids decided to hurry her away to the Toltec palace for rest and seclusion.

The prince was so moved by the vision of the princess clothed in white that he completed his business in the market place without enthusiasm. He bargained poorly. He desired only to see the beautiful princess whom he called Maravatia, meaning "precious treasure."

For the first time in his life the young prince had reason to be irritated at the barrier which the Toltecs had established between themselves and the dog-Chichimecs. According to the law of Teotihuacán, no Chichimec, not even a prince, was worthy of a Toltec princess. As his slaves carried him over the winding mountain paths to his own people in the pine forests, the prince resolved to erase the lovely Toltec princess from his memory.

As time passed, however, Prince Atapaneo found himself longing for a glimpse of the princess; her face hauntingly returned in his thoughts and dreams. After many restless days he returned to the Toltec capital. His slaves carried him past the Toltec palace. Framed in a low doorway laced with flowers stood the princess in her white robe lined with the plumed serpent emblem of her people, the symbol of Quetzalcoatl. Two heavy braids of black hair fell over her slender shoulders. Although she presented a picture of unsurpassed beauty, her eyes revealed an inner sadness.

Then suddenly Princess Maravatia beheld the prince. Her almond eyes immediately beamed and her lips formed a warm smile. As their eyes met she signaled him to come near. He jumped from his litter and strode towards her. The princess knew now that the tall, lithe Tarascan prince was the one whom she had always dreamed would some day find her.

Upon his head the prince wore a headdress of crimson-colored feathers. His handsome face, black eyes, and broad shoulders clothed in jaguar skin would have impressed even the most reticent maiden. Although they understood only a few words of the other's language, the prince told her of his love, while she whispered softly of her love for him. Then the maids-in-waiting arrived and forced the princess to withdraw into the castle.

The prince, puzzled as to what he should do, finally decided to contact the father of the princess. He sent a messenger to the Toltec palace, informing the king of his love for the princess and of his desire to marry her.

The king was furious. Waving his scepter with the blue worm motif, he haughtily rejected the messenger's proposal and commanded his daughter to appear before him. He rebuked the princess harshly for the first time in her life. When, through her tears, she revealed her love for the foreign prince, the Toltec king confined her to her palace quarters, believing that the passing of time would cure this childish fancy which she mistook for love.

One of the maids attending the princess sympathized with the plight of the two lovers. Unknown to the king the maid sent word to the Tarascan prince that she would arrange meetings for the two. Owing to her careful plans, the prince often met the princess in secluded places during the next several months. The king, believing his daughter had forgotten about the alien prince, relaxed his vigilance. Then the lovers daily met in a wooded area where the princess had roamed since childhood.

Finally during autumn the lovers decided to brave the king's displeasure. One evening at sunset the prince carried the princess away in his litter. Hoping that her father would sanction the marriage, the princess returned the next day to beg leniency and understanding.

But the young lovers had misjudged the king and the power of the Toltec taboos. The Toltec king was bitter and humiliated. He refused to see his daughter or to send her his blessing. The unwritten but well-understood Toltec law forbade intermarriage with other tribes. The princess, in Toltec eyes, had committed a double sin: first she had eloped without permission, and then she had chosen an outsider—a despised Tarascan.

The king issued a decree forbidding his subjects from giving the lovers any food, shelter, clothing, or other type of assistance. When the Tarascan royal household learned of the action of Prince Atapaneo, they too refused to help the lovers, for a Toltec princess was equally unacceptable to the Tarascans. The two lovers were forced to wander forlornly over the land.

Weeks lengthened into months. Weary and weak the couple wandered from place to place, eating berries from bushes and sweet roots dug from the earth. The silver streams of the forest provided them with drinking water. The *agua miel,* or honey water, from the maguey plant supplied them with energy and warmth.

As winter came and the wind grew bitter, both realized that at last they must die. One night while resting at the foot of two mountain peaks in an alien land far to the southeast of Teotihuacán, the young Tarascan prince told his Toltec bride that they must part at sunrise. The winter winds blew unceasingly, and they could no longer hope to survive.

He looked into her tired but beautiful eyes, and sadly spoke: "Tonight will be our last together on this earth. But we shall be together and happy in the spirit world. In that realm there are no laws of the two races, Toltec or Tarascan, to separate or punish us. The priests of our fathers have invoked the anger of the gods for the crimes we committed against the customs of our people. To atone for these, my beloved, we must pass through the valley of death.

"Tomorrow at sunrise," he continued, "we must part. Then you, my adored one, must ascend the lower of the two mountains in the distance. On its peak you will find your eternal resting place. The spirit of your god Quetzalcoatl will carry you safely to the top, where a bed of sweet smelling pine boughs will help you find a deep, lasting sleep. While you are doing this, I shall ascend the higher mountain, where I shall forever watch over your sacred form."

At the appointed time the following morning, as the sun showered its golden rays over the lakes and mountains, the Tarascan tenderly held his bride for the last time. Then he gently released her. Both turned away. Without backward glances they made the long ascents to their respective mountain peaks and took their eternal resting places.

Tradition tells us that the snows fell that day, covering the bodies of the lovers. The summit of the lower peak, named Ixtaccíhuatl or "Sleeping Lady" by the Toltecs to commemorate the mountain upon which their princess sank into her last long sleep, has been perpetually covered with a blanket of white snow since that day. It is the shroud of white eternally protecting their Sleeping Lady in death as her white robe clothed her in life.

The higher mountain, named Popocatépetl by the Chichimecs in honor of their prince who eternally watches on the summit, rumbles and sends forth great columns of smoke each year about the month of December. Even now, the Indian storytellers remind us, Popocatépetl or "Smoking Mountain" still gives vent to his sorrow as he mourns for his dead love, Ixtaccíhuatl, who sleeps nearby.

Our Lady of Guadalupe
by Frances Toor

The Virgin of Guadalupe is the most living legend in Mexico, the symbol of all that is most holy. Her basilica on Tepeyac Hill near Mexico City is built on the ruins of an Indian temple where rites were once held for the Aztec goddess of earth and corn, Tonantzin. Pilgrims by the thousands come to the shrine all year long to pray for health and happiness. On December 12 a magnificent fiesta is held at the shrine, with dancing and singing until dawn.

In other countries the First Lady of the Land is generally the ruler's or President's wife; in Mexico she is the Virgin of Guadalupe. She is the most widely known and beloved of all Mexican *santos*.

The Virgin of Guadalupe was the first of the various miraculous apparitions on Mexican soil. Immediately after the Conquest, Fray Juan de Zumárraga, first Archbishop of Mexico, ordered the destruction of all important pagan deities and their shrines. The one having the widest cult near the capital was that of the Aztec goddess of Earth and Corn, Tonantzin (also virgin and little mother) whose shrine was on Tepeyac Hill. The natives mourned her loss so deeply that the dark-skinned Virgin of Guadalupe was sent to take her place. In order that they might accept her with greater confidence, she appeared to one of their own humble sons.

Early on the Saturday morning of December 9, 1531, Juan Diego, a poor convert, was on his way to the Franciscan church at Tlaltelolco to receive Christian instruction. As he was crossing Tepeyac Hill on the way from his village, he heard heavenly music and a sweet voice calling his name. Soon he saw the Virgin, "radiant as the sun," her feet resting on the rocks, gleaming like precious jewels under them. She addressed him gently, calling him "my son," and said she wished him to tell the Bishop that she wanted a church on that spot—where the one for the Aztec goddess stood—so that she might be there near his people, to protect

189

and to love them, "For," she added, "I am the Mother of all of you who dwell in this land."

Juan promised to obey her commands. He had difficulty in seeing the Bishop, who listened to him incredulously and told him to come again when he was less occupied. So Juan returned sadly to the hill, where the Virgin awaited him. He reported the results of his interview and begged her to find a worthier messenger. But she insisted that he was the one she wanted and told him he must try again.

The following day, Juan went again to Tlaltelolco. After the religious services, he succeeded in seeing the Bishop. Juan knelt at his feet, with tears in his eyes, begging to be believed. The Bishop was impressed by the fact that Juan's story was exactly the same as on the previous day, so he sent him away more gently, and told him not to return unless he could bring a token from the Virgin. After Juan left, the Bishop ordered some trustworthy members of his household to follow him. They were able to keep him in sight until he reached the hill, when he suddenly vanished and they could find no trace of him. They reported this to the Bishop, saying that Juan must have dreamed or made up the story, and suggested that he be punished for doing so. In the meantime, Juan was with the Virgin, telling her what the Bishop had said. She told him to come for the token the following day.

On Monday, the next day, Juan had to stay home on account of the illness of his uncle. The doctor who saw the uncle said there was no hope, so on Tuesday Juan was sent to Tlaltelolco for a priest to administer the last rites. Juan had been so worried over his uncle, that he forgot all about the Virgin until he reached the hill. Then, fearing he had incurred her displeasure and wanting to avoid a scolding, he took a round-about path. But the Virgin came to meet him. She spoke to him gently and told him not to worry; that his uncle was already well again. Then she said he must go to the place on the hill where he had first seen her, and pick some roses, which were to be the token for the Bishop. Juan obeyed, and was astonished to find beautiful Castilian roses among the rocks, where previously only cacti had grown. Then the Virgin told him to hide the roses in his *tilma* or cape and to take them to the Bishop.

The attendants at the Bishop's Palace asked Juan what he had in his *tilma*. He tried to keep them from seeing the roses, but finally had to show them if he wanted to be announced. When the servants saw the roses they were as surprised as Juan but when they tried to take one, the flowers seemed to be part of the *tilma*. They told the Bishop about it, who immediately realized that this was the token from the Virgin. Juan was admitted at once. He knelt and in reaching for the roses to hand to the Bishop, he let his *tilma* fall. At that moment there appeared upon it the image of the Virgin of Guadalupe. Then the Bishop fell upon his knees to pray for forgiveness for having doubted Juan the first time. Afterwards he took Juan's *tilma* and placed it over the altar in his chapel and asked Juan to point out the place where the Virgin wanted her church. Juan did so, spending another day away from his home. On Wednesday, when he returned, he found his uncle perfectly well.

The news of the miracle spread with lightning speed. A chapel was constructed in which the *tilma* with the image of the Virgin on it was hung. Converts were made by the thousands. Yet in spite of that, the personalities of the Virgin and Tonantzin were so confused in the minds of the natives that some of the leading missionaries were in favor of abolishing the shrine. But the Virgin was so miraculous that she succeeded in establishing herself.

In 1544 there was a terrible epidemic in the capital in which thousands of people died. The Virgin was brought to the city and her presence abated the pestilence. In 1629, there was a flood, and her presence caused the waters to subside. In 1754, a Papal Bull declared the Virgin of Guadalupe Patroness and Protectress of New Spain. Now her image is seen everywhere—in churches, chapels, in niches on bridges and houses, even on liquor bottles; it is reproduced in paint, stone, metal, glass.

The Basilica of Guadalupe, situated at the foot of Tepeyac Hill, about three miles from the Mexico City Cathedral, is in the town of La Villa de Guadalupe Hidalgo. It is unimpressive architecturally, but of great human interest. On the hill stands an eighteenth-century chapel to mark the spot where Juan found the roses; below, about a block away from the big church, is La Capilla del Pocito, the Chapel of the Little Well. It is round and well proportioned, a lovely example of the Mudejar style of architecture, with its yellow-tiled dome shining like gold. Inside is the well of the Virgin, which opened under her feet during one of her appearances. Here come the healthy and the sick, the blind and the halt, to drink of its brackish waters from a little iron bucket. The sick pour it over their sores and take it home in bottles.

Formerly many pilgrims would crawl on their knees the distance of a mile or more from the edge of the city to the shrine, over the cobbled path along the fourteen stations of the cross, but since a railroad track has been laid there the handsomely carved landmarks are no longer used. Since then it has become a custom to go that same distance on foot along the tree-lined Calzada de Guadalupe. During the entire night of December 11 the wide sidewalk along this boulevard is filled with pedestrians, the young folks making a lark of it—singing, jesting, laughing.

Many a time I have seen the dawn at the Basilica on December 12, heard the *mañanitas* to the Virgin and seen the dancers perform reverently for the Virgin in the dimly lighted church. Afterwards I have followed them to the top of the hill to see them put up the three huge, freshly-painted crosses and dance around them, blow incense at them, and then offer it to the four cardinal points as in the days of the Aztec goddess. Then I have seen them dance for hours on a plaza at some distance away from the church, which has no atrium. But it was on the hill in the soft light of dawn that the dances were most beautiful.

Legends of the City of Mexico
by Thomas A. Janvier

These legends of the streets of Mexico City were set down nearly a hundred years ago. They were passed by word of mouth from grandmother to child, from a barber to his patron, from a waiter in a restaurant to his customer. They are in the best oral tradition, and have become part of the literary and folk culture of Mexico. The story of "Don Juan Manuel" has been made into a play. Other legends have been retold by poets and scholars. "The Obedient Dead Nun" belongs to the colonial period when the Church was all-powerful. "The Wailing Woman" is the oldest of all, going back to pagan days before the Conquest; in some form, it may be heard in all parts of Mexico, as persistent as the legend of Guadalupe.

THE OBEDIENT DEAD NUN

It was after she was dead, Señor, that this nun did what she was told to do by the Mother Superior, and that is why it was a miracle. Also, it proved her goodness and her holiness—though, to be sure, there was no need for her to take the trouble to prove those matters, because everybody knew about them before she died.

My grandmother told me that this wonder happened in the convent of Santa Brígida when her mother was a little girl; therefore you will perceive, Señor, that it did not occur yesterday. In those times the convent of Santa Brígida was most flourishing—being big, and full of nuns, and with more money than was needed for the keeping of it and for the great giving of charity that there was at its doors. And now, as you know, Señor, there is no convent at all and only the church remains. However, it was in the church that the miracle happened, and it is in the choir that Sor Teresa's bones lie buried in the coffin that was too short for her—and so it is clear that this story is true.

The way of it all, Señor, was this: The Señorita Teresa Ysabel de Villavicencio—so she was called in the world, and in religion she still kept her christened name—was the daughter of a very rich hacendado of Vera Cruz. She was very tall—it was her tallness that made the whole trouble—and she also was very beautiful; and she went to Santa Brígida and took the vows there because of an un-deceiving in love. The young gentleman whom she came to know was unworthy of her was the Señor Carraza, and he was the Librarian to the Doctors in the Royal and Pontifical University—which should have made him a good man. What he did that was not good, Señor, I do not know. But it was something that sent Sor Teresa in a hurry into the convent: and when she got there she was so devout and so well-behaved that the Mother Superior held her up to all the other nuns for a pattern—and especially for her humility and her obedience. Whatever she was told to do, she did; and that without one single word.

Well, Señor, it happened that the convent was making ready, on a day, for the great festival of Nuestra Señora de Guadalupe; and in the midst of all the whirring and buzzing Sor Teresa said suddenly—and everybody was amazed and wonder-struck when she said it—that though she was helping to make ready for that festival she would not live to take part in it, because the very last of her hours on earth was almost come. And a little later—lying on her hard wooden bed and wearing beneath her habit the wired shirt of a penitent, with all the community sorrowing around her—Sor Teresa died just as she said she would die: without there being anything the matter with her at all!

Because of the festival that was coming, it was necessary that she should be buried that very night. Therefore they made ready a comfortable grave for her; and they sent to the carpenter for a coffin for her, and the coffin came. And it was then, Señor, that the trouble began. Perhaps, because she was so very tall a lady, the carpenter thought that the measure had not been taken properly. Perhaps, being all so flurried, they really had got the measure wrong. Anyhow, whatever may have set the matter crooked, Sor Teresa would not go into her coffin: and as night was near, and there was no time to make another one, they all of them were at their very wits' end to know what to do. So there they all stood, looking at Sor Teresa; and there Sor Teresa lay, with her holy feet sticking straight out far beyond the end of the coffin; and night was coming in a hurry; and next day would be the festival—and nobody could see how the matter was going to end!

Then a wise old nun came to the Mother Superior and whispered to her: telling her that as in life Sor Teresa had been above all else perfect in obedience, so, probably, would she be perfect in obedience even in death; and advising that a command should be put upon her to fit into her coffin then and there. And the old nun said, what was quite true and reasonable, that even if Sor Teresa did not do what she was told to do, no harm could come of it—as but little time would be lost in making trial with her, and the case would be the same after their failure as it was before. Therefore the Mother Superior agreed to try what that wise old nun advised. And so, Señor—all the community standing round about, and the candle of Nuestro Amo being lighted—the Mother Superior said in a grave voice slowly: "Daughter, as in life thou gavest us always an example of humility and obedience, now I order and command thee, by thy vow of obedience, to retire decorously within thy coffin: that so we may bury thee, and that thou mayest rest in peace!"

And then, Señor, before the eyes of all of them, Sor Teresa slowly began to shrink shorter—to the very letter of the Mother Superior's order and command! Slowly her holy feet drew in from beyond the end of the coffin; and then they drew to the very edge of it; and then they drew over the edge of it; and then they fell down briskly upon the bottom of it with a sanctified and most pious little bang. And so there she was, shrunk just as short as she had been ordered to shrink, fitting into her coffin as cozily as you please! Then they buried her, as I have told you, Señor, in the comfortable grave in the choir that was waiting for her—and there her blessed shrunken bones are lying now.

DON JUAN MANUEL

This Don Juan Manuel, Señor, was a rich and worthy gentleman who had the bad vice of killing people. Every night at eleven o'clock, when the Palace clock was striking, he went out from his magnificent house—as you know, Señor, it still is standing in the street that has been named after him—all muffled in his cloak, and under it his dagger in his hand.

Then he would meet one, in the dark street, and would ask him politely: "What is the hour of the night?" And that person, having heard the striking of the clock, would answer: "It is eleven hours of the night." And Don Juan Manuel would say to him: "Señor, you are fortunate above all men, because you know precisely the hour at which you die!'' Then he would thrust with his dagger—and then, leaving the dead gentleman lying in the street, he would come back again into his own home. And this bad vice of Don Juan Manuel's of killing people went on, Señor, for a great many years.

Living with Don Juan Manuel was a nephew whom he dearly loved. Every night they supped together. Later, the nephew would go forth to see one or another of his friends; and, still later, Don Juan Manuel would go forth to kill some man. One night the nephew did not come home. Don Juan Manuel was uneasy because of his not coming, fearing for him. In the early morning the city watch knocked at Don Juan Manuel's door, bringing there the dead body of the nephew—with a wound in the heart. And when they told where his body had been found, Don Juan Manuel knew that he himself—not knowing him in the darkness—had killed his own nephew whom he so loved.

Then Don Juan Manuel saw that he had been leading a bad life: and he went to the Father to whom he confessed and confessed all the killings that he had done. Then the Father put a penance upon him: That at midnight he should go alone through the streets until he was come to the chapel of the Espiración (it faces upon the Plazuela de Santo Domingo, Señor; and, in those days, before it was a gallows); and that he should kneel in front of that chapel, beneath the gallows; and that, so kneeling, he should tell his rosary through. And Don Juan Manuel was pleased because so light a penance had been put upon him, and thought soon to have peace again in his soul.

But that night, at midnight, when he set forth to do his penance, no sooner was he come out from his own door than voices sounded in his ears, and near him was the terrible ringing of a little bell. And he knew that the voices which troubled him were those of the ones whom he had killed. And the voices sounded in his ears so woefully, and the ringing of the little bell was so terrible, that he could not keep onward. Having gone a little way, his stomach was tormented by the fear that was upon him and he came back to his own home.

Then, the next day, he told the Father what had happened, and that he could not do that penance, and asked that another be put upon him. But the Father denied him any other penance; and bade him do that which was set for him—or die in his sin and go forever to hell! Then Don Juan Manuel again tried to do his penance, and that time got a half of the way to the chapel of the Espiración; and then again turned backward to his home, because of those woeful voices and the terrible ringing of that little bell. And so again he asked that he be given another penance; and again it was denied to him; and again—getting that night three-quarters of the way to the chapel—he tried to do what he was bidden to do. But he could not do it, because of the woeful voices and the terrible ringing of the little bell.

Then went he for the last time to the Father to beg for another penance; and for the last time it was denied to him; and for the last time he set forth from his house at midnight to go to the chapel of the Espiración, and in front of it, kneeling beneath the gallows, to tell his rosary through. And that night, Señor, was the very worst night of all! The voices were so loud and so very woeful that he was in weak dread of them, and he shook with fear, and his stomach was tormented because of the terrible ringing of the little bell. But he pressed on—you see, Señor, it was the only way to save his soul from blistering in hell through all eternity—until he was come to the Plazuela de Santo Domingo; and there, in front of the chapel of the Espiración, beneath the gallows, he knelt down upon his knees and told his rosary through.

And in the morning, Señor, all the city was astonished, and everybody—from the Viceroy down to the cargadores—came running to the Plazuela de Santo Domingo, where was a sight to see! And the sight was Don Juan Manuel hanging dead on the gallows —where the angels themselves had hung him, Señor, because of his sins!

THE WAILING WOMAN

As is generally known, Señor, many bad things are met with by night in the streets of the City; but this Wailing Woman, La Llorona, is the very worst of them all. She is worse by far than the vaca de lumbre—that at midnight comes forth from the potrero of San Pablo and goes galloping through the streets like a blazing whirlwind, breathing forth from her nostrils smoke and sparks and flames: because the Fiery Cow, Señor, while a dangerous animal to look at, really does no harm whatever—and La Llorona is as harmful as she can be!

Seeing her walking quietly along the quiet street—at the times when she is not running, and shrieking for her lost children—she seems a respectable person, only odd looking because of her white petticoat and the white rebozo with which her head is covered, and anybody might speak to her. But whoever does speak to her, in that very same moment dies!

The beginning of her was so long ago that no one knows when was the beginning of her; nor does anyone know anything about her at all. But it is known certainly that at the beginning of her, when she was a living woman, she committed bad sins. As soon as ever a child was born to her she would throw it into one of the canals which surround the City, and so would drown it; and she had a great many children, and this practice in regard to them she continued for a long time. At last her conscience began to prick her about what she did with her children; but whether it was that the priest spoke to her, or that some of the saints cautioned her in the matter, no one knows. But it is certain that because of her sinnings she began to go through the streets in the darkness weeping and wailing. And presently it was said that from night till morning there was a wailing woman in the streets; and to see her, being in terror of her, many people went forth at midnight; but none did see her, because she could be seen only when the street was deserted and she was alone.

Sometimes she would come to a sleeping watchman, and would waken him by asking: "What time is it?" And he would see a woman clad in white standing beside him with her rebozo drawn over her face. And he would answer: "It is twelve hours of the night." And she would say: "At twelve hours of this day I must be in Guadalajara!"—or it might be in San Luis Potosí, or in some other far-distant city—and, so speaking, she would shriek bitterly: "Where shall I find my children?"—and would vanish instantly and utterly away. And the watchman would feel as though all his senses had gone from him, and would become as a dead man.

This happened many times to many watchmen, who made report of it to their officers; but their officers would not believe what they told. But it happened, on a night, that an officer of the watch was passing by the lonely street beside the church of Santa Anita. And there he met with a woman wearing a white rebozo and a white petticoat; and to her he began to make love. He urged her, saying: "Throw off your rebozo that I may see your pretty face!" And suddenly she uncovered her face—and what he beheld was a bare grinning skull set fast to the bare bones of a skeleton! And while he looked at her, being in horror, there came from her fleshless jaws an icy breath; and the iciness of it froze the very heart's blood in him, and he fell to the earth heavily in a deathly swoon. When his senses came back to him he was greatly troubled. In fear he returned to the Diputación, and there told what had befallen him. And in a little while his life forsook him and he died.

What is most wonderful about this Wailing Woman, Señor, is that she is seen in the same moment by different people in places widely apart: one seeing her hurrying across the atrium of the Cathedral; another beside the Arcos de San Cosmé; and yet another near the Salto del Agua, over by the prison of Belén. More than that, in one single night she will be seen in Monterrey and in Oaxaca and in Acapulco—the whole width and length of the land apart—and whoever speaks with her in those far cities, as here in Mexico, immediately dies in fright.

Also, she is seen at times in the country. Once some travelers coming along a lonely road met with her, and asked: "Where go you on this lonely road?" And for answer she cried: "Where shall I find my children?" and, shrieking, disappeared. And one of the travelers went mad. Being come here to the City they told what they had seen; and were told that this same Wailing Woman had maddened or killed many people here also.

Because the Wailing Woman is so generally known, Señor, and so greatly feared, few people now stop her when they meet with her to speak with her—therefore few now die of her, and that is fortunate. But her loud keen wailings, and the sound of her running feet, are heard often; and especially in nights of storm. I myself, Señor, have heard the running of her feet and her wailings; but I never have seen her. God forbid that I ever shall!

Glossary

(Spanish and Indian words which are not explained in context)

abrazo—embrace, a type of informal greeting between friends (men or women), involving much patting of each other on shoulders and back. A man may embrace a woman, or vice versa.

aguardiente—a strong alcoholic drink made from sugarcane.

ahuehuete—a tropical tree of the cypress family which grows only in Mexico.

braceros—day laborers, particularly agricultural workers, a common term for Mexicans who cross the border to work at unskilled jobs in the United States.

cacique—a pre-Conquest term for an Indian chief or governor of a small kingdom in pre-Hispanic times. The word is now applied to a person who exerts excessive influence in political and administrative affairs in a small town or village.

calmecac—an Aztec monastery school.

campesinos—country folk; peasants.

centavo—the smallest unit of Mexican currency. Ten centavos are approximately equal to one U.S. penny.

charro—a Mexican horseman in his holiday clothes. *Charro* also means loud or flashy.

chicha—a drink of fermented corn, used by the Guatemalan Indians.

coleta—a pigtail (sometimes fake) worn by bullfighters.

comadre—godmother [*compadre* - godfather] of one's child. The relationship between the parent and the godparent is very close.

comal—earthenware griddle.

compañeros—companions; comrades; fellow workers.

copal—a Náhuatl word for the resin from various tropical trees which is used in making lacquer and as a medicine and as incense.

corrida de toros—running of the bulls, or bullfight.

corrido—a ballad or satire in rhyme, often about a contemporary hero or villain or a current event, usually crudely printed on cheap paper and illustrated by a woodcut.

criollo—[creole] person born of Spanish parents, in Mexico or any other part of the Spanish Empire in America.

encomienda—a grant of land and Indian labor made by the Crown of Spain to the conquistadors as a reward for their services.

faena—the third act of the bullfight; the matador uses his *muleta*, the red cape, to bring the bull to the point where it can be killed.

gallo—a cock; or a serenade in early morning at the time when the cock crows.

gachupines—Spaniards living and doing business in Mexico; a derogatory term.

201

hacienda—a large ranch or plantation.

huaraches—leather sandals, commonly worn by men and women.

huipil—overblouse worn by women. Styles vary widely from region to region.

Indios—Mexican Indians.

jarano—Mexican sombrero.

lépero—professional beggar. Any crude and vile person.

maguey—one of several types of agave, a plant of the cactus family, from which the alcoholic drink, *pulque,* is made. Maguey fiber is twisted into rope or spun into thread. The leaves can be used for thatching and the thorns for needles.

mamacita—"little mother."

mañana—literally, "tomorrow." Also may refer to more distant future.

mañanitas—a morning serenade, on one's birthday or saint's day.

mariachis—traveling bands of six or more musicians playing stringed instruments, at times with a trumpet or two. *Mariachis* first appeared in the Guadalajara area during the French Intervention, as wedding musicians.

matador—the chief bullfighter, the one who actually kills the bull.

mestizos—people of mixed Spanish and Indian blood.

metate—three-legged stone, used to grind corn for tortillas.

México—from the Náhuatl name for the Aztec tribe which founded Tenochtitlán, now Mexico City.

milpa—a parcel of land on the edge of a village cultivated by a peasant for his own use. The main crops are corn and beans.

muleta—a small red cape used in bullfighting.

Náhuatl—the language of the Aztecs and some related tribes at the time of the Spanish Conquest. Náhuatl is still spoken today by about 200,000 monolingual Indians.

novia—a girl [*novio* - a boy] who is "going steady" or engaged to a member of the opposite sex. *Novia* also means bride; *novio,* bridegroom.

olla—a clay pot with a wide mouth, used to hold food or water.

papacita—"little father."

papas—Aztec priests.

peso—the basic unit of Mexican national currency. At the current (1973) exchange rate, a peso is worth about eight cents in U.S. money.

petate—a straw mat used primarily for sleeping. It can be rolled up during the day, or carried from place to place.

plaza—the main square or central open space around which a village develops. The plaza usually contains the church and on certain days the open market. Plazas are laid out with cobblestone walks, trees, flower beds, and sometimes a bandstand. There are benches where people wait for buses.

pronunciamento—the personal statement of an ambitious politician; a military uprising or revolt.

pueblo—a village.

pulque—fermented juice of the agave or *maguey* plant. A sacred drink of the Aztecs, *pulque* is a popular drink for all occasions. It is about as strong as beer. It is sold widely in *pulquerías*.

quechquemitl—a 4-pointed shawl made of two pieces of woven or embroidered material with a hole in the middle to form a poncho.

ranchero—the owner of a *rancho*, a medium-sized rural property. The term is also used for any person who works and lives in such a place.

real—a Spanish silver coin no longer in use. Eight *reales* made a dollar, or a piece of eight.

rebozo—a shawl worn by Mexican women. Developed from the Spanish mantilla, it is a long strip of cloth with a braided fringe. Women use it to cover their heads in church; it can be worn or draped in many ways. The finest *rebozos* are so sheer that they can be drawn through a wedding ring.

retablo—an altarpiece, or a small painting on wood or metal commemorating a miracle in which someone was saved from danger, disaster, or death by prayer to the Virgin or a special saint.

sarape—[in English, serape] a blanket worn by men, adapted from the Spaniards. Before the Conquest, men wore capes called *tilmas*. *Sarapes* are woven in distinctive tribal or regional designs.

soldaderas—women soldiers who accompanied their men during the Mexican Revolution, cooking their meals, loading their guns, and tending their wounds.

sombrero—a hat of Spanish origin, varying with region and use. Usually of straw, *sombreros* may also be made of felt or velvet.

telpuchcalli—an Aztec college.

teocali—an Aztec pyramid or temple where prisoners of war were sacrificed; literally, house of the gods.

tequila—a colorless alcoholic drink, similar to gin, made from the *maguey* plant.

tlacatecatl—"he who commands the warriors" (Aztec).

toreo—bullfighting. *Torero*—bullfighter. *Toro*—bull.

vaquero—a working cowboy.

vecindad—a neighborhood, or a multi-family dwelling.

verónicas—passes used at the beginning of a bullfight, in which the matador moves his cape back and forth in front of the bull as it charges.

zócalo—the main square or plaza in a large city.

zopilotes—buzzards.

Index